Latin American Plays in Translation

Latin American Plays in Translation

Modern Stories of Gender, Class and Society in Latin America

La Jana
A Ranch for the Lost Boys
The SAD Summers of Princess Diana
She
Nezahualcóyotl Dreams in Mictlan York
Extraordinary Life

Edited by GLOBAL VOICES THEATRE
With introduction by MALÚ ANSALDO

methuen | drama
LONDON • NEW YORK • OXFORD • NEW DELHI • SYDNEY

METHUEN DRAMA
Bloomsbury Publishing Plc, 50 Bedford Square, London, WC1B 3DP, UK
Bloomsbury Publishing Inc, 1359 Broadway, New York, NY 10018, USA
Bloomsbury Publishing Ireland, 29 Earlsfort Terrace, Dublin 2, D02 AY28, Ireland

BLOOMSBURY, METHUEN DRAMA and the Methuen Drama logo are trademarks of
Bloomsbury Publishing Plc

First published in Great Britain 2026

Copyright © Global Voices Theatre, 2026
La Jana Author © Juan Pablo Aguilera Justiniano, 2026
La Jana Translation © William Gregory, 2026
A Ranch for the Lost Boys Copyright © Sebastián Eddowes-Vargas, 2026
Published by arrangement with Sebastián Eddowes-Vargas. All rights reserved.
The SAD Summers of Princess Diana Author © Carla Zúñiga, 2026
The SAD Summers of Princess Diana Translation © Francisca Olivares Medina, 2026
She Author © Susana Torres Molina, 2026
She Translation © Gilda Bona, 2026
Nezahualcóyotl Dreams in Mictlan York Author © Xavier Villanova, 2026
Nezahualcóyotl Dreams in Mictlan York Translation © Roberto Cavazos, 2026
Extraordinary Life Author © Mariano Tenconi Blanco, 2026
Extraordinary Life English Translation © Catherine Boyle, 2026

The authors have asserted their right under the Copyright, Designs and Patents Act, 1988, to be identified as authors of this work.

For legal purposes the Acknowledgements on p. 257 constitute an extension of this copyright page.

Cover design by Jade Barnett
Cover illustration: Corazón by Soma / @somadifusa

All rights reserved. No part of this publication may be: i) reproduced or transmitted in any form, electronic or mechanical, including photocopying, recording or by means of any information storage or retrieval system without prior permission in writing from the publishers; or ii) used or reproduced in any way for the training, development or operation of artificial intelligence (AI) technologies, including generative AI technologies. The rights holders expressly reserve this publication from the text and data mining exception as per Article 4(3) of the Digital Single Market Directive (EU) 2019/790.

Bloomsbury Publishing Plc does not have any control over, or responsibility for, any third-party websites referred to or in this book. All internet addresses given in this book were correct at the time of going to press. The author and publisher regret any inconvenience caused if addresses have changed or sites have ceased to exist, but can accept no responsibility for any such changes.

No rights in incidental music or songs contained in the work are hereby granted and performance rights for any performance/presentation whatsoever must be obtained from the respective copyright owners.

All rights whatsoever in these plays are strictly reserved and application for performance etc. should be made before rehearsals by professionals and by amateurs to each individual writer of translator.

A catalogue record for this book is available from the British Library.

A catalog record for this book is available from the Library of Congress.

Library of Congress Control Number: 2025941917

ISBN:	HB:	978-1-3505-4227-3
	PB:	978-1-3505-4226-6
	ePDF:	978-1-3505-4228-0
	eBook:	978-1-3505-4229-7

Series: Methuen Drama Play Collections

Typeset by RefineCatch Limited, Bungay, Suffolk
Printed and bound in Great Britain

For product safety related questions contact productsafety@bloomsbury.com.

To find out more about our authors and books visit www.bloomsbury.com
and sign up for our newsletters.

Contents

Preface: On Process by Lora Krasteva, Robin Skyer and
Zhui Ning Chang of Global Voices Theatre 1
Introduction by Malú Ansaldo 2

La Jana by Juan Pablo Aguilera Justiniano, translated
by William Gregory 5
A Ranch for the Lost Boys by Sebastián Eddowes-Vargas, translated
by the playwright 33
The SAD Summers of Princess Diana by Carla Zúñiga, translated
by Francisca Olivares Medina 89
She by Susana Torres Molina, translated by Gilda Bona 141
Nezahualcóyotl Dreams in Mictlan York by Xavier Villanova, translated
by Roberto Cavazos 169
Extraordinary Life by Mariano Tenconi Blanco, translated
by Catherine Boyle 213

Outro: On Futures by Global Voices Theatre 255
Acknowledgements 257

Preface: On Process

By Lora Krasteva, Robin Skyer and Zhui Ning Chang of Global Voices Theatre

Latin American Plays in Translation is an anthology of plays by playwrights from Latin America, exploring modern stories newly translated into English. The plays included were all originally presented at two events run by Global Voices Theatre (GVT): *Global Female Voices* at the Arcola Theatre (2018) and *Global Latin American Voices* at the Roundhouse (2019).

GVT's flagship events aimed to amplify theatre and performance work by global artists that are underrepresented on UK stages. The texts came to us through our international callouts, and a selection of plays for each event were chosen by a curator: an established artist, who is a member of the community or group that the event focused on. For *Global Female Voices* (2018), this was Fauve Alice, a performance maker who has worked with various politically led theatre companies across Europe and Asia. For *Global Latin American Voices* (2019), this was Malú Ansaldo, an established Latin American producer with an international portfolio of work and, at that time, Head of Programming at the Roundhouse.

The curator for each event was supported by a panel of readers, who created a longlist for them. This reading panel included us three members of the GVT team and at least five other artists, writers, performers, or theatre makers who were members of the community or group that the event focused on (based inside or outside of the UK). For each of the plays chosen, an excerpt was read and performed by local artists at a GVT event.

Despite the wealth of significant and influential artistic creation in Latin America, this work has had a limited output in translation in English and Anglophone areas. The original *Global Latin American Voices* event aimed to engage diasporic Latin American creatives and the UK Latin American community, and to showcase to a UK theatre audience the unique theatrical talent from across the region. We are incredibly pleased that the work of that time will endure in print through Methuen Drama, and that we had the opportunity to collaborate with fantastic translators to bring fresh translations of these stories to a new audience. Alongside the five plays from the original *Global Latin American Voices* event, we have also chosen to include *She* by Susana Torres Molina, which was featured in *Global Female Voices*, to further demonstrate the excellent work yet to be recognized, read, and performed in Anglophone spaces.

Given the breadth of Latin American experiences across countries, communities, and cultures, each of the six plays in this anthology are accompanied by a brief translator's foreword, to better contextualize their specific geopolitical and cultural references and translation choices. We have also chosen to honor each playwright and translator's preference on language, whether that is British English, American English, or a third alternative; the spelling of Latin American, Latinamerican, Latiné; and so on, as long as it is internally consistent within the world of each play.

Through the publication of these plays, we endeavour to bring greater recognition to the playwrights, whose work is relatively unknown outside of their localities, and to share the multiplicity and complexity of Latin American experience demonstrated throughout the anthology.

Introduction

By Malú Ansaldo

When we first presented these plays in London in 2019, the world was a completely different place. Looking back and reconnecting with these stories, I can't help but notice how much is different, and how much remains the same. Unmoved. Unchanged. Still.

The global COVID-19 pandemic forced us to close venues, schools, airports. To stop the world and press pause. To isolate. It changed people's lives forever in many different ways. From the individual to the communal, from the personal to the political.

Personally, I was made redundant from a job I loved as Head of Performing Arts at London's Roundhouse. At the time, my aim was to programme work that would fill its Main Space and sell plenty of seasonal tickets, whilst also focusing on the various communities around London, attracting existing and new audiences with work that would truly speak to them on a big and small scale. We worked with established and emerging artists from London and around the world.

One of the first things I did at the Roundhouse was to make Global Voices Theatre an associate company. I was excited to connect with a vast array of international communities through showcasing plays and stories that would talk to them in a direct and open way: bridging the gap to UK audiences, working with translators and local migrant communities to bring it all together.

I was particularly excited, as a Latinamerican migrant myself, to work with the wonderful team at GVT to curate this event. Having started my professional career as a writer in Argentina, I spent my formative years in literary and playwriting groups where stories, ideas, and a strong sense of camaraderie filled our days and hearts. So we opened the call to plays from all across Latinamerica and to diasporic Latinx artists. Then, the stories started landing in our inbox.

Latinamericans from first and second generations, writing in their mother tongue, in English, in Spanglish. Translated plays, translations in development. Opposite from what we see many times onstage in the UK when you talk about a specific minority – in this case the Latinamerican community – these plays were exploring themes from domestic violence to power struggles, politics, art, death, family, dreams and friendship. They didn't simply engage in a self-referential way about the fact that they were – indeed – all written *by* Latinamericans. They were touching on global and intersectional stories, told and experienced *through the diversity of the Latinx eye*.

For many years now, we, the Latinamerican community, have struggled as an invisibilized minority in the UK. Even though it is now recognized as one of the fastest-growing minorities, and not a day goes by in London when you don't hear a Latin accent on the tube ... still, as creative practitioners and participants of the growing creative industries – with a clear economic impact in the UK – there was no data being collected about us for many years by Arts Council England. We were cornered into simply one box in all diversity forms: OTHER. This, of course, is not only reductive but also short-sighted: Latinamericans come in all shapes and forms, the diversity within our community is huge. There is not only one way of describing us, nor there is only one voice that can tell our stories.

The original GVT event at the Roundhouse in late 2019, *Global Latin American Voices*, was one shy but poignant attempt for a group of us to shed a light on the impact and importance of our stories, the diversity of our voices, the strength of our talent and the impact of our work in the UK. A place most of the participants in this event, for one reason or other, decided to call home.

What would have happened with these plays and their characters should the world not have closed down only a few months after? I guess we will never know. But re-engaging with them now brings me back to the actual issues they addressed and the power of storytelling. It reminds me that, even when we feel change can be fast and drastic, some things take decades to shift, they take collective effort, advocacy and faith. Faces and names might change in politics, but issues remain unsolved in various communities around the world.

As I type this, the effect of the recent floods in Spain have left thousands homeless and many dead. *La Jana* by Juan Pablo Aguilera Justiniano and translated by William Gregory could be a 2024 Spanish story, as much as it was a Chilean story back in 2019. Gender violence comes back to centre stage today – the day after the US election – as I try to avoid reading the news and postpone acknowledging the negative impact the Trump administration will have on women's rights in the US and across the world, through its impact on other fascist governments and right-wing global leaders. *The SAD Summers of Princess Diana* by Carla Zúñiga translated by Francisca Olivares Medina centres women's voices in its reminder of how violence against women and trans people at all levels of society keeps being normalized, and Susana Torres Molina's *She* reflects the dangerous flipside of that masculine obsession.

The fictional Soviet Union country went from being an almost utopic backdrop in *A Ranch for the Lost Boys* written and translated by Sebastián Eddowes-Vargas to a character in itself. The significance of staging this play, and sharing those experiences, would now be completely elevated and filled with new subtext. I'd be keen to see how a director might approach this particular challenge today.

Xavier Villanova's *Nezahualcóyotl Dreams in Mictlan York* translated by Roberto Cavazos could have been written during the 2020 global pandemic. It asks: What happens to all those who die alone? This took on a completely different dimension during the lockdown years, when people could not join their loved ones.

Stories and plays help us connect beyond language, ethnicity and geography. *The personal becomes political*, my good friend Mariano Tenconi Blanco has said to me many times. And fiction becomes a conduit of that. His gorgeous *Extraordinary Life* – Catherine Boyle's translation included in this anthology – shows how resistance can take the form of connection and friendship across kilometres and years. A true reflection of how thousands of people stayed alive, sane and connected during the darkness of lockdown.

It is interesting to sit back and reflect on how plays and stories interact with reality. How those interactions change with time and circumstance. The world is definitely not the same place it was when we launched this call-out. And still, stories written back then by Latinamerican writers can talk to us today. Here. At this precise moment when I type. Or there, wherever you are, in the exact moment when you read. God knows what will come next.

What I do know, though, is that we need theatre. We need stories. We need connection. A shared common space to process what happened, and dream about what is to come.

I hope you enjoy reading these plays. I am grateful for the wonderful team at GVT, not only for this specific selection of plays and the 2019 performance, but for the many other plays and events held during the years the company operated in the UK and globally. Spaces and platforms like this are rare: they exist in the margins of funding priorities (although one could argue that the intersection *is* indeed the place to shine). In a constantly evolving world, where migration, connection and cultural mixing will only become more prominent – not less, like the fascist and right-wing governments try to make us think – spaces like what GVT offered here in London are unique, invaluable and necessary.

The legacy on these pages and other publications are a true testament of Global Voices Theatre's commitment to their artists and communities through time, natural disasters and political outbursts. I hope these stories reach wide and far in this English version, like messages in metaphorical bottles floating across the world, through storms and sunny days.

London, November 2024.

La Jana

Juan Pablo Aguilera Justiniano

Translated by William Gregory

La Jana in English or 'Warning: Contains Strong Language'

By William Gregory

I was originally commissioned to translate *La Jana* in 2019. Global Voices Theatre (GVT), working with director María José Andrade, were planning on producing Juan Pablo's play as part of a season of Latinx theatre at the Tristan Bates Theatre (now the Seven Dials Playhouse) in London in 2020.

María José had a particular vision for the production, which informed the translation. Leaning into *La Jana*'s themes of social justice and the fight against erasure, as expressed particularly in the final scene, where La Jana riffs on the poem *Los Nadie* (*The Nobodies*) by Eduardo Galeano, the GVT production would reclaim space not just for the marginalized poor represented by the eponymous protagonist, but also for Latinx artists and the wider Latinx community living in twenty-first-century London. Following auditions in early spring 2020, two actors – one Chilean and one Spanish, Francisca Olivares and Fuen Vera – were cast jointly to voice La Jana onstage. Making a virtue of the play's direct-address style, and recognizing that a significant proportion of the audience would be Spanish speakers, a decision was made to weave linguistic identity into the piece, namely by leaving some sections in Spanish. Spanish has a good word for the objective of this approach: '*reivindicar*', meaning all at once to claim one's space, to defend one's position and to demand recognition. So the translation of 2020 was written with this in mind.

Then came the pandemic. Not unlike the tsunami referenced in the play, COVID swept away our plans, and although some online R&D took place that year, the difficult decision was made ultimately to cancel the production. Several years later, when the offer of publication came, a translation that had been held in suspension, originally intended for a particular purpose, needed to be revisited.

It is typical for the publication of a translated play in the English-speaking world, when a full production of the translation has occurred, to be a representation of what the actors onstage actually said. Doubtless this would have been the case had we been able to stage *La Jana* in 2020. But rather than publishing an unfinished text for a production that never took place, and which had a particular vision in mind, Juan Pablo was keen to focus back on translation in the stricter sense.

In the main, this meant reverting to the principle of translating every word into English, which presented challenges that I admit in 2020 I had been relieved to avoid. Although the vast majority of the play is written in a Spanish that almost any Spanish-speaker could understand readily, there are moments where the language used by La Jana becomes so specific to her geographical, cultural and socio-economic subject position that converting these into English became very difficult. In the 2020 version, it was these very moments that had largely been kept in Spanish, and included some great nemeses of the translator: swearing, proverbs, wordplay and rap. When La Jana declares that there are phrases 'only pronounceable by someone who belongs to the Chilean race', she's not wrong.

So, readers of this translation will find the Chilean expletive word-salads featuring '*huevón*' and '*conchetumare*' (*con perdón*) rendered more often than not using the Anglo-Saxon fail-safes 'fuck' and 'fucker'. Some of the proverbs have been translated literally, where the meaning is still fairly clear, such as 'asking for pears from an elm tree' (roughly similar to 'asking for blood from a stone'), but in other cases, I have opted for an English equivalent or – thank goodness for the direct-address form of this play – asked La Jana herself to explain (see the reference to 'Lieutenant Bello'). Wordplay hits extreme-sport levels in the list of pun-names in the campfire scene: how to carry across the double meaning of the Spanish-language equivalents of those gags favoured by Bart Simpson like 'Ben Dover' or 'Hugh Janus'? Any suggestions welcome!

I have erred on the side of caution when translating the scene in verse inspired by the late-1990s Chilean rap artists Rezonanzia. The present translation adheres more to the metre of English-language hip-hop from the period, rather than trying to follow the metre of the Spanish original. But my experience in this genre is very limited and I recognize that this rendering is far from perfect. In future productions, there will no doubt be others better qualified to create a version that sits more authentically.

What these knotty problems demonstrate, at the most daunting end of the task, is that any translation committed to print is only one set of solutions applied at the time to the best of the translator's ability. I'm glad to have had the chance to grapple with these ones, albeit with some regret that María José's GVT production of 2020 never took place.

* * *

Juan Pablo Aguilera Justiniano trained in acting at the Universidad de Desarrollo (Concepción) and in directing at the Universidad de Chile (Santiago). He has participated in over forty festivals, including Stgo a Mil (Santiago), the Buenos Aires International Festival, CASA (London), Pflasterspektakel (Linz) and ENTEPOLA, the Conference of Latin American Popular Theatre (Mexico), as well as travelling with his work to Germany, Italy, France, the Netherlands, Belgium, Luxembourg, Peru and Venezuela. Screen credits include the web series *El Desastre* (*The Disaster*), and *Real Heroes*, co-directed with Mauro Lamanna in Italy and Felipe Ipar in Uruguay, both made during the pandemic.

William Gregory's translations of Spanish and Latin American plays include *A Fight Against . . .* by Pablo Manzi (Royal Court, London), *B* by Guillermo Calderón (Royal Court), *Villa* by Guillermo Calderón (Prime Cut, Belfast; PlayCo, New York), *Cuzco* by Víctor Sánchez Rodríguez (Theatre503, London), Chamaco by Abel González Melo (HOME, Manchester) and *The Concert* by Ulises Rodríguez Febles (Royal Court; BBC). Translations with Bloomsbury include *The Oberon Anthology of Contemporary Spanish Plays*, *The Uncapturable* by Rubén Szuchmacher, *Selected Plays by Abel González Melo* and contributions to *The Methuen Drama Book of Contemporary Uruguayan Plays* (co-edited with Sophie Stevens), and *The Oberon Anthology of Contemporary Argentinian Plays*. He is a member of the Ibero-American theatre and translation collective, Out of the Wings, and Literary Associate at the Orange Tree Theatre, London.

La Jana High on a dangerous street light, the kind with its cables hanging loose, the kind where any moment you could fall, electrocuted, to the ground.
There's me: noble comrade of the trade, quick to leap, sleek, wildcat-fierce. Watchful worker of the Grey Cats.

La Jana Figueroa prowls the street lights.
La Jana. The only woman working as a Grey Cat.

Grey Cats is the name our gang is known by; grey is our colour and we're called cats 'cause of the skill each of us workers has as we jump down to steal from the fish trucks that drive through the streets of Talcahuano whipped by the rotten stench of fish.

Talcahuano, further south than Talca and fouler-smelling than actual guano.

I, La Jana Figueroa, prowl the street lights. I climb the porous corners up to the concrete peaks and there among electric cables and rusting iron girders I signal to the four other Cats waiting for the first truck to arrive, and then get stuck in with the stealing.

Joining this gang wasn't easy. It's the first time a woman's ever done it. It's always been said women should stay home cooking, cleaning and fixing the clothes fucked up by their pissed-up husbands.

I don't have a husband.

I live with my sick mum; money's tight here and there's no drunk fucker ruining his threads and needing them sewing. Come what may here, you have to earn your coin. There's no other choice. That's why I signed up with the Cats, 'cause there really was no other way. I had to fight the macho fuckers from the port, the filchers who wouldn't let me work and wouldn't even let me try, not me, not any woman.

And I spent a whole year fighting and fighting and showing them I was good enough, proving I had what it took to be in that gang.

And now I'm six years in.

Just 'cause you're a woman doesn't mean you can't be a Cat!

Besides, anyone can be a thief . . .

This is some criminal shit at the end of the day; none of the Cats like that word, but this is some criminal shit and anyone can be a thief . . .

Though when you think about it like that . . . Like getting kinda deep with it . . . The system always forces some people to steal; some people have to break the law.

I had to steal; I know it's bad, I'm not making excuses, but it had to happen to someone.

Plus, I'm not the only one who steals.

Even presidents are thieves these days, and they don't even need to dirty their hands with the stink of fish. They're fucking masters at it . . .

They just . . . do it.

No such fucking luck for me! I get filthy.

I do wash, though . . .

And even though the smell might always be there, seeped into my skin . . . I'm used to it now . . . I'm a Cat, after all.

I'm a Grey Cat . . .

Our work consists of filching. Also known as 'stealing'. Which, in Spanish, is '*chorear*'. Actually, maybe that's the reason people from Talcahuano are called '*choreros*'?

Maybe not . . .

Our work consists of filching, leaping from the street lights onto the backs of the fish trucks as they drive along filled with all the millionaire fish firms' merchandise.

Our work consists of filching, leaping from the street lights onto the backs of the fish trucks as they drive along and taking and taking fish and filling bags with them and throwing them onto the curb.

We do it in less than a minute . . . Cool and calculated.
The fish-filled bags are caught by a couple of Cats waiting in the dark alleyways of the port and taken to a cellar we've set up specially for storing our little treasures.
Then we sell them cheaper than the town traders do.
In some way what we do is kinda like Robin Hood, stealing from the rich to give to the poor, and even though we don't give the stuff away we do sell it cheap which is already doing a good deed.
You just have to see it from the other side.
Through other people's eyes . . .
Some people love us; they take us under their wings and watch our backs 'cause we save them a few pesos.
And some people hate us, 'cause they want those other people's pesos for themselves.

Our work consists of filching.

In this job you don't need to be violent, or aggressive; you just need to be quick with a good pair of kicks in case one of the braver drivers chases you down the stinking streets with his gun and you have to get the fuck outta there.

I belong to the land-based Cats; that is, we only hit the trucks and the cold stores where the fish is kept. 'Cause the Black Cats also exist; they go out to sea and attack the boats like pirates.
I don't really know how they work; I don't know them; I know they exist but I've never seen one.
No one knows us either; no one talks about us; they know we're there but no one's ever seen us.
But truth is, no one sees what they don't want to see, not in this country . . .

Our work is hard just like anyone else's and for that we deserve respect.

Our work consists of filching; we prowl the street lights and leap onto the backs of the fish trucks where each of us has just thirty-five seconds on the truck to take at least thirty fish and get them safely into our bags.
And there's five of us . . .
So, five times thirty . . .

It wasn't just Jesus who multiplied fish!

La Jana Figueroa is a master at it too.

Television[1]

La Jana We say it and we live it;
we say it, I repeat it:
here in Talcahuano,
life's not straight, hell no!
The city is filled
with screens all up the hills.
They turn them on again
but never comprehend.
I'll never understand
why the TV's in demand.
The more I reflect,
the more I object!
All they do is lie;
all I can do is try
to tell you it can't be
that the stations on TV
come and censor our minds
again. Not this time!
Books, culture, tunes
and hip-hop crews,
they've all been erased,
faded and replaced
with nothing on those stations.
Nothing but elections
for fuckers on TV
from the presidency
and the capital city,
throwing us shit. We
won't buy from the government.
Nothing but a front!
Telling us zip,
never speaking, saying squit,
while we're here tied up,
never knowing what's up.
What's going wrong,
when the poor struggle on,
earning eighty thousand pesos
and watching every one,
while they say nothing?
They front and do nothing!
Ignorant, incredulous,

---

[1] Inspired by the 1999 track 'La vida no es recta' ('Life's Not Straight') by the hip-hop band Rezonancia. For more on the English-language rendering of the rap in this scene, see the translator's note on page 8.

we respond, rebellious.
No, I wasn't selling it.
No, I'm not selling it.
I'll give you it now
for a few coins. How
many? How much? So what?
I'm not straight-up? So what?
Bling? I got nothing!
So what, when they do nothing?
It means nothing anyway
to us who have to pay
attention in our towns
that have been knocked down.
With this nothing we'll be made
into human grenades,
exploding in their face,
when all they do is waste
time in government.
Nothing but a front!
Scratching their ties
and snorting their lines:
happy white dust
setting to a crust
with their weird caresses.
Inhaling, on their asses,
and paying the TV
to do their work we
get hit by, we few.
That's us: me and you.
We say it and we live it;
we say it, I repeat it:
here in Talcahuano,
life's not straight, hell no!
And a rhyme that's strange
runs through our veins
with marginality,
originality;
the congeniality
of living up close to reality,
to rap. I won't sing
to Congress: they bring
us nothing, do nothing.
On TV, they say nothing,
say zip, offer squit,
nothing but bullshit.
My distance is pitiful

but I'm gonna spit it all:
my soul and my hands.
Here alone I stand,
saying out loud:
I'm poor but I'm proud.

The Sea

La Jana   I like the sea at Talcahuano . . . Lots of people may say it stinks, but I like it. I like going to the beach at night and seeing all the hillsides lit up and the dark sea in its infinite immensity . . . It's so big . . .
I like climbing the hillsides too 'cause you can see the whole port from there; from the top of the hill you can see all the sea; you can even see the whole Pacific Ocean . . .
Maybe that's why one of the hills is called Centinela! 'Cause it watches the whole of the ocean like a sentinel.
I think, if you wanted to, you could stay there watching the sea every day from Centinela's highest point.
I'd like to do that: sit there my whole life watching the sea 'til I get old, working out at sea, fishing 'til I'm old.
I like the sea; I like it 'cause it's huge and hides unfathomable mysteries and places. When I was a kid they told me there's a city hidden beneath the ocean, miles and miles down.
My grandma always made up stories for me . . .
My grandma was called Herminda, but for some weird reason we all called her María; I don't know why.
Over the years my Mapuche grandma María swapped her land in the south of Chile for a little house in a neighbourhood called Hualpencillo, swapped her life for bringing up four kids, swapped her name for housework, her life for the lives of others.

My grandma always made up stories for me . . .

I know that city doesn't exist, but I like remembering my grandma telling me the story of the people beneath the sea. She used to be so happy when she told me about that city. The people in that city lived happy lives; it was like a little village under the sea . . . A happy little village under the sea . . .

Grandparents are beautiful.
They're wise.
And they tell stories . . .

My grandma always made up stories for me . . .

Sea stories . . .
Marine myths . . .
Marine life
Life at sea
Out at sea
On the high sea
Marching waves
Tidal waves
Shit on the airwaves
Trawling the depths

The ocean depths
Crying an ocean
An ocean of tears
From ocean to sea
From confused sea
To an ocean of calm
The open sea
A sea of love
A sea of lovers
Mariners
Marinas
Mario
María
And to think of all the dead people taken by the sea . . .

Earthquake

La Jana   There I was, prowling on top of a dockside street light, when suddenly there was this really loud noise like a truck crashing, and I looked at the other Cats, all surprised . . .
The whole earth started to shake; I grabbed onto the lamppost and climbed down as best I could; I couldn't let one of the electric cables land on me so I climbed down while everything was still shaking and I heard my workmates freaking out at what was happening and screaming, 'Earthquake, earthquake! Jana, get down!'; one of the Cats fell from his lamppost and landed smack against the concrete on the street which was still shaking; I tried to run over to check he was OK, but the shaking was so bad I couldn't move my legs . . . Everything was moving so much, except my legs. The lampposts swayed from side to side, the heavy cables fell down from all sides, the adobe walls collapsed like dominos and landed on whichever unlucky fucker was passing by, the windows in the houses burst like firecrackers and people ran terrified through the alleyways screaming, crying, shouting for help, showing off their tragic flannel pyjamas and Chinese cotton slippers.
People prayed and asked God to stop the earthquake. To stop the earth from moving. 'Make it fucking stop!'
It was desperate, over-the-top horrific.
We managed to reach our fellow Cat and he got up like he hadn't even felt the landing and we all hugged each other; all we could think of doing was hugging each other. The old Cats were hugging me.
They thought I'd be scared . . . They thought right: I was shitting myself.
When everything finally stopped shaking, one of the old Cats said we should go up onto the hillside, 'cause a huge wave was coming; he knew about these things and the wave might suck us up and wash us away to the depths of the sea and never bring us back.

So then I felt a huge anxiety hit my chest; I thought of my mum and I panicked. She's sick; she's stuck in bed and she must have felt like shit at that moment and if a wave came now and washed away the few buildings that were still standing, she wouldn't survive.
I didn't even know if my house had survived the earthquake; I didn't know if I'd get home and find she was OK or squashed under one of the adobe walls.
But I had faith and I thought, 'She'll be fine.'
I just had faith in God . . .
I went straight to our neighbourhood to look for her; I needed to know what had happened. Don Franco said he'd go with me; Don Franco's a bachelor, he had no one to go see, so the old guy got his truck ready and we set off to look for my mum in a sea of desperate cars honking their horns out of tune to call for help.

People's faces were terrifying; there was panic in their eyes; everyone thought this was it, our time had come; it was a horror show seeing them running around in their checked dressing gowns looking for their families, their children.
We got to my neighbourhood, Luis Emilio Recabarren, I got out of the car, saw that my house was OK, and I sigh. I ran inside and there was my mum crying, praying in her bed, just waiting for death to come and claim her.

I cried so much to see her like that, so defenceless and sad, to see her little hands pointing up to God, searching for contact, like searching for an answer; it hurt me to my soul. I took her in my arms and got her up onto the truck. Then I went back inside to pick up a few things . . .

Don Franco honked his horn like a madman waiting for me to come back outside and I tried to collect as many warm clothes for my mum as I could. I said, 'Hang on, you old fucker,' like as a joke, to calm him down. Finally I came back out and we climbed up into the truck.

And amidst the desperate sobbing of the city and the mass of debris piled up in the streets, as if a giant had been playing dominos, we drove up one of the hillsides.

Everyone knows what happened next. Two hours later, from the top of Centinela, I watched the boundless sea flood into the city and wash away its pick of fishing boats, whipping away everything in its wake, killing with no mercy and with a sound like something beyond the grave, a sound like an endless, titanic thunder destroying my homeland, flooding my Talcahuano, my city. Which, as chance would have it, means 'city of thunder' in Mapudungún . . .

And I thought of all the people who couldn't get away; I thought of the old people, I thought of the kids, I thought of the people who trusted the words of their so-called leaders and went back down to their homes 'cause they'd said there was no risk of a tsunami.

Fucking politicians fucking it up . . .
They always fuck it up . . . I always finish up fuming at those fuckers.

Then, all the pandemonium calmed down . . .

But it was only just getting started.

Kids, this is the chronicle of the Chilean earthquake of February 2010!

Aftermath

La Jana   I'm sick of standing guard, watching out for looters coming here to my neighbourhood to steal from people's houses. They even say on the local radio that they're going 'round in gangs, burgling houses and blowing them up; I say 'blowing them up' 'cause they rob them then blow them up with Molotov cocktails. And they're scary and I'm sick of it.
I'm sick of the stink from the burning tyres in the streets and the alleyways where we live; I'm sick of sticking my finger up my nose and the bogeys coming out black from all the burning rubber I breathe in from clearing away the truck tyres from the streets. Those tyres that, before they were fires and after they were on trucks, used to be the seats and swings we used in the neighbourhood for our grandparents and children. And now folks set them on fire, trying to light up the wastelands in the dark shadows of the tower blocks General Pinocchio built.

I genuinely think the earth only moved the way it did 'cause it had something to say; I don't think things like that happen for no reason; I think the earth only cut off our water and electricity to make us understand the value of that shit. Life had just gotten so fucking easy over time, and having hot water was something normal . . .
And now there's no water and no electricity either . . .
And fuck do we need them . . .
Especially water. Some places have got their power back now . . .
Not where I live, though, obviously: our neighbourhood is poor.
But some places have got power back, but still it's still hard for them having no water.

Here in Luis Emilio, since the night after the earthquake, we've kept the gangs away; we all stand here every night, always the same fuckers, standing on the curb, sharing whatever smokes we can salvage from the lootings; it's February and it's cold, freezing cold.
All the neighbours take it in turns to stand guard. People say this like it's a fucking joke but the truth is it really did take an earthquake to make the neighbourhood come together how it did.
This is one of those neighbourhoods where everyone knows each other and all the old ladies have a past.
We've always been thick as thieves 'round here, united . . .

'This neighbourhood, kids, we were fighting for it from 1962 all the way through to 1968; it was our patch and another neighbourhood wanted to take it from us, but in '68 we finally fought them off . . .' That's what Granddad Pito-Pito used to say.

And now we were still there, all in it together; right there.
And even if we didn't really know each other, we were all still in it together; right there.
Looking after our home; right there.

Thanks to the earthquake I could even talk to some of my neighbours who I'd known by sight for years but never actually spoken to; I'd only ever waved at them.
So the earthquake kinda revolutionized the place.
Everything's been different since then; there was so much love in the street, man.

Like you could breathe the briny smell of humanity in the air, even though there were smells of disaster, smells of destruction, smells of desolation, smells of despair . . .
We could breathe the smell of humanity in the air with all its splendour through our nostrils filled with black burning rubber.

The earthquake, it was a whole fucking episode . . .

And not to mention the curfew, man . . . OK, the soldiers did help us protect our houses . . . But they're so violent!
One day, at like half past nine at night, when no one had thought yet of coming out into their front yards to start guard duty, some idiots broke into the Care' Muerto Bar.
El Chacho went running to the soldiers to tell them someone was looting the Care' Muerto; I grabbed my crowbar and went out looking for the fuckers, to kick them out of my neighbourhood. But just as I was on my way to that shit-hole bar, the soldiers just took the whole thing over, shouting and shooting everywhere. I heard a voice shouting from the darkness, louder than all the neighbours. The soldier shouting.
'Down on the fucking floor! I said down on the floor, you fuckers!' And he fired twice into the air.
I just froze there, stunned; I couldn't move with the sound of the gunfire, and this soldier is shooting at the looters' legs now . . .
Then he aimed at their heads to make them get down on the ground, 'Down on the floor, you piece of shit, or I'll motherfucking kill you!'
'I steal too,' I thought, and if they found out they'd come and pump me full of lead too, maybe they don't even need to know I steal for them to do that. They're just firing to make use of their military training, just for the sake of being at war and shooting their guns; they're desperate to use their guns; they're drooling like dogs as they pick up their guns.
That's the real reason they got there so quick . . .
How could they pass up the chance to shoot some poor fucker?!
I spent the whole night thinking about that moment; I couldn't forget the soldier's voice shouting, so aggressive; I get that they're trying to bring some order to the place and arresting fuckers who aren't from here and are going 'round stealing, and not only that, stealing our fucking booze, but I don't get how these experts in khaki can exercise their power with guns . . .

That's what we're so shit-scared of, in the end . . .
The law of the strongest and the most ruthless.

I couldn't stop thinking about it until I fell asleep, and that night I was awake until four thirty a.m.

Of course by this point the neighbourhood watch was fucking pointless, all standing smoking and pissing about, singing some song by the Little Green Men – that's a rock band from Argentina – while someone played the guitar . . .
And this was while there was a curfew.
Paradoxical shit, right?
I mean because of the Little Green Men . . .
Like the soldiers . . . They wear green . . .

Anyway, while everyone celebrated and had another drink and another one – because alcohol is a gift from Saint Isabel, the food of first resort and all that shit . . . Those old-fashioned songs and those cheery drunken chats came back out and we could hear them for the first time since the earthquake.
Completely incoherent.
Dumb as fuck but fun.

Jana *re-creates them.*

Guitarist . . . If the light of today
  Is just electric.
  If the magic of today
  Is just illusion . . . (*Cries.*)

Pancho Fuck, man. Chelo never finishes the songs!
He's always halfway through and something happens, fucker!

Guitarist But listen to the fucking lyrics, Pancho, it says the light is only electric . . . And we haven't had electricity for days . . . (*Cries.*)

Pancho Fuck, Chelo, have another drink and sing that one by Pablo Milanés.

Guitarist I don't know any songs by Pablo Milanés . . .

Pancho What do you mean, 'you don't know any'? What about that one you sang that time at Rucio Chico's place?

Guitarist Which one?

Pancho That one, man, the one that goes 'na na nana nana' . . .

Guitarist (*guffaws*) Which one's that then?

Pancho Yeah, Chelo, that one, 'na na nana nana' . . . Sing it to La Jana . . .

Guitarist Oh, but Pancho, it's not 'na na nana nana', it's 'nana na nana na' . . . And it's not Pablo Milanés, it's Silvio.

Pancho Well, they're like the same . . .

Guitarist OK, let's sing that one . . . 'This is our song, sung by the sands' . . . Silvio's a fucking weird name. (*Laughs hard.*)

Pancho See? You don't ever sing a whole fucking song . . .

Guitarist It's just it's a fucking weird name, like Solomeo Paredes.

[**Pancho** What's weird about Solomeo Paredes?

Guitarist Solo. Meo. Paredes. I only. Piss. On walls.

Pancho Oh, I get it . . .[2]

Guitarist Pato Carlos, Aquiles Baeza, Alma Marcela Silva . . .

End of the re-enactment.

La Jana It's a good job Pancho didn't sing me that song . . . I'd have been embarrassed . . .

While the drunk, out-of-tune voices are happily singing in their woollen hats, I drift away watching the flames rising up from that black tyre polluting and darkening the moonlit sky with its enormous cloud, and I think.
I'm still reeling from what that aggressive soldier did; his voice is still ringing in my head . . .

The guys have decided to celebrate every aftershock that comes in the middle of the night . . . Screaming in high-pitched voices every time the earth moves. (*Aargh.*) And as they celebrate my mum nearly dies from panicking that another earthquake will come and whip our lives away again.

And I'm still thinking . . .

And I think we should have listened to the earth before she frightened us.

---

2 Translator's note: A couple of lines have been added here to try to explain the wordplay to the English-speaking audience. For the remaining three names, the wordplay is, roughly: Pato Carlos: 'pa' tocarlos' ('to touch them'); Aquiles Baeza: 'aquí les va esa' ('they like that one here'); Alma Marcela Silva: 'al mamársela, silba' ('when you suck him off, he whistles').

Elephants

La Jana I saw a terrifying programme on TV today; it's not unusual for them to show these sorts of spectacles, but this one caught my attention a bit more. It turns out that in some city like in Guatemala or Ecuador . . . one of those weird places, some nutjob who'd raped some girls fucked off to Canada not really feeling sorry for what he'd done or really having paid for his crimes . . . The whole town was furious about what the stupid fucking pond life had done; they get together in a raging mob and go to look for him in jail and they knocked down the doors and went to find him right where he was and they beat the fucking shit out of him . . .
And then they lynched him.
They killed the fucker . . .
That shit really shook me up; I thought when people take justice into their own hands no fucker stands a chance . . .
That shit wouldn't happen here in Chile though; people are fucking lazy here.

They always say on the TV how the price of the metro and the bus is going up in Santiago but the people there never protest shit . . . They're lazy as fuck and they think they're so fucking special.
And I also thought if we did the same thing with the looters, taking justice into our own hands . . .
It'd be tough as . . .
I know in some places in other times they used to chop thieves' hands off . . .
Heavy shit, right . . .
All the important people I know use their hands . . .

All the workers for example, or the artists, the carpenters hammer with their hands, the painters paint with their hands, musicians play with their hands, singers sing with their mouths . . . but they still have to, like, hold the microphone!
Everyone uses their hands.
I don't know what I'd do if I lost my hands; I'd get depressed, I guess.
I'd have to try talking for a living, just using my mouth and my head and nothing else.

Still, there was that time I was watching TV one morning and there was a thing about South Africa where the elephants were painting with their trunks; that was some incredible shit . . .
It's weird enough not painting with your hands and painting with your nose instead . . .
But imagine an elephant's trunk!
This massive mammal picked up the paintbrush with its trunk and it could paint on a canvas with colours from the palette. And this elephant didn't just make random marks, it didn't paint random shit; no, man, it really painted.
It started with black paint on the paintbrush and painted this really weird shit, something that didn't make sense, but it was already entertaining, watching an elephant with a paintbrush in its trunk instead of a peanut, it's entertaining . . .
I say a peanut, 'cause that's the only shit elephants ever think about.

So there's Dumbo painting away when suddenly you started to see that the elephant wasn't just painting random lines, these lines were starting to make the shape of an elephant from the side, with a body and everything, with a tail and four legs and its trunk raised up to the sky, like an elephant praying . . .
An elephant praying, resplendent on the canvas of an elephant painter.
And all the people there clapping and celebrating this giant animal's self-portrait, but the cherry on the fucking cake is when the elephant painter takes another paintbrush and starts painting a flower in the praying elephant's trunk and then with a little orange paintbrush crowns it with all the little petals on the flower pointing up to the sky . . .
Mind blown . . .
It was fucking incredible, I got all the fucking feels, my heartbeat went really weird; I was totally in love with this elephant painter and the elephant praying.
They were fucking amazing . . .

But then I started thinking maybe behind all this beauty from the animal kingdom there was a secret story that was like torture for the poor animal; like I imagined the elephant's owners forcing the poor creature to learn to paint on those canvases and then selling them for a hundred dollars.
Plus I bet the poor little grey beast never saw any of the money.
So then I got really angry and I kept on thinking how shit the world is, 'cause even though this spectacle of the elephant is really sweet and gives you massive hope to keep on going through life, it's a horrible image of how animals get trained.
I just tried to put myself in the mind of that poor animal.
What would it think?
It must have to paint the same thing every day, and it must be sad that its life is the life of an elephant painter and not a free elephant wandering through the countryside like its ancestors.
That's why it paints that shit . . .
So sad . . .

Still, it was a fucking good painter though!
Well, they are very intelligent . . .
And they say they have a good memory, too . . .
Elephants are fucking amazing!
That's why on the other side of the world they're gods and people worship them.
In the land of Buddha, elephants are like gods . . .

Exchange

La Jana   It's really weird how we get given a nationality when we're born.
I didn't choose to be Chilean, but I was born here so I'm forced to meet all kinds of dumb obligations like paying tax . . . Why is that?
Money's stupid to begin with anyway; if the world worked by swapping things the cake would be different, bigger and tastier.
And I bet we'd all have a chance to taste it too, 'cause there'd be no people working for other people . . .
It's so unfair how nearly everyone in the world has to work just so some other people just get to do as they please . . .
They cut the cake into eight pieces but still only seven people eat.
The fuckers even cheat each other!

If we all just took care of our own needs and didn't work to earn a certain amount of money but just worked to meet our priorities, no one would go around stealing; people could produce things and we wouldn't have to wait for someone else to give our work value.
Say I've got some potatoes, for example.
So I go and I hand out sacks of potatoes in exchange for rice or other things I need, and I don't just mean food, you could get all sort of things you need, you could exchange your work for someone else's, it'd be that simple, no one would value any one person's work over anyone else's.
For example I could swap some sacks of potatoes for one of those king-size beds or a cute dress or cinema tickets or tickets for travelling, or some CDs . . .
People could choose whatever the fuck they like!
I think I'd get a dress or maybe tickets too, tickets to travel, to go see the world and get out of this country that's so far away from all the others.
And fly on a plane; that must be cool.
I'd go to so many places, Rome, Ecuador, Bethlehem . . .
I'd go to South Africa just to mess up the fucker who owns the painting elephant.
And I'd get out of Chile; people here think they're the shit, they think we're a European country but they do everything wrong, the fuckers sell off the land like they're sick in the head and then they leave us with nowhere to live.
And I've got a right to a little patch of land . . .
I was born here . . .
I'm here! Hello!
I'm alive! I'm from here! I should have a right to something.

Why do I have to buy a place to be able to rest? A place to take care of my mum in, a place to take care of my garden and my animals.
Is that fair? I don't think so; it's not fair to spend thirty or forty years paying for a shitty house when really, as a human being, if there's room for everyone, I deserve, we deserve to each live on our little piece of land, where we can grow our own vegetables and raise our own animals . . .
Or our own children, if you're into that.
And I mean land, not a room, not a crappy apartment in some building.

I think flats are the new global model for working-class living, people living piled on top of each other, floor on floor. Eternal floors going all the way up to twenty-five or more. Spaces stuck together with dreams and the muffled screams of their slave-driver bosses who live in houses that aren't houses but palaces where their butlers, cooks and chauffeurs line up when they're not at home in their working-class flat with three kids and their partner or in a working-class house in the ass-end of fucking nowhere.

It's not fair, there's no justice, there's no respect.

From Word to Deed

La Jana There's no respect.
But it's best not to speak; words carry in the wind.
I've got the gift of the gab, but best I keep it schtum.

The fish dies through its mouth, they say: careless talk costs lives.

And anyway, a word, to the wise, is enough . . .
To foolish words, deaf ears . . .
From word to deed is a long road indeed. Twixt ear and lips, little slips. A closed mouth gathers no flies. A mouth that's discreet keeps secrets in the street.

Although, they do also say silence gives consent . . .
And it's talking that helps us understand each other.

But that's not enough, with so many people blind from not wanting to see, or asking for pears from an elm tree, or trying to block out the sun with a single finger . . .
One-eyed men made kings in the kingdom of the blind.
I'd say to them: all that glitters is not gold.
One day we'll have to bite the hand that feeds us.
Because we reap what we sow.
There's no deadline that does not come and no debt that goes unpaid.

Enough of the biggest fish eating the smallest!
Enough of those who can doing and those who can't . . . being their bosses!
Why should we have to cry to get fed?
I say, they boil beans everywhere: everything's the same wherever you go. We all sit down to shit.
Everyone knows when their shoes are too tight: we all know our own weaknesses.

The crows have risen up and they're plucking out our eyes, but soon there'll be plenty of us killing two birds with one stone. And all of those people who humiliated us since we were kids and didn't let us grow will fall down. All those people who warned us: 'Eat sardines when you're young: shit fishbones when you're old'. Be grateful for the scraps of food you have.
All those people who ruined the beautiful bay of Talcahuano.
All those fuckers and their fucking mothers and their fucking daughters and the fucking blanket that covers them.
If you want peace, prepare for war!
'Cause he who lives by the sword dies by the sword.
I'll make sure of that . . .
I'll look the gift horse in the mouth, tempt fate, root out the problem, and work out who's pulling the strings.
'Cause one by one they'll start to appear, the ones who'll get rid of the big fish swimming in the seas of ignorance and money.
They'll start to appear, the ones who'll wipe out the shade-hoggers keeping the best trees for themselves and telling us to keep our feet on the ground, not to look up at the sun in case it blinds us.

I don't believe it takes a thief to catch a thief.
I'm a thief.
And those fucking thieves haven't caught me! I'm not that stupid . . .
Besides, the thief who robs a thief is forgiven for a hundred years. And if there's no harm in asking, there's no crime in taking.

I know every saying there is, all by the book.
And I use them in any situation.

A good cockerel will crow in any henhouse.
'Cause curiosity doesn't kill this cat.
'Cause a bad weed never dies.
'Cause not all cats look black in the night.
Some of us are grey . . .
Some of us just steal.
The rabbit said, 'This warren sucks', so he jumped to a new hole. If it stops being funny, jump out like a bunny.
The way this system shares things out, we're going nowhere fast.

This sharing out – where the person doing the sharing out gets the biggest share, and which is fucking unfair – fucked all of us over, bit by bit, so many of us, 'cause we never made it to captain, only to sailor.
In this world, where if the sea were made of wine everyone would be a sailor . . .
Where from swimming and swimming so much we'll end up on the shore drowned by a tsunami or cirrhosis caused by the tax system.

'Cause right now we're really fucked . . .
We're more lost than Lieutenant Bello.

[Lieutenant Bello was a Chilean pilot who got lost in his plane . . . Never mind.][3]

No to injustice, I say . . .
Things should be fair for everyone!
Everything for everyone, or nothing for anyone.
No more short-lived happiness in the house of the poor man.
Don't give me that bullshit!
Throw that bone to some other dog!
Thing should be fair here.
Let's call a spade a spade, bread, bread and wine, wine.
To every sheep her mate, and nothing more . . .
We're all brothers and sisters in the end.
In lean times, let's be thick as thieves.
The house is small but the heart is big.
And there it is . . . With you through thick and thin.
So we can do it together . . .
Let's sow parsley in May and have it all year round!
Yeah, one hand washes the other, man. And together, they can wash the face!

---

3 This line does not appear in the Spanish original. For more on the translation of the proverbs and sayings in this scene, see the translator's note on page 8.

The Gawping Fish

La Jana I was at work one day . . . This was really freaky.
Something weird happened.
It was late already and we hadn't done a single truck.
Suddenly one started appearing through the mist; slowly, silently, lights off, trying to sneak by unnoticed.
It must have been a new driver; all the new drivers are scared of us so they turn their lights off when they go through the hairiest streets to try and sneak under the radar. They're so fucking stupid . . .
Those are the drivers we fuck up most of all, to make them respect us right from the start.

We made the usual signals and jumped down to start stealing.
I jumped down onto the truck, sleek, fast as a wildcat, picked up my first fish . . .
But then like a flash of lightning hitting my eyes, the fish stared at me.
It looked me in the eyes like it was wanting to say something and as this fish was staring at me with its fishy eyes I froze.
Six years I've been doing this job and this was the first time a fish had looked me in the eyes.
And the fucker just stared at me, fixed.
Its eyes piercing into mine.
I felt paralysed.

I heard someone say 'Thirty', so it was nearly time to jump down and I'd only picked up one fish. One with a singular stare, but still only one. One fucking staring fish.
Don Pedro said 'Five', and we all jumped off together.

I jumped down with this goggle-eyed fish in my trouser pocket while the other Cats had their bags full; they hurled a whole salad of insults at me, a salad only pronounceable by someone who belongs to the Chilean race: 'My sister's pussy, motherfucker!'
And I had to agree with them. They were right, the night was nearly over already, we'd only attacked one truck, and there was me, the silly fucker with only one fish.

And after they'd finished shouting 'The whore that popped me out!' and 'Filthy, soap-dodging fuck-hole!' I left without saying a single word. I walked back to Luis Emilio with the fish in my trouser pocket. It was cold, sticky and wet, all its stink trickling down my leg, all its stench of death.

I always smell of fish because of the job I do, but the smell of this fish was different. The smell of this fish was inconceivable . . .

I got home, walked through the yard and went straight to my room.
I turned on the light . . . The stink was unbearable.
I took the fish out from my trouser pocket and put it on the table.

I stared it in the eye for a while.
The fish was still looking at me.

And I kept staring back at it; it was something so mysterious when I looked at it; there was something in that fish that frightened me, intimidated me, so much so that I didn't want to go on looking at it.

I don't think anyone had ever looked at me that way in my life before. I mean, OK, my dad looked at me like that, especially when he was pissed off with me. And I always avoided his gaze when he was pissed off with me.
I remember one time he caught me stealing a ten-thousand-peso note from his wallet and he looked at me right in the eyes with this furious look . . . I tried to slip away without saying anything, unnoticed; I just wanted to turn around and get out of there. But he kicked me so hard up the ass that I had to sleep face down for four nights until the pain eased off.

And the truth is . . . now I think about it . . . that fish reminded me of my dad . . . It's stupid, but it reminded me of my dad.

Maybe 'cause both fuckers were dead!

The fish was still there and I felt so stupid because I was scared of a shitty fish. And so just like my friends had done to me, I hurled a whole salad of insults at it, a salad only pronounceable by someone who belongs to the Chilean race.

Fucking fish motherfucker!
What are you looking at with those fucking eyes of yours? What are you looking at, shit-brained fucking monkey, motherfucking toad, thousand-whore-fucking rat, sonofabitch fish?

And after that I thought, why do all our swear words have to do with animals?

The Ending

La Jana   But the fish was still there . . .
And I was still there staring at it like someone stupid.
And it's no big fucking deal; a dead fish is just a dead fish . . . Maybe if it was alive.
But this fish was dead, for fuck's sake!

I think maybe the fish has been looking at me all night because it didn't want me to forget my dad when he caught me stealing and 'cause now I was stealing again it was looking me in the eyes like he looked at me.
Why do these things have to happen to me when I steal? It's like someone's watching me from beyond Centinela Hill and sending me signs and trying to tell me something through the medium of a fish.
I steal because I have to.

That fish has burst into my story and given it endings I never expected; that fish looking at me straight in the eyes has come to do something else to my hands; things don't happen for no reason, they don't happen just because. That sonofabitch fish came to me straight to tell me something I shouldn't forget; it came to see me from beyond its death, its animal death.
Maybe it came because I steal . . .
But I don't care what the fish might think of me.
I might even say I don't care what all of you think of me.
I steal and I'll keep on stealing, 'cause I don't wanna be part of your system; I wanna stay an undercover criminal 'cause that way I can live in peace; 'cause that way I can do something for my people, selling to them at a different price; 'cause I don't want this fish to lose its head at the hands of the thieving fish company.
It's better for me to take care of my people.
Besides, I steal from a company that sets the price of the fish up in the clouds.
What, so it's better for some fuckers to pay the local fishermen three pesos and then sell the fish for up to five times what they bought it for?
Isn't it better to take work away from those companies, who exploit the old women who fillet hundreds of hake every day and only earn five fucking coins at the end of the month?
'Cause that's how the whole system works. So I'm out; I don't wanna stay here sunk in this fucking neo-capitalist-liberal model of life. Or whatever it's called . . .
That fish staring at me made me realize I really don't want anything from this place.
I don't want laws, or examples, or morality, or religion, or nationality.

I don't want this shitty country that thinks it's such a shining example when it doesn't so much as glimmer, because they even fuck up the countryside, building power stations, cutting down trees, mercilessly deforesting the mythological forests that have done nothing to us except let us breathe with patience and eternal silence.
This miserable state that fucks up our education and forgets that learning and studying are a human right . . .
This ridiculous nation that hands its seas over to the boats from Hong Kong that come to dump their black shit alongside the multinationals selling kerosene.

And even so we accept it . . . Of course.
It's like the song says: you'll see how in Chile they love any friend who's a foreigner . . .

> This shitty country that mimics the great capitals of the world, destroys its land, sells off its minerals, its water, sells its customs and denies us our identity. Banning the wisdom of myths and legends, burying the native heroes and heroines who die in aboriginal silence.
>
> And as for the few indigenous people who do remain, who, by the way, were the first inhabitants of these lands, they make them slaves of a capitalist regime that exploits them like cattle and lines them up under a single constitution.
>
> Indigenous people who can no longer have a religion because what they practise is now called superstition; their art isn't art, but traditional crafts; their language isn't a language but a dialect; they're no longer human beings, they're human resources. Made for producing.
>
> To all of them, those forced out by neglect, forced to become beggars, prostitutes and criminals . . . thieves with open veins and twisted hearts.
>
> The persecuted, those scorned by the conquest. They, only they, those poor, small people who have known how to keep the best of these lands not for themselves but for all humanity, the memory of community as a possible way of life.
>
> America, the centre of the empire of greed and ambition, could have been the centre of a home for the whole world and not a concentration camp. A world that perhaps the world itself wanted to be before it was even the world.
>
> To those who have known how to preserve the indispensable memory of things, so that the adventure of the universe, the walk of the everyday, is not a continuous invitation to pain and death. Those who believe in that balance between identity and nature. And not in a world like ours where the water, the land, the air and our souls have been poisoned.
>
> How could the legacy of the indigenous people not be important? They were the only ones who knew how to take care of nature. Theirs are cultures that can't understand how land can be sold, because they can't understand how anyone could sell their own mother.[4]

Isn't it time finally to listen to what really matters, to what the earth is trying to say, to what the earth wants to shout out, shaking the whole planet?

Wake up! Life is not the future; it's happening now.

Gullible motherfucking cock-sucking fuckers!
I'm the only one with a monster in my heart!

But I'm no one.
To this world, I'm no one.
All I am is me.
Just me.
La Jana.

---

4 Based on the poem 'Los nadie' ('The Nobodies') by, and interviews with, Eduardo Galeano.

A Ranch for the Lost Boys

Sebastián Eddowes-Vargas

Translated by the playwright

A Palace Made of Debris

By Sebastián Eddowes-Vargas

When I was fourteen, I was obsessed with films. I could understand movies but I couldn't understand life, so I looked at the world through the screen.

I grew up in Perú during the dictatorship of Alberto Fujimori. But even if the people around me discussed politics all day long, I couldn't grasp what was going on. I didn't get why everyone was so scared, why everyday life had to be so violent. Movies happened on the other side of the screen. It was easier to cry for the pain of others than look into our own wounds.

Perú doesn't have a film industry. It has grown in the last years, but it is still small. Foreign films allowed me to see the world through the eyes of others. I will never forget the afternoon I saw Stanley Kubrick's *2001: A Space Odyssey*, lying in bed with my eyes glued to a small screen, my heart pumping in my throat and thinking, "I want to do this too." Not having to disconnect HAL in space, of course, but making movies.

Michelangelo Antonioni became my favorite director, so I watched *L'Eclisse* obsessively. I had an aesthetic rapture watching a close-up of tomatoes in Pedro Almodóvar's *Mujeres al Borde de un Ataque de Nervios*, and I sang *Soy Infeliz* as if it was me who was abandoned by my man. Watching movies was something I'd do alone. But sometimes I would get high with friends and watch Alan Parker's *Pink Floyd – The Wall*; force my classmates to appreciate the cinematography of *A Clockwork Orange*; organize field trips to see Satoshi Kon's *Perfect Blue*; or spend the night with my best friend Shanti, watching *Grease* first and then Bob Guccione's *Caligula* until dawn. The uncensored version. We were fifteen and had no idea what we were watching, but of course we had the best time. My parents tried to keep the movies age appropriate but my hunger for film was bigger.

I loved movies so much I needed to make my own, but there was no money and I had no idea how to start. Cellphones were rudimentary and we couldn't afford cameras. We borrowed one or two and tried, but failed. I had amazing friends, crazy enough to try weird projects that were never finished. Later, I discovered theater. It was cheaper. All we needed was time, stubbornness, and stealing furniture from our families.

A Ranch for the Lost Boys is built over these memories. I created Benjamin Murieta as a surrogate of teenage Sebastián, overwhelmed by unfulfilled passions that devour him. Both of us have this urge to create stories to shape the chaos we inhabit, because we can't keep seeing life only through the eyes of others. That is one of the consequences of living in a post-colonial land: we've been taught to think of ourselves as subaltern, with words that are not ours, with ideas forged to talk about others. We gotta create our own languages, not *ex nihilo*, but with rags and leftovers. *A Ranch* is a palace built with debris and proud of it. Like Oswald de Andrade, the characters of the play cannibalize culture, and like Vicente Huidobro, they yell, "*Non serviam*!", all while wearing dresses, like Copi's characters.

I started writing *A Ranch* in 2014. I've written many plays, and none of them have demanded so much as this one. It's a beast that keeps asking to be fed. The first draft was fifteen minutes long, then I wrote a terrible three-hour version. And I kept rewriting.

In 2019, it was produced in Perú for the first time and read in London thanks to the excellent work of Global Voices Theatre. In 2021 I rewrote it for a new production, this time directed by my sibling Rosa Victoria Chauca Gutierrez, one of the most extraordinary artists I know. Her work made this play so much better. It had another production in 2022. Having three professional productions of the same play in four years is very uncommon in Peruvian theater. And *A Ranch* is always looking for new homes.

To be born and to grow, this play needed lots of co-conspirators. The list is huge. I must lovingly mention Rosa Victoria Chauca Gutierrez (always), Almiro Andrade, Fabricio Ascárate, Jorge Black Tam, Valeria García Cannock, Nae Hanashiro, Karl Hawkins, Luis Alberto León, Sylvia Majo, Sergio Maggiolo, Juan Osorio, Javier Quiroz, Sebastián Ramos, Gonzalo Rodríguez Risco, Claudia Sacha, Carlos Victoria. And even if they did not directly work on the play, it owes a tremendous debt to my parents, Espalda de Bogo, Andreas Andreou, Sharnelle Branyon, Luis Daniel Cárdenas, Arturo Dávila, Krista Dobson, Charo Francés, Pilar Millones, Chantal Rodriguez, Margarita Saona, Catherine Sheehy, Puka T'ika, Arístides Vargas, Gina Vargas, Mario Zanatta, Renzo Zegarra. I'm blessed to collaborate with extraordinary humans.

* * *

Sebastián Eddowes-Vargas (he/they) is a Peruvian theater artist and scholar, author of *La Muerte Danza* (with Espalda de Bogo), *Nunca Estaremos en Broadway* (with Rodrigo Yllaric), *Fronteiras* (with Colectivo Âmbar), *Hasta Que Choque El Hueso* (with Mario Zanatta), *Debut* (with Caro Black Tam), *Una Historia de (Poli)Amor*, *Can The Peruvian Speak?*, among others. His academic and artistic work has been presented in Belgium, Brazil, Canada, Colombia, Costa Rica, Ecuador, Peru, UK, and USA, receiving several awards. Currently, they are a DFA candidate at the David Geffen School of Drama at Yale, with the dissertation *Post-National Dramaturgies of the Américas, or, The Nation Fails*, and a Lecturer at Boston University.

World Premiere

El Rancho de los Niños Perdidos, at Casa Amaru (Lima, Perú), October 2019, directed by Sebastián Eddowes-Vargas and produced by Fabricio Ascárate.

Additional Productions

El Rancho de los Niños Perdidos, at Centro Cultural Ricardo Palma (Lima, Perú), April 2021, directed by Rosa Victoria Chauca Gutiérrez.
El Rancho de los Niños Perdidos, at Casa El Grito (Trujillo, Perú) in June 2022, directed by Gustavo Ramos.

Additional recognition includes:

Sala de Parto Award, 2015 (Lima, Perú)
Script published by Teatro La Plaza, 2019 (Lima, Perú)
Global Latin American Voices, 2019 (London, UK)

Characters

This is a play written for three actors.
Actor B, *who will turn into* **Benjamín Murieta**
Actor S, *who will turn into Alexander Porfirievich Zinatov, also known as* **Sashka**
Actor M, *who will turn into Francesco Rossi, now known as* **Michel**
*All other characters (***Ingmar Bergman***, ***Wim Wenders***, ***Anita Ekberg***, ***Hans Butzer***,* **Hosts**, **Interviewer**, *etc.) will be played by these actors.*

There MUST be obvious differences between the bodies of the actors and the bodies of the characters in terms of age, race, gender, national origin, etc. The decisions you make will tell different stories.

NOTE ON MICHEL: Michel is an impossible character, who does not want to be categorized in any way. Michel wants to divest from history. Some days this is easier than others. If clothes are used to perform gender, culture, age, convention, Michel's costumes must break with these.

Place

A Ranch for the Lost Boys, an impossible place somewhere in what was the USSR. From here, the characters will go across Europe.

Time

Now. 1989. 1984. And also before that.

Notes on Staging

A Ranch for the Lost Boys *tells impossible love stories in an impossible space. What we will see on stage is three bodies gathered to tell them. The actors must speak as themselves, and won't pretend to be others. They will occupy the space and borrow words and characters. An audience must feel they could be any of these characters. I don't want them to be seen as "others." Also, the cosmopolitanism in this play is intentionally absurd. Avoid accents for the three protagonists. Speak with your voice.*
    This play can be staged with very little design. Most clothes and objects should be borrowed from other productions, found at vintage stores, or brought from the houses of the artists (or their families).
    One last note, about the music. This is a play about how three kids expelled from history got into spaces that were never meant for them. The same is true about the music. Don't use it to create an illusion of being in the USSR. Invade the stage with sounds. Maybe Rubén Blades. Maybe Ana Gabriel. Or Britney Spears.

Prologue

The doors open. The audience enters. The music is loud.

Choose a song we all know. Is this a day for ABBA? Beyoncé? Bad Bunny? What are you feeling?

*The three **Actors** are ready to welcome the audience. They are not yet playing characters.*

They sing. They start conversations with the newcomers. They invite them to dance.

They are not "acting"; they are creating a shared space.

Take photos, post them on social media. Destroy the distances between audience and the performers. Create a space for shared pleasure and complicity. We'll play together. Make this party happen.

*When we are ready to start, the **Actors** call the stage manager and ask them to stop the music.*

***Actor B** stands on the stage and asks for silence.*

They ask for a volunteer, who will read the next lines for the whole audience.

> Good evening. Welcome to *A Ranch for the Lost Boys*, a two-act play, written by Peruvian playwright Sebastián Eddowes-Vargas.
> The show you'll see tonight is directed by _____ and produced by _____. It has a running time of _____ minutes.
> Please, take a moment to turn off or silence your cellphones and other devices.
>
> Thank you.

Actor M   We are the cast of tonight's production.

Actor B   My name is _____. Tonight,[1] I'll be Benjamín Murieta. A twenty-one-year-old boy, born and raised in Perú.

Actor S   My name is _____. Tonight, I'll be Alexander Porfirievich Zinatov, also known as Sashka. The best filmmaker in this world. My character is around fifty-five years old.

Actor M   My name is _____. Tonight, I'll be Michel. Someone who was Italian and who was an actor.

An abrupt change in rhythm. The next lines are fast, fast, fast.

Actor B   The story you'll see never happened.

Actor S   Because it can't happen.

---

[1] If the show is not performed at night, change "tonight" in these lines to "today," "this morning," or "this afternoon."

Actor M   We'll tell you an impossible myth.

Actor B   Every myth starts in an exotic, faraway place. We begin in a land lost in the middle of South America.

Actor S   Perú.

Actor B   In the political and economic center of the country.

Actor M   Lima.

Actor B   We'll take you to a time before time. The end of the first administration of former president Alan Damián García Pérez.

Actor S   1989.

Actor M   Perú just hit rock bottom! One of the worst crises in its history!

Actor B   Hyperinflation. War. Scarcity. Military repression. Curfews.

Actor S   Benjamín Murieta is twenty-one years old.

Actor B *becomes* **Benjamín** *and speaks to the audience.*

Benjamín   Everything started in the Cinematógrafo de Barranco. An old, small movie theater. Lost between the small streets of a big city, a couple of blocks from the ocean. With ancient seats that shriek in the dark.
This is where you go when you're done with Hollywood. It's a place that dreams.
Once, I blew the candles of my birthday cake, and wished that every movie theater was as special as this one. One should not share their wishes, but it's OK. It will never happen.
My Lima is a harsh city. Grey, dirty, smells like pee. It can blow up in your face at any time. Someone must have designed it to crush your bones every day.
I miss it every fucking day. As if I lack a part of my body. But I'll never return.
One night, the Cinematógrafo showed a movie with a German name: *Tiefblauen Morgen*. The director was Polish, Alexander Porfirievich Zinatov, and it was filmed in Belarus. It is the best movie ever made. I saw it three times.
When you find something this precious, there is only one thing you can do.
Pack your bags, walk across the screen, and meet the artist on the other side.

Act One

Scene One

Sashka *working in his private office.* **Benjamín** *enters.*

Actor M *is somewhere on stage. They will be present during most of Act One.*

Benjamín   Alexander?

Sashka *stops to see who is there. Beat.*

Benjamín   I'm here. Finally.

Sashka   Who is this?

Benjamín   Sorry. It's me, Benjamín Murieta. So nice to meet you in person.

He tries to shake **Sashka**'s *hand.* **Sashka** *does not.*

Sashka   This is a private space . . .

Benjamín   I didn't want to bother you, I'll see you later. Where is my room?

Sashka   Can you tell me who are you and what are you doing in my office?

Benjamín   Benjamín Murieta. Remember? The Peruvian who wrote from Lima to visit you.

Sashka   I don't know who you are. You don't have an appointment and you are not welcomed.

Benjamín   Apologies. I didn't mean to . . .

Sashka   I am a busy man, Mr. Murieta. The boys will show you the way out.

Benjamín   You invited me, Mr. Zinatov. Don't you remember? I sent you a script I wrote. *The Malaise of Dawn.* Your letter praised my work. Remember?

He gives **Sashka** *a letter.* **Sashka** *reads it.*

Sashka   Mr. Murieta. What is the date in this message?

Benjamín   February, 1989.

Sashka   That was how long ago?

Benjamín   Five months?

Sashka   Almost seven, Mr. Murieta.

Benjamín   I'm sorry. I couldn't come earlier. Coming to Europe takes time.

Sashka   Did you cross the ocean just to see me?

Benjamín   You invited me to stay.

Sashka   Reread the letter, please.

Benjamín   What?

Sashka   "If you happen to be around in the following weeks, feel welcome to *visit* my Ranch."

Benjamín   So?

Sashka   No one invited you to stay. Have a coffee, maybe, but that's it.

Benjamín   How else could I get here if I was not staying?

Sashka   I tried to be polite. I answer a couple of hundreds of letters each month. I didn't remember yours.

Benjamín   Could I at least have some of that coffee?

Sashka   I don't have any right now. This is a busy time. Please, leave.

Benjamín   No, no, no. You can't do that!

Sashka   Who do you think you are? This is my house and you have no right . . .

Benjamín   What do you expect me to do?

Sashka   I don't give shelter to random kids knocking on my door.

Benjamín   I thought that was why you created a Ranch for the Lost Boys.

Sashka   It doesn't work like that.

Benjamín   Please, sir. I beg you. I have nowhere to go. I don't have any money.

Sashka   You should have thought of that before.

Benjamín   You don't know how hard it was to get here . . .

Sashka   I don't care!

Benjamín   My country is in a crisis. People stand in infinite lines to get some food. Bombs are exploding in the streets. Perú will collapse at any time!

Sashka   Mr. Murieta . . .

Benjamín   And you can't make movies there. We don't have the money, Mr. Zinatov! I can spend my life dreaming with film but that will never happen. It fucking sucks. The thing I care about the most in this life is directing movies, but I'll never get to do that. And one day I discovered your work . . .

Sashka   Kissing my butt won't . . .

Benjamín   Nobody cares about it in Perú, just me. I fell in love with your films. So I sent you a letter. And I receive a response. A way out of that impossible country where I had to be born.

Sashka   That letter was not . . .

Benjamín   Nobody believed in me. Then, the best filmmaker *in this world* says yes, you are a good writer, come see me . . . I did everything I could. I worked my ass off, but in my country you don't earn enough to leave. I tried sex work, but only made pennies. You know how expensive it is to migrate? You know only the fucking bourgeoisie can do it? I did what anyone would have done. I stole money from my grandfather. He saves dollars in his mattress; he can't trust the banks. My grandfather filed a police report. For stealing money he didn't need. He has enough to live until he dies, but that fucker never gave me a penny. He wants to die with that money! And won't give it to me! So I took it. If I return to my country I'll go to jail. I have no home, Mr. Zinatov. I got on a plane, got lost in Europe. And got to the most wonderful place in the world! And you want to kick me out? I have no home, Mr. Zinatov. I have no home.

A beat.

Sashka   How can I know you are not lying?

Benjamín   I wouldn't.

Sashka   You could be a spy.

Benjamín   I can show you documents . . .

Sashka   They could be fake. These are hard times, Mr. Murieta. You don't open the doors of your house in a war. Even if your heart is moved.

A beat. **Benjamín** *points to a pocket watch on the table. This is his last chance.*

Benjamín   Is that the clock from *Tiefblauen Morgen*?

Sashka   What?

Benjamín   On your table. Is that the clock from your movie *Tiefblauen Morgen*?

Sashka   Yes.

Benjamín   Critics claim it is a symbol of time. They are wrong.

Sashka   You think you know better than the critics?

Benjamín   I might. Claiming it is a symbol of time is too easy, and doesn't make sense with the scene after the wedding, when the clock is buried. You can't get rid of time. No. It is a symbol of an absent father. The model must be Swiss, or German, produced just before World War II, where the father fought. Your character does not have anything else from him, and carries it to feel less alone. Less . . . plucked off. I cried so much with your movie. I don't have a dad. The son of a bitch left me and didn't leave anything. Not even a clock. I haven't read anyone claiming that but I'm right. I must be. Am I? Please tell me. Am I right?

An impossible silence.

Sashka   Tomorrow, breakfast will be served at four. At four thirty we'll be outside to film the dusk. Take the room under this office. Don't be late. Now leave. I really need to work.

Benjamín *smiles, scared.* **Sashka** *doesn't.*

Benjamín Thanks. This means a lot. Thank you.

Sashka *won't answer. He is back to the documents.*

Scene Two

Actor M   Ten days after his arrival, Benjamín breaks into Zinatov's office. Again.

Benjamín   Mr. Zinatov?

Sashka   I am busy right now, boy.

Benjamín   I'm sorry to interrupt . . .

Sashka   Then don't.

Benjamín   I've been trying to talk to you for some days but you never seem to have time.

Sashka   I don't have time now.

Benjamín   There is a problem with your script.

Sashka *gets increasingly angry as he speaks.*

Sashka   Five whole years working on *Le Scoglieri nella Baia*. Five years of writing with a brilliant team of artists. This is the best script that . . .

Benjamín   *Tiefblauen Morgen* is better.

Sashka   Excuse me?

Benjamín   *Le Scoglieri nella Baia* won't be better than *Tiefblauen Morgen*.

Sashka   Get out.

Benjamín   In scene three . . .

Sashka   You don't understand the script. It is written in Italian.

Benjamín   I borrowed a dictionary from the library.

Sashka   OK. OK. Two minutes. I'll listen. But if you're wrong, you won't talk to me for two weeks.

Benjamín   I don't buy the beginning. The father stays too long with his son. He should have left before.

Sashka   Human motivations are strange.

Benjamín   Why does the father abandon his family?

Sashka   Because he looks at his offspring and sees they have nothing in common. He hates the child, he must renounce everything he wants to take care of him. He only stays for his wife. When she dies . . .

Benjamín   The wife dies eight months before. He wouldn't stay so long.

Sashka   No one abandons a son in a day.

Benjamín   He must have made up his mind before. You wrote a reckless character who doesn't think, he just acts, acts, acts. Like me. You need to start the movie two scenes later and cut the breakfast sequence.

Sashka   There is important information in that sequence . . .

Benjamín   False. I revised the whole script with that hypothesis. Nothing really changes if the audience doesn't know the backstory. The problem with the film is that you want to say things in the name of Alexander Porfirievich Zinatov. They become annoying. There is a conflict between the needs of the work and the needs of the author and that is damaging your baby.

A beat. **Benjamín** *realizes he fucked up.*

Benjamín   Shit. Sorry. I mean . . . I didn't want to be disrespectful. Your script is brilliant, it will make a wonderful movie. The thing is that . . .

Sashka   Shut up.

A beat.

Tomorrow we begin filming at ten. Meet me at six, sharp, in the projections room. You should start your film education. Now, out.

Benjamín   Will you follow my advice?

Sashka   OUT!

Scene Three

Sashka *is in the projections room. We just need two chairs facing the audience.* **Sashka** *sits down. After a moment,* **Benjamín** *enters running.*

This scene must be fast, fast, fast. It is a duel between two sharp minds.

Benjamín I am so sorry, Mr. Zinatov. I . . .

Sashka Eight minutes late.

Benjamín I had a problem with the shower . . .

Sashka Wake up earlier. You don't have to take a bus to get here . . .

Benjamín It won't happen again . . .

Sashka I could be doing something else. I could be resting . . .

Benjamín I understand perfectly, Mr. Zinatov.

Sashka You know how valuable my time is?

Benjamín Yes. I don't understand why you want to waste it discussing this.

A beat. **Sashka** *smiles a little bit, for the first time in the show.*

Sashka Don't get too clever with me, boy.

Speaks in Portuguese to the person in charge of the projections, who we don't hear or see.

Nelson! Projeta o filme que eu selecionei.
Eu sei. Eu sei. Desculpe pelo atraso. O menino idiota chegou tarde demais.

Benjamín Menino idiota?

Sashka Nelson is pissed at you. I made him wake up early and you arrived late.

Benjamín *sits. They start watching a movie that we don't see. But you can project the sequence.*

Sashka Do you know what this is?

Benjamín Of course. *Battleship Potemkin.*

Sashka (*starts lecturing*) Directed by Sergei Eisenstein in 1925. Produced by Mosfilm. Real cinema! Unlike American films. American films are corrupted at their core. Built over the illusion of the power of the individual. The cultural production of capitalism focuses on a heroic or paradigmatic subject, ignoring that a person is an abstraction and what is real is the people. Think of *Star Wars* . . .

Benjamín *Star Wars*?

Sashka Trash!

Benjamín I liked it.

Sashka Your taste is corrupted by the Empire.

Benjamín Isn't that an exaggeration, Mr. Zinatov?

Sashka How many Palm d'Ors do you have?

Benjamín None.

Sashka I happen to have a couple. (*Beat.*) Think of the title: *Star Wars*. It suggests cosmic conflicts. And what do you get? The stupid idea that a man can change the world.

Benjamín Luke Skywalker leads the Rebels. A whole community facing an Empire.

Sashka A community that fails until they get a savior.

Benjamín Vladimir Illich Ulianov.

Sashka Lenin was just the face of the people.

Benjamín Just as Luke Skywalker.

Sashka Are you comparing Lenin with Luke Skywalker?

Benjamín Would that be so bad?

Sashka Yes!

Benjamín I guess you won't let me complain about Stalin.

Sashka What do you want to say about Stalin, Benjamín?

Benjamín He was a genocidal dictator.

Sashka He did what he had to do.

Benjamín Are you defending Stalin?

Sashka Socialist films don't center the individual, but the whole community.

Benjamín Wait. In *Tiefblauen Morgen*, the camera never stops following Francesco Rossi.

Actor M I will be Francesco Rossi. Just not yet.

Sashka What is the name of the character?

Benjamín He doesn't have a name.

Sashka He is a man void of content. Anyone. Or no one.

Benjamín No critic wrote that.

Sashka The capitalist critics, they didn't. You probably don't read Russian, though. The socialists understood everything.

Benjamín Is that wonderful thing possible? To belong to a community?

Sashka It is what the Soviet experiment is trying to achieve. Turn this flesh into New Soviet Men. A body that prioritizes community over individuality.

Benjamín That sounds amazing. But I'm skeptical, I'm sorry. Imagine that: a world where you are never alone. You find yourself in the eyes of others. We are so fucking lonely, and that scares the hell out of us. I've only spoken with you since I arrived to the Ranch. I've always felt like an asshole nobody understands. I arrive here, to the utopia I've always dreamed of, and I'm alone all day. You say in communism I won't feel disposable. I saw that movie, *Potemkin*. I didn't understand shit. These folks feel death breathing down their necks and they become one. You need to be dying to care for someone else. Such a stupid species we are. We want the same, but we kill because we want it in a different way. Why are we so messy if loving each other is easy? How can I stop feeling alone, Mr. Zinatov? I'm sorry. I talk too much. I want to listen.

Sashka I ask myself this every day. You said it so candidly . . .

Benjamín Can I become a Soviet man?

Sashka Why not?

Benjamín I'll invent a new species, then. *Homo Sovieticus Peruviensis*. The South American version.

Sashka *smiles. A beat.*

Benjamín Mr. Zinatov?

Sashka Yes?

Benjamín Can we watch together *Tiefblauen Morgen*? Here. Now. While I ask questions.
There is nothing I would want more.

Actor M Benjamín and Alexander watch *Tiefblauen Morgen* together. They find how erotic the gaps in a film can be. Their knees touch. They pretend they don't notice.

Scene Four

A camera in the middle of the stage. This is theater. We just need a box, maybe a gesture.

Actor M   August, 1989. The filming of *Le Scoglieri nella Baia* is almost over. Dozens of men on the film sets of the Ranch, ready for the final shot. Zinatov has rehearsed hours with the young Ladislao Grgurovich, from Yugoslavia. It is cold as hell but Ladislao is naked, ready to have his body trapped by the film. A small grin on his face. He's ready to deliver the best performance any of them has ever seen. Ladislao doesn't want to think this can bring them all back to Cannes. But he can't stop thinking it. The stakes are high, nothing can go wrong. Action. Ladislao acts. But Sashka interrupts. He yells in Russian. I don't speak Russian. We'll do the scene in English.

Sashka *looks through the eye of the camera. It is not working. He yells.*

Sashka   Cut! Ladislao, stop. The shot is not working. You're great, the problem's with the camera.
Well, boy. Sorry, but there is nothing I can do. We need to stop.
You're an actor, I'm your boss. Who decides? You or me?
Stop!
I won't waste time with a spoiled brat. I said shut the fuck up! Quiet!

He goes to the camera.

Stop moving. I said, stop moving. I can't figure this shot if you keep moving! Quiet! I want everyone here to acknowledge we're wasting valuable time because the lad doesn't know how to be a professional.
Benjamín. Come. Come! Look. Tell me what's wrong.

Benjamín   How would I know?

Sashka   Look through the camera. Where's the problem?

Benjamín   I've never done this.

Sashka   You said you wanted to make movies?

Benjamín   Yes!

Sashka   Tell me what's wrong.

Benjamín *looks. Guesses.*

Benjamín   We need more light.

Sashka   More light brings more shades. I don't want that. What else?

Benjamín   The camera is too close to the actor. We need more space.

Sashka   The set design won't let me open it more.

Benjamín   Sorry. I don't know.

Sashka   Was I wrong about you?

Benjamín   I'm not a wizard!

Sashka   You've trained for two weeks. You should know better.

Benjamín   Could we have this conversation later? Everybody is looking at me right now.

Sashka   Get your sorry ass out. OUT!

He pushes **Benjamín** *with too much violence.*

You don't deserve shit. You're just like all these parasites. Those with talent rely on instinct.

Benjamín   I have instincts!

Sashka   Where the fuck are they?

Benjamín   Do you think this is fair?

Sashka   Life ain't fair, you stupid boy. Either you have something to offer or you're screwed.

Benjamín *looks again. Tension. Too many eyes on the boy.* **Benjamín** *moves the camera.*

Sashka   I didn't tell you to move the camera.

Benjamín   You asked me to solve this problem.

Sashka   I asked you to *tell me* what was wrong! Nobody gave you the right to mess with . . .!

Benjamín   Shut up and look!

Sashka, *angry, looks. The frame is perfect. He tries to conceal his shock.*

Sashka   Team! Get ready! Ladislao, positions. We'll start again. Three. Two. One. Action!

Benjamín *is on the top of the world. He just beat God at his own game.*

Scene Five

Actor M Alexander is a tyrant, but he's good at his game. The Ranch celebrates. After some drinks, Zinatov and Murieta grab a bottle and go to the room of the Peruvian kid.

Benjamín *and* **Sashka**, *singing. Choose a song that feels very out of context!*
Benjamín *steps into the bed. Again, this is theater. You can have the bed, or not.*

Benjamín Hip hip!

Sashka Hurray!

Benjamín Hurray for Alexander Porfirievich, the best filmmaker in this world. No, no. Hurray for Zinatov and Murieta. The hottest new thing in Peruvian–Soviet film. Or whatever. Hurray!

Sashka You're really drunk.

Benjamín Not at all, Mr. Zinatov! Just a bit. A tiny little itsy bit. And you?

Sashka In the perfect moment to be happy without falling down.

Benjamín I love that. Me too. But falling down. Come, come. Sit down. We can sit on the bed; I don't have a couch. I don't have shit, really. Not even this bed. It is yours. Sit!

A beat, almost uncomfortable. Eye contact, laughter. Tension. They don't know what to do. So, they drink.

Benjamín Mr. Zinatov.

Sashka Yes?

Benjamín What do you think about me?

Sashka What do you want to know?

Benjamín That you won't kick me out. I don't wanna be left alone in the Soviet fields . . .

Sashka Life is unpredictable, Benjamín.

Benjamín You don't trust me.

Sashka I don't trust anyone.

Benjamín I trust too much. My grandpa took me to Disney on my birthday. I loved it. But my dad left us while we were away. Grandpa took me for a reason. You don't have a dad either, right?

Sashka Why do you say that?

Benjamín Your movies.

Sashka I don't film autobiographies.

Benjamín   Tell me where they come from. Let's exchange our secrets, ok?

Sashka   What?

Benjamín   Shit. That was dumb. Ignore that. But really, tell me. Did your dad abandon you too?

Sashka   Why do you want to know that?

Benjamín   Because I am a nobody having vodka with God. Did you drink with Andrei Tarkovski?

Sashka   Oh, no. Andrei was a Russian without emotions. He was ice cold and I know he loved me. Ah. Without him, I wouldn't be here.

Benjamín   Where were you born, in Russia? Are you from Moscow?

Sashka   You think I'm Russian?

Benjamín   Your name is super-Russian, isn't it?

Sashka *smiles. He decides, for once, to be sincere.*

Sashka   You can call me Sashka.

Benjamín   Sashka?

Sashka   Sounds more human, right? Alexander Porfirievich Zinatov is the name of the best filmmaker in this world. But that is not the only thing I am.

Benjamín   Sashka. I like it.

Sashka   I was born in Poland. Not Russia.

Benjamín   Yeah. Kind of the same thing.

Sashka   Bolivia and Perú are kind of the same thing, right? Brazil, as well?

Benjamín   You know what I meant.

Sashka   Yeah. You said something stupid. My dad was Russian, my mom French. We lived in Poland when the war came. I fled to Spain, but I had to run away from there.

Benjamín   You were too communist for them, right?

Sashka   I was a communist already. But it was not because of that.

Benjamín   Then?

Sashka   I committed acts against the good morals of society.

Benjamín   Meaning?

Sashka   I tried to fuck a man.

Salvador. We met in the Communist Party. A wonderful Spaniard, thin as a stick, with long hair over his shoulders. He looks at you and your belly jumps and you know you'll never be good enough. One night, we were in the attic where he slept, drinking and singing to the moon. I kissed him. He pushed me away, I insisted. Minutes later I was in the streets of Madrid, my face red with blood and tears. He spread the word. I left, traveled around Europe, got to Russia. Married Masha Ivanova, the most gorgeous woman in the world. I drove her crazy. One night I get back home, she has a gun. We yell, I say the most horrible things I've ever said and slap her with a hate she never deserved. A struggle. A shot. I don't know who fired. Her face red with blood and tears. Her brains on the wall. I never wanted to marry. I had to. This world does not trust a man alone. Some days I wake up and feel Masha's brains in my hand. You should never touch the brains of another human, but what do you do when you need to clean them? You cry, and it doesn't go away. You remember it. In the shower, during sex, in your sleep. After vodka.

Benjamín It was not your fault . . .

Sashka Of course it was. I hope you never have to understand. No one pressed charges. I claimed self-defense and left Russia. The streets of Moscow reminded me of Masha. I was working for Andrei Tarkovski. I told him everything. He gave me a beautiful recommendation letter, and, with it, I tried my luck with the government. It worked. I created a Ranch for the Lost Boys, a land for those without a land. A mythical place that is nowhere, a utopia outside of the world. Somewhere that is nowhere. That does not belong. I am not Polish, Spanish, Russian. I have no home.

Benjamín Like me. How did you choose the name?

Sashka A ranch is a place that produces goods. Cotton and tobacco, maybe meat. Cheese. Or movies.

Benjamín Like a plantation?

Sashka Yeah. Why not?

A beat.

This world was not designed for people like me, Benjamín.
We needed a place outside the laws of men. Where I can make the laws.
You know that in this country it is illegal to commit homosexual acts?

Benjamín Can you do that? Make it illegal?

Sashka Is it legal in Perú?

Benjamín Of course!

Sashka Your nation must be very progressive.

Benjamín No, not at all. It is legal but it may as well not be. In Perú is dangerous to be . . . that.

Sashka What?

Benjamín That.

Sashka Name it.

Benjamín Doing thingies with guys.

Sashka   "Thingies."

Benjamín   Don't mock me.

Sashka   It's OK to be a virgin at nineteen.

Benjamín   Twenty-one. And I'm not a virgin.

Sashka   You sound so scared of talking about sex . . .

Benjamín   Yeah. I'm Peruvian. I've had girlfriends, Sashka.

Sashka   Oh, you're not a boy. You are a man! A man who does thingies with guys?

Benjamín   I told you.

Sashka   I don't remember discussing your sex life.

Benjamín   I had sex for money when I decided to come. I thought I could make some coin. It was never enough. I couldn't even get to Ecuador with that.

Sashka   Right. You shared your life to move me.

Benjamín   I convinced you.

Sashka   Were you manipulating me?

Benjamín   I was desperate.

Sashka   Shit.
Who is mad enough to chase his favorite film director?

A beat.

Benjamín   I'm sorry. I'm just weird, Sashka. Here and there. In Perú it is dangerous to be like I am. Here it is illegal! Shit. There is no place for me. I can't go back, I don't have money. I have no home, Sashka. I have no home.

He tries not to cry. This time, he's genuine.

Sashka   You need a hug?

A beat. **Benjamín** *nods quietly.*

A deep hug between two men who finally feel seen. **Benjamín** *cries.* **Sashka** *protects him.*

It must be a beautiful encounter. Then, they look at each other in the eye.

Sashka   Are you OK?

Benjamín   Yeah.

Sashka   You sure?

Benjamín   I don't like to be seen like this.

Sashka   You can't be strong all the time.

Benjamín *is overwhelmed. He is not great with emotions. He tries to deflect and move forward.*

Benjamín   Do you have more vodka?

Sashka   You've had enough.

Benjamín   Not enough. Never enough.

Sashka *gives him a bottle.* **Benjamín** *drinks too fast. Smiles. It's obvious he's breaking down.*

Sashka   Calm down, boy.

Benjamín   Wanna listen to music?

Sashka   What kind of music?

Benjamín   Surprise me!

Out of the blue, coming from nowhere, an upbeat song starts playing.

Benjamín   I love this song!

Lights change. The music sounds louder.

Reality is broken.

If you can get a disco ball, use it. **Benjamín** *laughs and sings. Dances trying to be sexy, but he is clumsy as fuck. In this conversation, they need to yell a bit to listen to each other.*

Sashka   Francesco Rossi and I danced this song in the Hungarian joints.

Actor M   I will be Francesco Rossi, just not yet!

Benjamín   I've never danced with a man!

Sashka   Really?

Benjamín   In Perú? Come on!

Sashka   We're not in Perú anymore!

Benjamín   Is it illegal if we both dance?

Sashka   Kinda. Let's be criminals. May I have this dance, boy?

Benjamín *blushes.*

Sashka *offers his hand.*

They dance and they feel in heaven.

Actor M *dances as well. A party.*

When the dance sequence ends, the three smile, and take a moment to process.

Sashka   How did it feel?

Benjamín   Heaven. Earth won't ever be enough. I must walk on air from now on.

A beat.

Tell me more. How did you create this Ranch?

A change.

Actor M   It all started with an audience between Sashka and a president.

Sashka *talks to the audience. It looks like a very rehearsed speech by a politician.*

Sashka   Capitalism destroys thousands of European kids! Born without parents, begging for coins to get bread. No dignity, no future. Let's rescue them, comrade! Educate them in modern filmmaking and the values of the Motherland. Cinema forms the mind. Makes us who we are, teaches us how to live. Let's turn a generation of agnostics into serfs of the Party!

Benjamín   You tricked him.

Sashka   I wasn't lying.

Benjamín   You needed a studio, so you got state funding! I don't think you'd be lucky having that conversation with my president.

Sashka   You want to hear my story?

Benjamín   OK. I'll shut up.

Actor M   The Ranch is a well-oiled machine and everyone knows their place in it. The head, of course, is Alexander Porfirievich Zinatov. The best filmmaker in this world.

Benjamín   The executive, legislative and judiciary powers of utopia.

Sashka   Your country lacks a head to shape the body. That is why everyone kills each other. Here, hierarchies are clear. Everyone knows their role and fulfills it without question.

Benjamín   Is Francesco Rossi the prince? I mean, after his work in *Tiefblauen Morgen* . . . Is he in the Ranch? I don't think I've seen him.

Actor M   I will be Francesco Rossi. Just not yet.

Sashka   He was.

Benjamín   What happened?

Sashka   Life happened.

Benjamín   Why haven't you filmed another movie after *Tiefblauen Morgen*?

Sashka   I've been busy with other projects. And the creation of *Le Scoglieri Nella Baia* took so much.

Benjamín   What happened with Francesco?

Sashka   I work with Ladislao Grgurovich now.

Benjamín I don't get it. Your movie *and* your protagonist won the Palme d'Or in Cannes. The whole world was ready to follow the steps of Rossi and Zinatov. But the five-year silence was loud. Now you tell me Francesco was a prince but not anymore. What happened?

Sashka I don't think this is any of your business, Benjamín.

Benjamín You're hiding something.

Sashka Everybody hides their stuff.

Benjamín But I know your soul. You poured it into *Tiefblauen Morgen*.

Sashka You didn't understand my movie.

Benjamín Excuse me?

Sashka What is it about?

Benjamín A boy abandoned by his father.

Sashka That is you. Not my movie.

Benjamín Films can be interpreted in different ways.

Sashka That is postmodern bullshit. *Tieflabuen Morgen* is about a boy without a land. Like me. That is why he travels. You didn't understand it.

Benjamín Your interpretation is no better than mine.

Sashka It is my movie.

Benjamín Now it's mine as well.

Sashka Whatever you say, kid. I'm going to bed.

He gets up to leave. **Benjamín** *stops him.*

Benjamín How do you climb the hierarchies of the Ranch?

Sashka Each person has a different path.

Benjamín You have rituals? You skin a goat and paint your bodies with blood?

Sashka Don't be foolish.

Benjamín I don't see you drinking the blood of Christ.

Sashka There's no blood.

Benjamín Every ritual has blood.

Sashka Coming to your room was a bad idea.

Benjamín Stay.

Sashka No.

Benjamín Your serfs never talk back to you, right?

Sashka　Talking back is a privilege, not a right.

Benjamín　I thought all men were created equal.

Sashka　That is not true.

Benjamín　Communism should be that, right? But you break it when you want to control it. You wanna be the perfect leader! The one with all the answers! You are a fucker. But don't get me wrong. I love it. You run the cheapest studio in the world with the most submissive crew. Do you need bodies that won't resist you?

Sashka　Benjamín.

Benjamín　Are you afraid of the truth?

Sashka　What truth?

Benjamín　You live surrounded by serfs.

Sashka　The youth is never docile.

Benjamín　They are if you know how to make them.

Sashka　Apologize.

Benjamín　Why?

Sashka　You are disrespecting the man who welcomed you when you had nothing!

Benjamín　Communism claims that property belongs to the community, not the individual. And, I should remind you, this institution belongs to the state.

Sashka　Your ideas are pretty, but regulating resources . . .

Benjamín　Oh, you lied to me. You are as selfish as the gringos you hate so much.

Sashka　My spirit . . . !

Benjamín　Oh please. Your friend Charlie Marx believed in materialism.

Sashka　History has spiritual laws . . .

Benjamín　You fuck the lost boys, don't you?

A beat.

You can tell me. I won't judge.

Sashka　Of course not. Now go to bed.

Benjamín　You hate adults, right? I'm scared of them.

Sashka　Aren't you scared of me?

Benjamín　Why would I? You're just a boy.

He tries to kiss **Sashka**. **Sashka** *pushes him too hard against the floor.* **Benjamín** *is hurt and ashamed. A silence full of tension.*

I'm sorry. I'm so sorry. Please don't leave. I said too much. Don't leave me.

Sashka   We can talk tomorrow.

He is leaving, but **Benjamín** *runs and hugs him from behind.*

Benjamín   I like you.

Sashka   You're being a prick.

Benjamín   I don't know how to do this!

Sashka   I'm trying to do things right with you. Just this once. I always fuck everything up.

Benjamín   I just wanted a kiss. Unless you think I'm ugly. I may not be that hot. Others are hotter than me. But I am not ugly. Or do you think I'm ugly?

He gets desperate. He feels so rejected and doesn't understand why, poor child. He takes all his clothes off and looks at **Sashka**.

Benjamín   Don't you like me? Not even a bit?

Beat. **Benjamín** *suddenly feels all the shame in his body. He grabs his clothes, but doesn't wear them.*

I'm sorry. I shouldn't have done that. I don't know what's wrong with me.

Sashka   I am your mentor. You could be the son I never had.

Benjamín   Is that what's stopping you?

Sashka   I've never been a good guy. I've tried. Really. I thought things would get easier with age.

Benjamín   I stole my grandpa's savings. I could be the villain of this story.

Sashka   I don't want to destroy you.

Benjamín   I'm not fragile.

Sashka   Don't underestimate me.

Benjamín *drops his clothes. He is naked. Looks at* **Sashka** *and smiles.*

Benjamín   Now *you* are underestimating me.

A beat. They look at each other.

Sashka *comes closer, caresses his face tenderly.* **Benjamín** *closes his eyes. Smiles. Surrenders to the touch. Then,* **Sashka** *puts his hands on* **Benjamín***'s neck. Abruptly, violently, gets the boy on his knees in front of him. The lights change. Both* **Actors** *freeze while* **Actor M** *talks to the audience.*

Actor M   Young Murieta smiles. His god desires him. No one has touched his skin in months. Not even his mom when he left. It feels so good. But then Benja remembers that guy. The one that paid him, did things to his body that he will never tell. He can't. That night, he ran out of a cheap motel, so scared he was shaking. He looked at the sky and realized that no one would ever protect him from life. And that

was terrifying. He cried and screamed at 3 a.m. in the middle of a park, until a cop sent him away. But now he's far from home and there's nowhere to run. Benja remembers those nights when his body was not his. He washed his skin with detergent, but he could still smell the sweat of strangers on it.
Sashka finishes and has nothing to say. He says nothing.

Sashka *leaves.* **Benjamín** *in bed, hiding in the sheets.*

Actor M   Benja realizes. He is drunk and alone. He doesn't know who he is. He is alone, he feels alone. Needs a fucking hug. When he was a kid and panic invaded his guts, his dad sang lullabies. But dad is not here anymore. Benja sings to himself.

Benjamín *sings a lullaby. His voice is broken.*

After a few verses, the other **Actors** *join him.*

The three sing, with the terrible loneliness of being a migrant.

Benjamín *gains confidence, and when he gets to the end of the song, his fear has become anger.*

Actor M *kisses his forehead and leaves the stage. We won't see them until Act Two.*

Scene Six

Sashka *works in his office.* **Benjamín** *enters holding a bunch of papers.*

Benjamín   Sashka?

Sashka *welcomes him dearly. As if nothing had happened.*

Sashka   Good morning, Benjamín! Did you sleep well?

Benjamín   I apologize. I don't know what happened to me.

Sashka   All is well, kiddo.

Benjamín   It was the vodka, you know?

Sashka   Did you have breakfast? I didn't see you at the table.

Benjamín   I'm not hungry.

Sashka   Sit down. I'll get you some coffee. Some eggs?

Benjamín   I'd rather not.

Sashka   You have to eat, Benjamín. You're growing up.

Benjamín   I'm twenty-one.

Sashka   I have the best German bread. Only for government officers.

Benjamín   I don't want it, Sashka. Thank you.

Sashka   You should take care of yourself.

Benjamín   I'm old enough to make my own decisions.

Sashka   Could you just eat, please?

Benjamín   No. What I want is . . .

Sashka   For fuck's sake, EAT! Shut up and eat!

Benjamín *eats, furious, looking at* **Sashka** *in the eye.*

Sashka   OK. If you don't want to, don't eat.

Benjamín   Oh, this coffee is sooooo good.

Sashka   I didn't want to force you.

Benjamín   No. Now I want to.

Sashka *tries to take the plates away. They struggle for them.*

Sashka   Give this to me . . .

Benjamín   OK. I didn't come to talk about food. Can we chat?

Sashka   OK. OK. What's on your mind?

Benjamín Remember my script?

Sashka Which one?

Benjamín *The Malaise of Dawn*. I sent it to you. You praised it. I spent the night rewriting it.

He puts the papers in the table.

Sashka Congratulations, boy! Your first script. I love the name: *The Malaise of Dawn*. Something that can't grow up because it's wounded.

Benjamín It is my best work. A symbolist short film.

Sashka Excellent. You want me to read it? Give you feedback?

Benjamín You'll notice your influence on my writing is very strong. You direct it, I will assist you. Francesco can be the star.

A small beat, to notice the absence of the actor.

Sashka These are very busy days. I'm editing the new film while filing budgets.

Benjamín It's thirty pages long. It won't take much time.

Sashka Leave it, I'll try to find some space. Now, if you excuse me, I need to go back to work.

Benjamín You won't produce it.

Sashka We're not done with *Le Scoglieri nella Baia*.

Benjamín You will find the time.

Sashka You know how expensive it is to make a movie, Benjamín?

Benjamín You created this Ranch to make it easier.

Sashka The resources belong to the state.

Benjamín The state will love it.

Sashka It is too much money. No. You want to take the day off?

Benjamín You wanted this to be easier for others. It was so hard for you.

Sashka You'll understand when you're older.

Benjamín I'm an adult.

Sashka Then behave like one.

A beat.

Benjamín You said homosexuality is illegal here.

Sashka It is.

Benjamín The Ranch is an impossible place with its own rules. But the laws of the state apply to it.

Sashka Nations are stupid inventions.

Benjamín The president disagrees.

Sashka Are you threatening me?

Benjamín (*without hiding the irony*) Of course not, Alexander.

Sashka You'll need proof. No one will speak against me.

Benjamín You think I'm capable of such a thing?

Sashka Of course you are. Finish your food and leave. The resources of the state won't fund caprices. The president and I agree on that.

Benjamín You rejected my film without reading it.

Sashka I'll find time to reject it after reading it.

Benjamín You think I don't have talent.

Sashka How do you think this world works? That your pretty face makes you worthy of what? You need to shed blood to *earn* these things.

Benjamín Is this because I'm Peruvian?

Sashka Nonsense.

Benjamín How many Peruvians have you read?

Sashka I don't have time for tests.

Benjamín You Europeans have written about us for centuries. Deciding what we are. What we can be. But we can't do the same. We can't write about you. You invaded us and wrote pages and pages about it. Since Columbus' journals. Dissecting who we are. And it's gotten worse, now. What are communism and capitalism, but European inventions? You gather at a table to decide the future of our flesh and soil.

Sashka When did your country became independent?

Benjamín That doesn't matter.

Sashka Answer me.

Benjamín A hundred and sixty-eight years ago.

Sashka A hundred and sixty-eight years ago you could claim victimhood. Now it's too late.

Benjamín You can't free someone after crushing their spirit for hundreds of years and hope things turn out alright. Our gold was stolen and it keeps crossing the ocean.

Sashka You think this Europe is a utopia? We've had two massive wars in half a century. The Spanish monarchs fucked your lands, boy, but this is not Castilla. Our Eastern countries are similar to yours. And my name is not Christopher.

Benjamín OK, let's play a game. Let's forget history. You and I are not responsible for what our ancestors did. We're two creatures who just came into being, without original sin. Alright? Ready! In this corner, the owner of the plantation! Black hair, five foot two, fifty-something years, played by the actor _____, having infinite resources . . .

Sashka They are not infinite.

Benjamín OK, plenty of resources. Don't ruin my act! On the other side, poor old me. Benjamín Murieta, the migrant boy, played by _____, without coins, without a country to call his own. Today, here, now, at this table, five centuries of history are at stake. Five centuries in which your continent has ravished mine. You wrote everything you wanted, but never read our words. You have the power to undo five centuries.

He turns to the audience.

Five whole centuries, dear audience. This man says yes, renounces a tiny little bit of his power, and poof! History vanishes. Tell me. Tell *them*. What are you going to do?

A beat.

Sashka You may be talented, Benjamín. To tell you the truth, I don't know. Three smart comments don't make you a genius.

Benjamín I've learned to see my face in the face of Hamlet. I learned to see my face in your movies. Now, I want Hamlet to see himself in *my* face. And you. Can you?

Sashka I can. But you need to prove your worth. Alone.

Benjamín You didn't do it alone!

Sashka I earned my right to be here!

Benjamín Tarkovski. The president. Cannes.

Sashka You think I don't deserve the throne.

Benjamín I say, loud and clear, you had the chance. I don't.

Sashka You are being a cocky brat.

Benjamín You are being a stubborn patriarch.

Sashka Get out.

Benjamín I don't want to.

Sashka This is my Ranch. I give the orders.

Benjamín Say you'll produce my work, *master*, and I'll leave.

Sashka No!

Benjamín It's a short film! It is not that hard. But I am no one and you, the best filmmaker in this world. You just love to be the master in power. You're so selfish that . . .

Sashka *grabs* **Benjamín** *from his shirt.*

Sashka   You go to your room. Think about what you've done. Then you'll come and beg for forgiveness. And if you don't want to be kicked out of *my ranch*, you'll have to clean the floors and do the dishes for the month as a punishment.

Benjamín   I don't want to.

Sashka   My roof, my rules.

Benjamín   You have no right!

Sashka *throws* **Benjamín** *to the floor. They fight with the desperation of five centuries.* **Sashka** *is stronger.*

Sashka   Are you done with your tantrum?

Benjamín   You are not my father. Understand? I HAVE NO FATHER!

He runs away. **Sashka**, *alone, furious. He kicks a chair.*

Act Two

Scene Seven

Sashka *on stage.*

Offstage, **Michel** *sings Schubert's* Ave Maria. *The voice is loud, broken, off key. But so powerful we feel goosebumps. It is a yell, coming from the cracks of the belly. With the wisdom of someone who's at peace now.*

Sashka *leaves.* **Michel** *enters, wearing impossible clothes. The robe of a Franciscan priest. But it could be a dress. High heels. As if gender doesn't have meaning anymore. Goes to the front of the stage and kneels.*

Benjamín *enters. He watches, fascinated, moved.* **Michel** *sees him and stops.* **Benjamín** *doesn't know what to say. He knows the land in front of him is sacred.*

Michel   You are the Peruvian, right?

Benjamín   You know who I am?

Michel   We all do. I'm Michel.

Benjamín   Benjamín.

They come closer to shake hands.

Francesco.

Michel   It is Michel now.

Benjamín   Francesco Rossi. Protagonist of *Tiefblauen Morgen*.

Michel   I was Francesco. But not anymore.

Benjamín   Sorry for interrupting. I just . . .

Michel   Some mornings I come here to pray.

A beat.

Benjamín   I like your clothes.

Michel   You do?

Benjamín   They're cute.
You're blushing.

Without thinking (as always), **Benjamín** *touches* **Michel***'s face, softly. Both are confused.*

Benjamín   I'm sorry. I never thought I'd meet the incredible Francesco Rossi.

Michel   Michel.

Benjamín   That happens with actors, you know? You see them through a screen but don't touch them. When you see them in the flesh you think you know them. You know nothing of me, I feel like I know you. And you must know everybody, don't you? Have you met Malcolm McDowell? Is he like Alex in *A Clockwork Orange*, like, rebel, evil, so freaking sexy? I am Peruvian, I don't know these people. Do you? Are you like your character in *Tiefblauen Morgen*? Or is that just the movie?

A beat. **Michel** *smiles.*

Michel   You talk a lot, don't you?

Benjamín   I'm sorry. I'm nervous. I never thought I'd actually meet you. When I get anxious I talk my ass off. I am the worst, right? What happens is that . . . see? I was starting again.

Michel   It was nice to meet you. I need to get some breakfast.

Benjamín   Francesco.

Michel   Michel.

Benjamín   Michel. Can we go out sometime?

Michel   Out where?

Benjamín   Like a date, I mean.

Michel   I've never been on a date.

Benjamín   Me neither. That's better, right? We won't have standards.

Michel   Will you talk all the time?

Benjamín   I swear I won't. The filming of *Le Scoglieri de la Baia* finished already, but the sets are still there. The dining hall of the palace looks beautiful. I can't take you to dinner. There are no restaurants around. And I don't have a penny. But I can steal bread and water from the kitchen. What do you say?

Scene Eight

Benjamín *grew up watching films from faraway countries, like the USA or France. Now he wants to imitate what he has seen on screen. He sets everything for the date in front of the audience, while* **Michel** *dresses in a fabulous outfit.* **Benjamín** *wears a suit that is too big for him. A tie with a poorly made knot. Sets a table with a tablecloth, a plastic rose placed in the most hideous vase you can find. Two mismatched glasses. Two pieces of bread. It looks ridiculous. Also, cute as fuck.*

Benjamín   I did my best.

Michel   I'm impressed.

Benjamín   It looks horrible.

Michel   You don't know how to put a tie on.

Benjamín   I've only had to wear one once. My mom did the knot.

Michel *approaches him seductively and fixes the knot.*

Michel   Attaboy.

Benjamín   Sit! We have bread that is not too old and tap water. Fancy.

They sit down. Silence. They exchange looks.

Now what?

Michel   I dunno.

Benjamín   Why Michel and not Francesco?

Michel   Francesco is the name of my family, my house, my land. I'm not any of that anymore. I have no home.

Benjamín   I've heard Italians are like that. Rebels! Without a cause!

Michel   Are you like every other Peruvian? Representing your country in a foreign land?

Benjamín   Of course not! I'm weird as fuck.

Michel (*this phrase is key. – make it important*)   Communities are illusions, Benjamín.
I'm no one.

Benjamín   Do you always dress like that?

Michel   Like what?

Benjamín   Weird.

Michel   When people see you, they categorize your flesh. Man or woman, White or Brown, queer or straight, young or old. From Japan or from Nigeria. Things you do and things you don't. Categories. You dress to show those categories. I don't wanna be a category. I'm no one. I want to be no one.

Benjamín Damn. That's cool.

They share a smile.

The following conversation is a duel, fast, with the precision of brilliant folx who don't need to check Wikipedia to write smart lines.

Didn't you do another movie after *Tiefblauen Morgen*?

Michel I couldn't.

Benjamín Yeah, it is a masterpiece . . .

Michel It is not too bad.

Benjamín Best movie ever made.

Michel I prefer *Some Like It Hot*.

Benjamín That is imperialist cinema.

Michel Yeah, with Marilyn Monroe.

Benjamín Oh, you like Norma Jean?

Michel Who doesn't?

Benjamín I prefer Anita Ekberg and Anouk Aimée.

Michel *La Dolce Vita* is the most boring movie ever made, Benjamín.

Benjamín That is the point!

Michel It's a terrible point!

Benjamín It shows the ennui of postwar Italian bourgeoisie. Soulless and tedious.

Michel Three hours of fucking ennui!

Benjamín Wonderful ennui!

Michel You love the movies.

Benjamín There's nothing I like more.

Michel Why?

Benjamín Movies make this world make sense.
Maybe, if my life would be a movie, all would be easier. I would blame the screenwriter and not me for all the shit I do, Francesco.

Michel Michel.

Benjamín Michel. In the movies, the lives of others look cuter than mine. Making one must be fantastic.

Michel It's not a big deal.

Benjamín Michel, you're the best actor in the world in the best movie ever made.

Michel (*not fake modesty – actually, triggered*) Oh, shut up.

Benjamín   Don't give me that fake modesty. You got an award at Cannes.

Michel   It was for the movie.

Benjamín   And another one for you.

Michel   There wasn't.

Benjamín   Why didn't you go to Cannes?

Michel   Zinatov only got one invitation. They said the movie was brilliant, but the actor was hideous.

Benjamín *freezes. He gets it. He speaks slowly.*

Benjamín   Michel. *Tiefblauen Morgen* won the Palme d'Or in Cannes. And an award for best acting for its protagonist, Francesco Rossi. You beat Marcello Mastroianni! Jean-Pierre Léaud! The most discussed award of the decade, won by a really young actor. The best men in the business gave you a standing ovation.

Michel   Alexander Porfirievich said I couldn't go. That I was a mistake, that my performance ruined the movie . . .

Benjamín   You didn't see the newspapers?

Michel   We don't get newspapers at the Ranch.

Benjamín   You got the most important award in the world, Michel. And you didn't know.

Michel   You're lying.

Benjamín   Why would I?

Michel   Because there is no way this is true!

Benjamín   I don't have proof. But it is true.

A beat.

Michel*'s universe has just crumbled.*

Michel   Years ago, I failed the man that loved me. I almost destroyed the most important movie of his life, because I didn't have the talent he saw in me. I betrayed him. You didn't see the sadness in his eyes. I failed the man who saved me from death. Who the fuck do you think you are? You come out of the blue, from a country I can't find on a map, to tell me that five years ago Alexander Porfirievich Zinatov lied to me. And you want me to believe you?

Benjamín   Yes.

Michel   Shit.

Benjamín   I thought you knew.

Michel   He should have let me go. But Alexander is good, he doesn't want anything to happen to me. If he is the evil fucker you say he is, why didn't he kick me out?

Benjamín If he did that, you'd know he lied.

Michel Benjamín.

Benjamín Yes?

Michel Bitch, I'm falling apart and you are not holding me.

Music.

Slowly, **Benjamín** *stands up.*

Puts a hand on **Michel**'s *shoulder.*

Michel *breaks down. And then stands up.*

Both look at each other in the eyes.

A hug. They break down together.

And then, they dance in silence.

Their bodies learning how to take care of each other.

Scene Nine

Michel's Story

A change.

This scene and the following have a lot of text. Stage them with movement, dance, projections, sound, music.

Push them as far as you can. Be outrageous.

Realism, from here to the end, will be destroyed.

This world, like our world, is absurd. But the feelings are very real.

Actor M   Michel is an impossible character. Descended to hell and climbed to heaven in thirty years. Saw Death in the eyes and sitteth at the right hand of the Father. Michel was a saint. But none of that remains. Now it's just cleaning. Cooking. Doing laundry. Whatever is needed. Michel reads. Paints. Dresses and undresses with clothes from the movies. Sometimes prays. We don't know to who. Michel thinks this is happiness. The happiness of not having to struggle. Not even for a piece of bread.

Actor B   Francesco Rossi was born in Turin, Italy, near the Alps. The youngest of five kids, his parents were bougie as fuck. Lots of money, inherited for ever and ever.

Actor M   Amen.

Actor B   They wanted him to become a priest.

Actor S   At seven he wore Mom's dresses. His small feet walked in high heels like a pro.

Actor M   Francesco liked the idea of becoming a priest. Of course. He wanted to live surrounded by men wearing dresses. Room, board, pray.

Actor B   Well, just one dress. And it was brown. It is not *that* cool.

Actor S   But it is what it is.

Actor M   Francesco was the best altar boy. Sang *Ave Maria* with the voice of an angel. But let's be honest: his skin was white as milk, the body of an ephebe, blue eyes, the blondest hair you've ever seen. In this fucked-up world, these things matter. He was also really cool.

Actor S   Picture your granny meeting him. She would say, "Oh, this boy is so cute! Clean, polite. He must come from a great family. And Catholic! I'm dead. Be like him."

Actor B   No friends, no girlfriend. Then he fell in love with another altar boy. Federico.

Actor M   They didn't know how to love each other. At sixteen, they loved too much. Hours in bed, listening records in silence. That was happiness. Until Mom found them. Their bodies inside of each other. Dad hit them until they bled and threw them out. Walked through Europe without money. To eat, they fucked others. Sometimes alone, sometimes together. Depending on how much the strangers could pay.

Actor S   One day, they were attacked. Francesco saw Federico's guts falling out of his body in the outskirts of Budapest. There was no time to cry. He had to work. Not even twenty, a widow and an exile! Then, he had a client unlike any other. In Bucharest, he met Sashka.

Actor B   They made love and Sashka begged him to stay. He paid more. Francesco didn't know he was fucking an important man. Until Sashka took him to his place.

Actor M   They loved each other. Wild sex all night until dusk, and then canceled filming to navigate their skins. Sashka was a boyfriend, lover, father, master, symbiote. God.

Actor S   And gods devour their creatures.

Actor B   Sashka didn't want to take Francesco to Cannes. He said he had only one invitation.

Actor M   He was lying.

Actor S   God was afraid.

Actor M   Awards were invented to change the course of history. In May 1984, the lives of these three people whose stories we're telling became something else.

A change.

Actor S   Benjamín and Michel spent some days together.

Actor M   They shared their deepest secrets.

Actor B   And learned how to love each other.

Benjamín   Can you dress me like you?

Michel   You know that goes against everything I'm trying to achieve.

Benjamín   I'll look like you.

Michel   I would stop being no one.

Benjamín   *We'll* be no one. Together.

Music. **Michel** *smiles.*

Benjamín *dresses with* **Michel***'s clothes.*

Now both have old, impossible dresses.

Michel   Have you ever been in Sashka's room?

Benjamín   Never.

Michel   I haven't returned since 1984.

Benjamín He must have some clippings around.

Michel I wanna see them.

Actor S Michel breaks the lock with a hammer. The boys find the diaries, the boxes with newspapers. They read the secrets of God.

Scene Ten

The Secrets of God

*The **Actors** perform the diaries in first person, as if they were **Sashka**. On stage, old papers and notebooks.*

Actor M Nineteen sixty-two. Sunday. Living in Italy is not bad. Quiet. Working at Fiat is not bad. I never imagined I'd become a proletarian and assemble cars. It's not bad. It's not good. Every morning I hear my father's voice.

Actor S Petit bourgeois to proletarian. Petit bourgeois to proletarian. Petit bourgeois. Proletarian.

Actor M I won't ever stop being petit. I'll never be a grand bourgeois.

Actor S Filthy declassed. You should have increased the fortune, right? And now? Filthy declassed.

Actor M Father. Two world wars. Exile. Crisis. What did you expect?

Actor S The economy grows like it never has and you are a proletarian. A disgusting proletarian.

Actor B And I'm afraid. Of my body. Of disease. War. Poverty. This world these fuckers created. You gotta amass wealth. If you don't, you fall in the infinite void. How do you stop being poor?

Actor M I spend my days alone. Nobody notices me. Lunch. I sit next to the window and see people walk. Ladies in beautiful dresses. Men I want to fuck. I see them. Nobody looks back. I go to the movies. *Cléo de 5 à 7*, by Agnes Varda. The movie is pretty good, until Michel Legrand comes in and I feel a fire in my chest. My dick gets hard and I forget about the movie. I picture myself ripping his clothes off and seeing his butt. The most perfect ass in this world. I'm alone, in the last row, I grab my cock and my eyes fuck Legrand. I look at him. He doesn't look back. I cum on my shirt. I'm dirty. Ashamed. I ran. Another Sunday. *L'eclisse*, by Michelangelo Antonioni. I look at Alain Delon. He looks at Monica Vitti. I hate Monica Vitti. My eyes fuck Delon. My clothes are dirty. Another Sunday. Another movie. *Jules et Jim*, by François Truffaut. I look at Oskar Werner. He doesn't look back. My clothes, dirty. 1963. *Otto e Mezzo*, by Federico Fellini. I look at Marcello Mastroianni. He doesn't look back. My clothes are dirty. I make phone calls. I write letters. I ask Cineccità, the biggest studio in the country. But they don't look back. I'm a migrant proletarian. We don't exist. Nobody looks back. I want those naked men at my feet. Adoring me. Like their god. But they don't look back. What if they make a movie about migrant, sodomite proletarians? Would anyone look?

Actor S It's the world that these fuckers created. If you don't amass wealth, you fall in the infinite void. How do you stop being poor?

Actor B May. 1968. I spent the night with François. Whores bore me after a bit, but I like how he smiles. His body makes my cock really hard. He says he's twenty-two, he's not even twenty. I don't know if he likes me or if he's just good at his job. But he sleeps here and doesn't steal. There is not much to steal. We have breakfast and I ask if he has a girlfriend. Boyfriend. He avoids my question and asks me. No. I pay. It's easier. I see photos of Paris on the papers. Proletarians and students are protesting. Could I be there?

Actor M   It's the world these fuckers created. If you don't amass wealth, you fall in the infinite void. How do you stop being poor?

Actor B   June. 1968. All my savings, some pickpocketing. I go to France to be part of the revolution. But the revolution is over. Nobody looks back. I'm a migrant, sodomite proletarian. I knock on the doors of the Cinémathèque française. Asked Henri Langlois for work. I want to be like Godard, Truffaut, Varda. Langlois hired me as a janitor. He didn't look back. But I can watch as many movies as I want. September. 1968. I can jerk off in the seats of the Cinémathèque.
I am not ashamed anymore.

The **Actor** *looks at the audience, and challenges them.*

Why should I be ashamed?

A beat.

Actor M   I read Marx. I read Marx again and again. As if reading Marx could save me from this world. I believe every word he writes. And dream of a world of equals.

Actor S   But I have doubts. Can I doubt? They told me to have faith.

Actor M   To destroy class struggle you need a revolutionary process where the state concentrates power to reorganize society.

Actor B   A revolution. A wildfire to destroy the social structures that sustain horror. The system that devours our flesh.

Actor S   An almighty state.

Actor M   But Marx writes that this state should transform it all, then disappear.

Actor S   Disappear. Or power will corrupt us.

Actor M   What if you hold power to transform it all but then you don't want to leave power? What if authority is sweeter than utopia? What if you use power against those you defend?

Actor B   I need peace and to get peace I need power without power there is no peace. I need peace and to get peace I need power without power there is no peace.
No power, no peace.
What if power is sweeter than utopia?

Everyone   I solemnly swear all power will taste bitter.

Actor S   What if power is sweeter than utopia?

A beat. And now, the last part of the play.

Of course, A Ranch for the Lost Boys *never cared about mimesis.*

Now, we'll go to the Cannes awards of 1984, where Alexander Zinatov and Francesco Rossi were honored for Tiefblauen Morgen. *But* Tiefblauen Morgen *doesn't exist. The Palme d'Or went to Wim Wenders for* Paris, Texas. *The best actors of the year were Francisco Rabal and Alfredo Landa for* Los Santos Inocentes *by Mario Camus. This is all a lie. Isn't it?*

The sequence is totally over the top. Music. **Actor B** *and* **Actor M** *play the hosts. It is a joke, but* **Sashka** *can't understand it. He's totally serious. We should feel a bit sorry for him.*

All Hell must break loose.

Host One   Good evening, and welcome to the most important event in showbusiness! The Cannes Film Festival!

Host Two   An Olympus for the rich and famous. The most talented people in the world, gathered under the same roof.

Host One   This year, we have a constellation of stars.

Host Two   Wim Wenders, James L. Brooks, Werner Herzog, Lars von Trier, Ingmar Bergman, Satyajit Ray, John Huston, Mario Camus, Woody Allen, Sergio Leone, Gerard Depardieu . . .

Host One   And of course, our favorite. The prodigy of Soviet film. The enlightened of a new proletarian art.

Host Two   Alexander Porfirievich Zinatov, presenting *Tiefblauen Morgen.*

Host One   Stay with us, while we discover who is the best filmmaker in the world!

Suspended, **Sashka***.*

Sashka   I spent a week choosing a suit. It had to be perfect.

Interviewer   We are here with the wonderful Alexander Porfirievich Zinatov. Is this your first time in the festival, Mr. Zinatov?

Sashka   Indeed, it is.

Interviewer   But you have a long list of excellent films! Why you didn't come with *La Danse de la Mort,* or *Wir Werden Niemals in Broadway Sein*?

Sashka   You are aware of the political tensions of our time.

Interviewer   But you are here with us now. And this is historical, Mr. Zinatov: you've been an exile and a factory worker. You bring the voice of the oppressed. What a noble mission! Ennobling us, the most privileged classes. Please tell us. What is your motivation for filming? Do you want to portray the gaze of the contemporary working man?

A light change. **Sashka** *is very convinced of his words. He is opening his heart.*

Sashka   I create movies to wash the mold that rot our souls. To break the History of the West, a virus devouring our hearts. The only way of achieving a life of plenitude is to pervert and pulverize European heritage. Start anew. The world we received is not real. Let's create a new one!

Back to the interview.

Interviewer Aw. That sounds so cute! Why didn't you bring Francesco Rossi?

Sashka He had personal business to attend. Back to *Tiefblauen Morgen*.

Interviewer Such a brilliant performance.

Sashka A good director can guide the young, so they can offer a decent work.

Interviewer Oh, Mr. Zinatov. This goes beyond your directing.

Sashka Rossi is a complex character.

Interviewer He is enlightened.

Sashka A lucky boy.

Interviewer Some think he can receive an award for best acting.

Sashka Oh, they think that?

Interviewer Yeah, they do.

Sashka *smiles.*

Sashka It would be a sin to snatch it from Mastroianni.

A beat.

I grew up watching the Cannes Festival through a small screen. But I didn't have a visa to visit that land. Now my body is on the other side of the screen. On the red carpet. I became an Olympian.

Actor M And the best movie of the year is...*Tiefblauen Morgen*!

Sashka *receives the award.* **Actor M** *gives him the most ridiculous object you can think of.* **Sashka** *delivers a speech with total conviction, holding this object. He looks absurd. Or tragic.*

Sashka Beloved European siblings. You can't even imagine how important this award is for me. A stateless man who ran away from war and fascism. Who belonged to the proletariat of this continent and found a small home in the Soviet family. But this award . . . *this* shows I have a home now. I'll never be an exile again. Cannes is my nation! A land of men who create the worlds that life denies them. Thank you!

Applause. Change.

I thought I won. And then the party started.

The party. Music. Everyone wants to talk with **Sashka**.

Wim? Wim Wenders!

Wim Wenders Alexander Porfirievich, your work is sublime. SUBLIME!

Sashka Coming from you . . . Your *Paris, Texas* is a masterpiece.

Wenders It is nothing, *nothing* next to *Tiefblauen Morgen*, maestro.

Ingmar Bergman Don't trust that German asshole. He's been stolen by the gringos. But he's right about one thing, you motherfucker. *Tiefblauen Morgen* is the best movie I've ever seen. The Soviet geniuses would be jealous. I promise you: Eisenstein, that bitch, he would give you an ovation.

Sashka Ingmar Bergman. Coming from you . . . I don't know what to say.

Bergman Of course you don't know what to say, you asshole. I am fucking Bergman praising your shit.

Sashka And you just screened the beautiful *Fanny och Alexander*.

Bergman I've had my years. And I'll have many more. You know, I'm the shit. But this is your night!

Sashka Excuse me, Madam Ekberg . . .

Anita Ekberg Please call me . . . Anita.

Sashka Can I have this dance?

Ekberg It would be my honor, Alexander Porfirievich.

Actor B After dancing with Anita Ekberg, Sashka sees a boy. Must be around twenty. Sashka thinks he is the hottest guy around.

Sashka How is your martini?

Hans Butzer It isn't terrible.

Sashka This wine is excellent. But I need something stronger now.

Hans Which grape?

Sashka Tempranillo.

Hans Disgusting.

Sashka This one is good.

Hans I only drink good cabernets. This life is too short for bad wines.

Sashka Hans Butzer. From the new movie by Nikolai Grundtvig.

Hans You know me. I'm flattered. Did you see it?

Sashka Excellent. Movie of the year.

Hans Better than that piece of crap. *Tiefblauen Morgen.*

Sashka Oh, you didn't like *Tiefblauen Morgen*?

Hans Boring and pretencious. This bunch of imbeciles give awards to shit. But I don't know you. You come often?

Sashka Weren't you in the ceremony?

Hans Why would I? People come to get bored and feel important. Jesus Christ, you get me?

Sashka I think so.

Hans Everyone here is so vulgar. Mediocre, uncouth. Nobody knows authenticity! They take shits in front of each other and applaud their sorry asses.

Sashka Then why are you here?

Hans Free booze. And you can always fuck a hot dude in the bathroom. Speaking of hot dudes. Francesco Rossi, from the shitty movie. Goddamn! He is the best actor ever. And that ass looks perfect. Not the script, not the cinematography, none of that. That ass is the best part of the movie. Oh, no, no, no. Did you like *Tiefblauen Morgen*?

Sashka It wasn't bad.

Hans You are one of them.

Sashka Them, who?

Hans Those who think they're smart when they feel bored. Who won Cannes five years ago?

Sashka I don't remember.

Hans Nobody does! This is a temple for banality! Also, by the way, your name?

Sashka Benoit.

Hans I don't hear a French accent.

Sashka I'm Swiss.

Hans No Swiss accent either.

Sashka I travel a lot.

Hans Do you work in film?

Sashka I'm a producer. Looking for an exciting new project.

Hans I have exciting new projects in need of funding.

Sashka Let's go to the beach, then. We can keep chatting.

Actor B Sashka now only wants the body of that German boy. The one who denied his divinity. On the beach, they drink.

Sashka Tell me about you.

Hans No much to tell. I just want to fuck, drink and make movies. But society eats our guts.

Sashka You can move to the communist side.

Hans You're joking.

Sashka I've visited Soviet land. Its wonders are real.

Hans Soviet socialism is the biggest hypocrisy ever made.

Sashka You say capitalism is perverse. Well, go to where they dismantle it.

Hans You are a utopian, Benoit.

Sashka And you are here to get hold of my millions.

Hans But not a hypocrite. I believe in authenticity! Money makes you free. Elevates you from mundane concerns to release your pulsion. God made us perverse, and I want to be a servant of my body. Not follow the Party or the Capital. I obey the desire that the Divinity planted on my chest. No one is going to control my desire to fuck, destroy and get drunk.

Sashka Nobody controls you, Hans.

Hans The world never ceases to repress us!

Sashka Is your father too strict?

Hans I'm talking 'bout the world, not my father.

Sashka Just making a guess.

Hans A stupid one.

Sashka *smiles. He won.*

Sashka You seem affected, boy.

Hans I'm not.

Sashka Dads destroy their sons. That's their mission. But it still hurts. Do you need a hug?

Hans I'm telling you I'm fine.

Sashka You can trust me.

Hans I don't trust people.

Sashka What did he do, that hurts so much?

Hans Don't talk about my father.

Sashka Mine was a piece of shit.
Maybe us, who have been hurt by the world, can take care of each other.

Hans Are you a Catholic or a socialist?
Or just a liar howling clichés at the sea?

Sashka I'm just a human.

Hans Humans are beasts, Benoit. Christ said "murder thy neighbor."

Sashka What is your solution?

Hans Authenticity!

Sashka Yeah, you said that.

Hans Submit to my nastiest desires and forget about politics. Infinite orgies! Cruising on docks! Getting under sweaty male bodies. Mindless violence, to break the hypocrisy of society! Drinking with strangers, getting naked on the beach singing like crazy. The only balm for the pain of existing.

He looks at the sky. He is playing it cool. But he is affected.

God! Can you hear me? Why did you made us horrible and ask us to be good? Can't you see that's fucked up?

Sashka You want to get naked and sing like crazy? Let's do it.

Hans Will you do it with me?

Sashka *gets as naked as he feels comfortable and starts singing a song.* **Hans** *follows him. He was not really expecting that, but he likes it. They sing together, naked. When they're done, they look at the ocean.* **Hans** *gets close to* **Sashka** *and puts his head in his shoulder.*

Sashka All good?

Hans I've never done that. That was nice.

Sashka It was.

A beat.

Hans Why is God so perverse?
He wants us to need our parents and our parents are monsters.
They devour you. You murder them.

Imitating a sportscaster.

Chronos against Oedipus! The historical duel happening eeeeeeevry day, eeeeeeeverywhere.

Plays with his hands and makes stupid voices.

I'll kill you!
No! You will die!
I'm drunk.

Sashka Me too.

Naked as they are, they hug. Look at each other in the eye. **Sashka** *kisses him.* **Hans** *kisses him back.*

They have sex on the beach.

Then, they lay on the floor. Is smoking a cigarette too cliché?

Hans I like the sea.

Sashka It's nice.

Hans The sand gets on your ass though.

Sashka True.

A beat.

You fucked me for my money, didn't you?

Hans (*thinks about it – he sounds very honest*) No. I came for your money. We fucked because I wanted to.

Sashka You wouldn't fuck me if I didn't have it.

Hans Are you're not a millionaire, Benoit?

Sashka Your movie was terrible, Hans. And you're not a good actor. I would never give you money.

Hans Oh, you'd want to fund shit like *Tiefblauen Morgen*.

Sashka I directed that movie.

Hans Zinatov?

Sashka I gave you a chance. But all you have to offer is teenage anxiety with words you don't understand.
Authenticity? What the fuck is that?
You cry because your daddy doesn't love you. Please grow up.

Hans You know your movie is trash, don't you?

Sashka Cannes disagrees with you.

Hans This is a political prize. Guys with power offer alms to the poor, and the poor think they can join us. You are a token.

Sashka Talk, kid, if it makes you feel better. Your rich ass fucked a proletarian.

Hans *talks as he gets dressed. He is extremely calm.*

Hans Not the first one, not the last one. Tarkovski saw you and thought you were a curiosity. A proletarian watching movies at the Cinémathèque française. He turned you into the voice of the European working class. A brilliant publicity stunt, I'll admit. The voice of the people! But nothing is more vulgar than the people. Communists care about the most abject humans. Look at you. Cannes invited you to party, but you're not one of us. You're filthy. An exotic attraction to entertain bored rich bastards. They use you to claim this system is fair. As if merit meant shit. You tell people that if they are good enough they'll make it. So, *some* of you make it. But you believed the lie, poor thing. You were condemned since birth, Zinatov. So different from Rossi. You're not a sinner because you're here. You are a sinner because you think you deserve it.

Sashka *feels these words are truer than he wants to admit.*

He stands up and looks at **Hans** *in the eye. He is naked,* **Hans** *is fully dressed.*

Sashka   Your only merit was to born in the right place.

Hans   Do I need anything else?

Sashka   You are trash. Your class is trash.
History will prove me right.
History will scorch your culture and disappear your memory. Parasites of the surplus value.
Destroying the world just to build another mansion.

Hans   Yes. I'm not ashamed, though. You spent the most important night of your life trying to fuck me. Years trying to be like me. Don't tell *me* I'm pathetic.

A beat. A smile. A final stab.

Tonight, the masters invited you to the party. I hope you had fun. They won't have you again.

He leaves.

Sashka *is alone, naked, with a bottle. He's been broken.*

We hear the sea. Or a song.

Actor B   The next morning, *Tiefblauen Morgen* was on all the European newspapers.
All the headlines.
All of them.
Mentioned Francesco Rossi. A revelation. The future of cinema.
Nobody cared much about an exiled director coming from the Italian factories.
A week later, Sashka called Ingmar Bergman. Maybe he'd have some advice.

Ingmar Bergman   That's life, my man! Don't be sad.
You work on your little movie for years and that kiddo had the glory.
But glory is fleeting. You made a cute movie, Sashka. Isn't that enough for you?
Do me a favor.
Give my number to Rossi.
I have the best role for him.

Finale

Actor B Sashka opened the door.
Saw the boys with his papers.
And the longest silence choked the air.

Sashka You know it all now.
Is there anything I can say?
I haven't slept in weeks.
I thought. If I save Benjamín, God may forgive me.
But I couldn't. I can't.

Michel There was a cold night, some months ago.
I went to the projections room at 2 a.m.
Watched *Tiefblauen Morgen* alone, under four blankets.
It starts with the boy running naked through the beach.
That scene is beautiful. The Lumières invented movies to film that.
I cried seeing my young body.
Only you could make utopia with a piece of film.
Tiefblauen Morgen is the best movie ever made, Zinatov.
It brought this boy across the ocean.
I never cared about movies. I wanted a home. And the most brilliant filmmaker in the world found me on the streets and hugged me like only Federico hugged me.
You were my home, Sashka. My land. My nation.
Remember the night you asked me to act?
When you showed me your script?
We read it together. Made love over the pages.
You were inside me and I was you and we were the same. I felt your beard on my lips and we belonged to the universe. I moaned and angels sang from my throat.
I gave my body to you.
Cannes was nothing!
Glory was nothing!
Power was nothing!
And I am broken, Zinatov. You broke me.
The movie is testimony of the love I had for you. A movie that will outlive us.

He leaves. A beat.

Sashka You could get lost with Michel in the middle of nowhere.
Or stay. Prepare for the throne. We can do better than *Tiefblauen Morgen*.

Benjamín I don't want your throne, Sashka.

Sashka Stay.
Let's make this studio great. Shame Cineccittà. Humiliate the Hans Butzers of the Earth.

Benjamín It won't happen.

Sashka Why not?

A beat.

The illusions in **Benjamín***'s head are burnt, now.*

So he has the power.

He approaches **Sashka**. *Grabs his chin. Looks at him in the eye.*

Benjamín   Because the master's house was never made for us, Sashka.
If I stay, I'll become you.

Sashka   You were always a boy, Benjamín.

Benjamín   A lost boy.
And I will never understand the ways of the world.

Beat.

I want to tell you that everything will be alright.
That the future holds peace and happiness for all.
But it is not true.
We're fucked.
We'll leave everything we believed in to live in a capitalist world.
It will be terrible, Sashka.
Our biggest fears will become our daily bread.
We'll have to rebuild everything again to survive.
It is my turn to leave my father, his house, his god, his fatherland.
And find mine.
Or, who knows? Maybe I can learn to live without any of that.

He hugs **Sashka**. *Kisses him on the forehead. Then, leaves the stage.*

Sashka *is alone. Broken.*

Music.

Maybe, **Benjamín** *and* **Michel** *sing.*

Maybe, both of them hold hands.

And become a community of two.

The End.

The SAD Summers of Princess Diana

Carla Zúñiga

Translated by Francisca Olivares Medina

A Theatre-Maker Translates

By Francisca Olivares Medina

Translating *The SAD Summers of Princess Diana* has reshaped the way I understand language, voice, and storytelling in my creative practice. As the first play I ever translated, it shaped my approach both as a theatre director and translator. For me, translation isn't just about finding the right words in another language; it's about bridging cultures, amplifying marginalised voices, challenging norms and offering new perspectives.

I began translating this play in 2018 while studying for my MFA in Theatre Directing at East 15. At the time, I had no formal training as a translator – and to be honest, I still don't – just a bit more experience now, and a better sense of what I'm doing (most days). What I did have was a deep desire to bring this powerful Chilean story to British audiences. *The SAD Summers of Princess Diana* spoke to me profoundly. It's a raw, bold and unapologetically political play that confronts the grotesque and the tender alike. It captures the violence imposed on women and gender-diverse communities in ways that are heartbreakingly poetic and brutally honest.

Though the play references Princess Diana and Anne Boleyn, this story is not about them. Their public images are reimagined through a Latinx lens, becoming entry points into a broader conversation about how shame, control, and silencing are imposed on women and gender non-conforming people. These figures are explored as mythologised icons, shaped by the fantasies and projections of a society that imposes rigid ideas about what it means to be a woman, who qualifies, who doesn't, and how those meanings are enforced. This anti-fairy tale resists the mould of princess stories and exposes the violence beneath it. For me, sharing this play with UK audiences felt urgent, not just because I'm also Chilean and want to share our incredible stories and Carla Zúñiga's fascinating and unique voice, but also because it represents the kind of cross-cultural dialogue that I strive to foster in my own work.

My process has been far from traditional. As a migrant theatre-maker working in a second language, I've approached translation in a hands-on, collaborative way, rather than following academic methods. It's been slow . . . sometimes frustratingly so. Over the years, I've conducted more than ten workshops with actors, creatives, friends and peers to refine this translation. I've tested scenes with bilingual actors, British actors and those completely new to Latin American texts. They weren't just about refining language; they were about exploring how this story resonates across different cultural contexts and understanding what gets lost or gained in translation. They became spaces for me to delve deeper into the play, as well as the cultures I am bridging and navigating in my work.

One of the most rewarding parts of this journey has been working closely with Carla. Her insight was invaluable in adapting her voice while keeping its integrity. Together, we navigated the cultural particularities that make this play what it is. The process mirrored my own identity as a migrant artist, with one foot in each culture. It deepened my belief that translation is a creative act, not just a technical one.

As a director and translator, staging this play has always been my intention. I know it may be difficult to produce, especially in the current UK theatre context, where resources are limited, casts are expected to be small, and work in translation is still rarely produced. This play does indeed have a large cast, a complex, stylised structure, and politically charged content. But these are also the very things that give it strength and urgency, and I remain hopeful. The fact that it's a Chilean play engaging with British icons speaks to the heart of cross-cultural collaboration, not as tokenism but as a way to break boundaries, spark exchange, and find common ground in difference.

I hope this translation does justice to Carla's remarkable work and opens up space for international stories to be valued, for work in translation to be produced, and for urgent conversations about gender-based violence and the continued erasure of women, particularly women of colour, as well as queer, trans, and migrant voices in public discourse.

* * *

Carla Zúñiga is a celebrated Chilean playwright, renowned for her bold and satirical exploration of societal norms. A graduate of ARCIS University and the University of Chile, she has developed her craft through workshops with the late Juan Radrigán and the Royal Court's international programme. Her repertoire includes *La Trágica Agonía de un Pájaro Azul*, *Prefiero que me Coman los Perros* and *Los Tristísimos Veranos de la Princesa Diana* – a play commissioned by the British Council in 2016. Twice awarded the Critics' Circle of Chile Award, she co-founded the influential theatre company La Niña Horrible, shaping contemporary Chilean theatre.

Francisca Olivares Medina is a Chilean theatre director, translator and theater-maker based in London. She graduated from ARCIS University and holds an MFA in Theatre Directing from East 15 Acting School. Passionate about feminist practices and cross-cultural collaboration, Francisca bridges Latin American stories with English-speaking audiences, amplifying underrepresented voices. Her work explores themes of identity, gender and migration, creating socially engaged and accessible theatre. She has collaborated with organizations such as Out of the Wings, CASA Festival, CLACS, Latinx Actors UK and Icarus Theatre to create transformative work that connects communities and challenges boundaries.

World Premiere

Los Tristísimos Veranos de la Princesa Diana, at Espacio Diana (Santiago, Chile), August 2017, directed by Javier Casanga.

Additional Productions

Los Tristísimos Veranos de la Princesa Diana, at Teatro Nacional Chileno – Festival Santiago Off (Santiago, Chile), January 2018, directed by Javier Casanga.

Los Tristísimos Veranos de la Princesa Diana, at Teatro Sidarte (Santiago, Chile), August 2018, directed by Javier Casanga.

Characters

Princess Diana
Brunilda, *a maid*
Dorotea, *another maid*
Guillermo, *a prince*
Enrique, *another prince*
Journalist
Tom, *a* travesti[1]
Fatima, *a girl*
Jester
Narrator
Guard

---

[1] The term travesti (lit. 'transvestite') in Latin America refers to a gender identity that resists traditional binaries. It is not directly equivalent to 'transvestite' or 'transgender' in English-speaking contexts. In Chile, travestis often embody a politicised femininity shaped by marginalisation, performance, and survival. The figure of the travesti has been powerfully explored in the work of Pedro Lemebel, particularly in *Tengo miedo torero* (2001), translated by Katherine Silver as *My Tender Matador* (Grove Press, 2020), which offers a powerful literary portrayal of the travesti figure in Pinochet-era Chile. This identity also features prominently in his crónicas, where the travesti emerges as a symbol of rebellion, defiance, and resistance against patriarchy and state violence.

Scene One: The Princess has vomited all over her bedroom

*The **Princess**'s bedroom. The **Princess** has just woken up from a long and confusing dream. She is covered in vomit. **Brunilda** and **Dorotea**, her maids, are cleaning the vomit off her clothes, her hair and her bed.*

Narrator   That morning, the Princess woke from a long, bewildering dream, with no memory of the night before. She had dreamt of monsters, that was all she could remember.

Princess Diana   I couldn't make it to the toilet. I vomited over the whole bed.

Brunilda   You are unwell, Princess.

Princess Diana   No, I'm not.

Dorotea   So, why did you vomit?

Princess Diana   I don't know.

Dorotea   How don't you know?

Brunilda   Leave her alone, Dorotea. The Princess is tired.

Princess Diana   I'll get some water.

Dorotea   No! Don't worry, I'll bring it for you.

Princess Diana   No, I'd rather go myself.

Dorotea   No, you're unwell. I'll fetch it.

She exits.

Brunilda   Has the Princess been vomiting for a while?

Princess Diana   No.

Brunilda   I thought I heard the Princess vomiting yesterday.

Princess Diana   No, I didn't vomit yesterday.

Brunilda   Are you sure?

Princess Diana   Yes.

Brunilda   How strange! I could've sworn I heard you vomiting.

Princess Diana   I didn't vomit.

Dorotea *enters.*

Dorotea   Here's your herbal tea, Princess.

Princess Diana   Thank you.

Dorotea   Has the Princess been vomiting for a while?

Brunilda   I already asked her that.

Dorotea   And what did she say?

Brunilda   She said no.

Dorotea   No? But I thought I heard her vomiting yesterday.

Brunilda   I heard her too.

Princess Diana   I didn't vomit yesterday.

Dorotea   How strange!

Princess Diana   I need fresh air.

Brunilda   Why?

Princess Diana   I don't feel well.

Dorotea   Shall I fetch the fan?

Princess Diana   No, I'd rather walk outside.

Brunilda   You're pale as death, Princess.

Dorotea   You might faint.

Princess Diana   No, I already feel better.

Dorotea   You don't look it. You look dreadful.

Princess Diana   Do I really look that bad?

Brunilda   Of course you look awful. You lost a great deal of blood yesterday.

Dorotea   Litres of blood.

Brunilda   I don't know how you even have the strength to vomit after losing so much blood.

Princess Diana   I just want some fresh air. I think it would do me good.

Brunilda   You're too weak, you shouldn't go outside, Princess

Dorotea   I'll fetch the fan, Princess.

Princess Diana   I'd like to walk a little.

Brunilda   You look terribly unwell, Princess.

Princess Diana   I'm not unwell.

Brunilda   Dorotea, bring the fan for the Princess.

Dorotea *leaves.*

Princess Diana   Brunilda.

Brunilda   Yes?

Princess Diana   Did something happen last night?

Brunilda Something like what?

Princess Diana I don't know . . . Something strange.

Brunilda No. Why do you ask?

Princess Diana I can't remember what happened.

Brunilda Nothing happened, Princess. We came straight from the hospital to your room. You fell into a deep sleep. You'd lost so much blood, you couldn't even stand.

Princess Diana When I fell asleep . . . I have this . . . shadowy memory of people being in my room. Shapes moving. But perhaps it was just a dream.

Brunilda No one came to see you, Princess. No one wanted to, not after what happened yesterday.

Dorotea *appears with the fan.*

Dorotea Here's the fan!

Princess Diana Thank you, Dorotea, but I'm going to see the boys.

Brunilda Why do you want to see the boys?

Princess Diana I want to see them. Where are they?

Dorotea They're playing in the garden.

Princess Diana Brunilda, pass me a cigarette.

Brunilda A cigarette?

Princess Diana Yes.

Brunilda You shouldn't smoke, Princess.

Princess Diana Where are my cigarettes? They were here on the vanity.

Brunilda I don't know.

Princess Diana Who put those bars on the window?

Brunilda What do you mean, who put them there?

Princess Diana They weren't there before.

Dorotea What do you mean, Princess?

Princess Diana My window didn't have bars.

Brunilda Your window has always had bars, Princess.

Dorotea Are you sure you're feeling well?

Princess Diana Who put those bars there?

Brunilda Princess, they've always been there.

Princess Diana I've never seen them before.

Dorotea   Your window has always had bars.

Princess Diana   No . . . I used to let the birds in.

Dorotea   You never did that, Princess.

Princess Diana   Why is the door closed?

Brunilda   What's wrong with the door being closed?

Princess Diana   It's always open.

Brunilda   It's always closed, Princess.

Princess Diana   I don't understand what's happening.

Brunilda   Nothing is happening.

Dorotea   Shall I open it for you?

Princess Diana   Yes, please.

Dorotea *walks to the door but does not open it.*

Brunilda   Let me take your temperature.

Princess Diana   Why?

Brunilda   You're probably feverish, Princess.

Princess Diana   No, I feel fine.

Dorotea   You don't look it.

Princess Diana   I want to see my boys.

Brunilda   They're playing outside.

Princess Diana   I want to see them.

Dorotea   They don't want to see you.

Princess Diana   Why not?

Brunilda   They're angry with you.

Princess Diana   Why?

Brunilda   After what happened yesterday, they were devastated. They didn't sleep a wink last night.

Dorotea   They did nothing but cry and cry.

Brunilda   They're traumatised, I don't think they'll ever recover from this.

Dorotea   They saw you face-down unconscious, they thought you were dead.

Brunilda   They watched your blood pooling across the floor.

Dorotea   They kept asking us what had happened, but we didn't know what to say. We had no words to explain such a terrible tragedy.

Princess Diana   Do they know that I . . .?

Brunilda   Everyone knows, Princess.

Dorotea   They hate you, Princess.

Princess Diana   Who?

Brunilda   The boys.

Princess Diana   How do you know?

Brunilda   Because they told us.

Dorotea   Enrique said he wishes you were dead.

Brunilda   And Guillermo said he wishes you had never been born.

Princess Diana   I have to go find them . . .

Dorotea   They don't want to see you.

Brunilda   They hate you, Princess.

Princess Diana   They don't understand what really happened . . .

Brunilda   Oh they understand, Princess. Everyone does . . .

The **Princess**'s *face turns pale. Suddenly, she rushes out to the toilet to vomit.*

Brunilda   Don't tell her anything.

Dorotea   Why would I?

Brunilda   Just don't.

Dorotea   I won't.

Brunilda   Did you hear how she spoke to us?

Dorotea   Unbelievable.

Brunilda   She thinks she's better than us.

Dorotea   I pity her.

Brunilda   So do I.

Dorotea   She's going straight to hell.

Brunilda   And she'll rot there for all eternity.

The **Princess** *re-enters, pale and trembling. Her movements are slow, disoriented.*

Brunilda   How are you feeling, Princess?

Dorotea   Did you vomit again?

Brunilda   We heard you retching.

Princess Diana   Did someone cut my hair?

Brunilda   What?

Princess Diana   My hair, it's short.

Brunilda   You've always had short hair, Princess.

Princess Diana   No, I've always had it long.

Dorotea   No, Princess.

Princess Diana   Yes. How could I not know how I wear my own hair?

Brunilda   You're scaring me.

Princess Diana   Why?

Brunilda   You are acting . . . strange.

Princess Diana   I've always had long hair. Look, someone's hacked it with a knife. There's blood on me.

Dorotea   But you're always cutting yourself, Princess.

Princess Diana   What?

Dorotea   You cut yourself.

Princess Diana   What are you talking about?

Dorotea   You slice your legs with blades. It makes you feel better.

Princess Diana   Why are you saying that?

Brunilda   Everyone says you cut yourself.

Princess Diana   What's that got to do with anything I'm saying? Someone cut my hair! They cut my skin! There's blood on my clothes!

Brunilda   That blood could be from anywhere. You had a terrible haemorrhage yesterday . . .

Princess Diana   There are wounds on my head!

Brunilda   Didn't you make those wounds yourself, Princess?

Princess Diana   What? No! Why would I do that?

Brunilda   Because sometimes . . . you cut yourself.

Princess Diana   That's a lie.

Brunilda   How strange. Everyone says you cut yourself.

Princess Diana   Are you sure no one came to see me last night?

Brunilda   We already told you, no one wanted to see you.

Princess Diana   What happened last night?

Brunilda   Nothing.

Princess Diana Someone came in the early morning . . . I saw shadows, I'm sure . . . someone did something . . . someone did something to the room . . .

Dorotea Go to bed.

Princess Diana I don't want to go to bed.

Brunilda You look dreadful, Princess.

Princess Diana Why didn't you open the door?

Dorotea What?

Princess Diana I asked you to open the door ages ago.

Dorotea Yes.

Princess Diana So?

Dorotea So what?

Princess Diana You didn't open it.

Dorotea No.

Princess Diana Why not?

Dorotea I got distracted, Princess. What do you think is happening?

Princess Diana It's locked.

Brunilda What?

Princess Diana The door is locked.

Brunilda Why would we lock the door?

Princess Diana Are you keeping me locked in?

Dorotea You're delusional, Princess.

Princess Diana What's going on?

Dorotea What's wrong with you, Princess? You're so pale.

Brunilda You're confused because you lost so much blood yesterday.

Princess Diana Open the door!

Brunilda Alright, Princess. Calm yourself.

She crosses to the door and opens it. The **Princess** *tries to step out, but abruptly turns and rushes to the toilet.*

Dorotea What's wrong, Princess?

Brunilda You're not going to vomit again, are you? People might think you're bulimic.

She closes the door.

She's beginning to suspect.

Dorotea Yes. Soon, she'll piece it all together.

Brunilda Did you see her face when I said the word?

Dorotea What word?

Brunilda Bulimic.

Dorotea She nearly died.

Brunilda She thinks we haven't noticed.

Dorotea She thinks we're fools.

Brunilda But the fool is her.

Dorotea She's such a fool.

Brunilda I don't understand why people love her so much, I hate her.

Dorotea After what happened, no one will love her.

Brunilda Everyone says terrible things about her, I don't know how she stands it.

Dorotea If I were her, I'd join a convent or kill myself.

Brunilda If I were her, I'd throw myself onto the train tracks and let the train run over me.

Dorotea If I were her, I'd dig a hole in the ground and bury myself alive.

Brunilda I think she's so thin and pale because she has AIDS.

Dorotea You think so?

Brunilda That's what happens when you spend too much time with homosexuals. What's the appeal of spending time with the homos, anyway?

Dorotea Did you know that butler she was so friendly with? He's a homosexual now. He used to be normal, had a wife, kids, and then one day, poof, he turned gay. It's like a cat waking up tomorrow and deciding it's a dog.

Brunilda That wicked Princess is going to hell. She'll rot in hell for all eternity.

Princess Diana *enters.*

Dorotea Did you vomit again, Princess?

Princess Diana I'm sorry.

Brunilda Why?

Princess Diana For behaving like this. I've been a bit paranoid . . . after everything that happened yesterday.

Dorotea Don't trouble yourself, Princess.

Princess Diana Will you get the boys?

Brunilda Of course, Princess.

Princess Diana Tell them their mother is calling. We need to pack.

Brunilda   Pack? For what?

Princess Diana   We're going to a place where it snows.

Dorotea   Why would you go to a place where it snows?

Brunilda   That's no place for a woman alone.

Princess Diana   I'm taking the dogs.

Brunilda   The dogs?

Princess Diana   Did you close the door?

Dorotea   Yes.

Princess Diana   Why?

Dorotea   I must have closed it by accident.

Princess Diana   Leave it open, please.

Brunilda   You're still bleeding Princess, you've stained your dress.

Princess Diana   I'll change . . . don't worry.

Dorotea   Try to get some sleep, Princess.

Brunilda   Let us know if you keep bleeding so we can call the doctors. We wouldn't want you to bleed dry overnight and wake up dead tomorrow.

Dorotea *and* **Brunilda** *exit. They slam the door. The sound suggests they've locked it.*

Narrator   The Princess awakens at dawn and tries to open the door, but it doesn't budge. Her worst fear is confirmed: the door is locked. She screams in desperation, hurling a bottle that shatters against the wooden door, but no one seems to hear her. She realizes there is no one in this world who can hear her pain.

She sinks to the floor, defeated. 'Life is shit and should be shorter,' she thinks. Suddenly, one of the curtains shifts. The Princess freezes, her breath catching, her heart pounding. From between the fabric, a child's foot appears.
Perhaps, in this cruel, dark world, someone still loves her after all.

From behind the curtains, her son **Enrique** *appears. Moments later, from out of the closet, her son* **Guillermo** *steps forward.*

Guillermo and Enrique   Mother!

Both children run to her and hug her tightly.

Scene Two: The Princess is treated like a dog

Same room, but in slightly more disarray. **Princess Diana** *talks to her children,* **Guillermo** *and* **Enrique**.

Princess Diana   Did my mother refuse to help me?

Guillermo   No, she said we shouldn't see you anymore.

Enrique   If only fairy godmothers were real, Mummy, they could help us.

Princess Diana   Did she say anything else?

Guillermo   She told us you were crazy.

Enrique   I don't think you are crazy, Mummy.

Guillermo   And she said that under no circumstances should Enrique or I become like you when we grow up. Especially me, since I'm going to be king.

Enrique   I'd love to be like you, Mummy.

Guillermo   She said you're an embarrassment.

Enrique   I don't think you're an embarrassment, Mummy.

Princess Diana   That's what she said?

Guillermo   Yes. That's all she said. But she seemed strange.

Princess Diana   Strange how?

Guillermo   Like she was hiding something from us.

Enrique   Everyone's acting so strange.

Princess Diana   Why?

Enrique   They talk to us weirdly and look at us weirdly. This morning a woman hugged me and started crying. She said she was very sorry.

Princess Diana   Why was she crying?

Enrique   I don't know, but she wouldn't let me go. She said that she had done the same thing you did, but I shouldn't tell anyone.

Guillermo   Is it true what they say?

Princess Diana   What do they say?

Guillermo   That the other day you fainted and started bleeding because . . . I don't know how to say it . . .

Enrique   They say you killed someone.

Guillermo   Enrique!

Princess Diana   I didn't kill anyone.

Enrique   They say someone was living inside of you . . . Was it a fairy godmother?

Princess Diana   No, darling.

Guillermo   When are they letting you out, Mother?

Princess Diana   Nobody tells me anything.

Enrique   They say you won't be a princess anymore.

Princess Diana   Is that what they're saying?

Guillermo   Why did they lock you away?

Princess Diana   Because I did things . . . things princesses aren't supposed to do.

Guillermo   I want things to go back to how they were before.

Princess Diana   That's not possible, Guillermo.

Guillermo   Why not?

Princess Diana   Things have changed.

Guillermo   What changed?

Princess Diana   Everything.

Enrique   How can we help you, Mummy?

Princess Diana   I need you to find Tom.

Guillermo   Tom? Your butler?

Princess Diana   Yes.

Guillermo   He was fired.

Princess Diana   Fired?

Guillermo   Yes.

Princess Diana   Why?

Guillermo   Because he started dressing as a woman.

Princess Diana   So?

Guillermo   What do you mean, 'so'?

Princess Diana   What's wrong with that?

Guillermo   No one liked that he dressed as a woman.

Princess Diana   Why not?

Guillermo   Because it's weird.

Princess Diana   I need you boys to go find him.

Guillermo   Who?

Princess Diana   Tom.

Guillermo   No.

Princess Diana   Why not?

Guillermo   Because he's weird.

Princess Diana   We're all weird, Guillermo. Besides, he's my friend. He's my only friend.

Enrique   Do you know where he lives?

Princess Diana   On the other side of the city.

Guillermo   How will we get there? We can't go alone, something could happen to us . . .

Princess Diana   I need your help, boys.

Enrique   I'll go with you, Guillermo, I will protect you.

Princess Diana   Do you remember those animal costumes you got for Christmas last year? Put them on and go there. Don't let anyone recognize you. Don't talk to strangers, keep your heads down, walk quickly and don't make eye contact with anyone. When you get there, tell him what's happening. He's my friend; he can help me escape. Please . . . be careful.

Enrique   Alright. We'll do what you need us to do.

Princess Diana   The maids are coming!

Guillermo   Let's go, Enrique.

Enrique   Mummy, you look beautiful with your short hair.

Princess Diana   Thank you, my love.

Guillermo   Quickly, Enrique!

Princess Diana   Boys, please, be very careful!

Guillermo *and* **Enrique** *exit.* **Brunilda** *and* **Dorotea** *enter.*

Brunilda   Good morning, Princess. I see you didn't die overnight.

Dorotea   Good morning, Princess.

Princesa Diana   Good morning.

Brunilda (*handing her a tray*)   Here, Princess, your breakfast.

Princess Diana   What is this?

Brunilda   What do you mean?

Princess Diana   There, floating in the milk . . . Oh God! It's a dead rat!

Brunilda   What are you talking about, Princess? It's just breakfast. Eat it.

Dorotea   I don't see anything.

Princess Diana   It's there, floating! Get it out! Get it out!

Brunilda   You're skipping breakfast again, Princess. You didn't eat yesterday either.

Princess Diana   There was a rotten frog yesterday . . .

Brunilda   You always complain about everything, Princess.

Dorotea   There are people starving in this world, and here you are, throwing away perfectly good food.

Princess Diana   Please bring me something else, I'm hungry.

Brunilda   I'll see if there's something you might like.

Princess Diana   Someone's tampering with my food.

Dorotea   You're being paranoid again, Princess.

Brunilda   I'll bring the Jester to lift your spirits.

Princess Diana   Why? I don't want to see him.

Brunilda   Why not?

Princess Diana   I don't like him.

Dorotea   How can you not like him, Princess?

Brunilda   I've already sent for him.

Princess Diana   I told you, I don't want to see him.

Brunilda   It's very rude to reject artists like this.

Princess Diana   I don't want to see anyone.

Brunilda   Alright, I'll tell him he's not welcome. Dorotea, dress the Princess and air this room. It smells like a wet dog.

Princess Diana   Please, bring me something to eat.

Brunilda   Of course, Princess.

She exits.

Dorotea   Which dress would you like to wear, Princess?

Princess Diana   Dorotea, I need your help.

Dorotea   No, Princess, I'm sorry, they'll hang anyone who helps you.

Princess Diana   I beg you.

Dorotea   No, Princess. After what you did, no one will help you. What you did was terrible, Princess. You're a murderer.

Princess Diana   I'm not a murderer.

Dorotea I won't help you, no matter what, Princess.

Princess Diana Please, I'll give you anything you want.

Dorotea Really?

Princess Diana Yes.

Dorotea How about that sea-green dress I like?

Princess Diana Take it, it's yours.

Dorotea And that bracelet with the diamonds?

Princess Diana Yes, take it.

Dorotea What do you want to know, Princess?

Princess Diana When will they let me out of here?

Dorotea Never.

Princess Diana What do you mean, Never?

Dorotea I can't say anything more, Princess.

Princess Diana Please, Dorotea . . .

Dorotea Everyone's furious with you.

Princess Diana Because of what happened?

Dorotea Of course. No princess in the whole of human history has ever done such a thing. Never ever.

Princess Diana That's not true, Dorotea, many princesses have done it . . . but in secret, no one ever knew about it.

Dorotea Don't be ridiculous.

Princess Diana Please, help me. I need a phone to call someone who can help me . . . I'm begging you.

Dorotea No, Princess. I shouldn't have even told you this much.

Princess Diana Please.

Dorotea No.

Princess Diana Take whatever you want.

Dorotea Whatever I want?

Princess Diana Whatever you want.

Dorotea Really?

Princess Diana Yes.

Dorotea Your crown?

Princess Diana Yes, take it.

Dorotea Your wedding dress with that long train and puffy sleeves?

Princess Diana Yes.

Dorotea And that citrus perfume I like?

Princess Diana Yes, take it.

Dorotea Alright, Princess. I'll help you. Tonight I'll bring you a phone. But please, I beg you, don't tell anyone I helped you.

Princess Diana You have my word.

Dorotea Princess?

Princess Diana Yes.

Dorotea Would you like me to tell you more?

Princess Diana Yes, please. Dorotea, tell me everything you know. I beg you . . .

Dorotea But I'd like to ask for something in return.

Princess Diana Whatever you want.

Dorotea Promise you won't laugh at me.

Princess Diana I won't.

Dorotea It's a bit strange . . .

Princess Diana Just tell me.

Dorotea I'd like to see you naked.

Princess Diana What?

Dorotea I'd like to see you naked.

Princess Diana Why?

Dorotea I don't know. I just . . . want to.

Princess Diana Now?

Dorotea Yes, now.

Princess Diana Alright.

She begins to undress, slowly and with shame. She stands completely bare. **Dorotea** *watches, unflinching.*

Dorotea They're going to kill you, Princess. This afternoon, you were sentenced to death.

Princess Diana *faints.*

Scene Three: A journalist gets stuck in the window

The same room, now emptier and filthier. **Princess Diana** *looks paler and more haggard.* **Guillermo** *and* **Enrique**, *dirty and bruised, stand before her.*

Princess Diana   My goodness, boys! . . . Who did this to you?

Guillermo   The people in the street . . .

Princess Diana   What happened?

Enrique   We went to the other side of the city to find Tom. We wore the costumes, just like you told us, but . . . someone recognized us.

Guillermo   People gathered around us. They started talking, asking questions. We got really scared.

Enrique   We tried to run, but they chased us. We couldn't get away.

Guillermo   I don't understand why they were so angry. They pushed us around . . .

Enrique   Some of them were taking photos, recording us.

Guillermo   Others spat at us. They threw us to the ground and said awful things about you.

Enrique   They touched our hair, our faces . . . Everyone was shouting so loudly.

Guillermo   I don't even know how we managed to escape. We got lost and walked all night.

Princess Diana   My God . . .

Guillermo   Finally, we found Tom's house.

Enrique   We rang the bell but . . . no one answered.

Princess Diana   What did you do?

Guillermo   We went inside. I was so scared I could barely feel my legs.

Enrique   There was a strange smell in the house. We called out to see if anyone was there, but no one answered.

Guillermo   We kept walking . . . and then we saw him.

Enrique   It was so dark. We tried talking to him, but he didn't respond.

Guillermo   Tom was dead.

Princess Diana   Dead?!

Enrique   Yes, Mummy. He hanged himself from his bedroom ceiling.

Princess Diana   Oh God!

Guillermo   We cried and ran away.

Enrique   We found a letter he left.

Princess Diana What did it say?

Guillermo It said he did it because he was ill and didn't want to suffer anymore.

Enrique He mentioned you in the letter.

Princess Diana What did it say?

Enrique That he loved you very much . . . and that true freedom doesn't exist.

Guillermo After that, we left the house and started walking back.

Enrique But we got lost again. It took us an entire day to find our way home.

Princess Diana I'm so sorry, my children . . .

Enrique We'd do anything for you, Mummy.

Princess Diana I can't believe Tom is gone.

Guillermo I'm so sorry, Mother.

Princess Diana Why would he do such a thing?

Enrique He must have been so sad, Mummy . . . he must have felt very lonely . . .

Princess Diana What are we going to do now?

Enrique We need help . . . the three of us can't do it alone. I wish fairy godmothers were real.

Guillermo Mother, please go back to the way you were before . . . that's why they've locked you up in here.

Princess Diana What are you talking about?

Guillermo You used to be different. You were happier, you didn't vomit. We used to go to the sea together. You were a normal mother.

Princess Diana I wasn't happy before, Guillermo.

Guillermo Yes, we were happy! We laughed all the time . . .

Princess Diana What are you talking about? I used to lock myself in the bathroom just to cry.

Guillermo That's not true.

Princess Diana Yes, it is.

Guillermo Why can't you be like other princesses?

Princess Diana Because I'm different . . .

Guillermo Why do you have to be so different? I hate that you're so different! If you were normal, we'd be swimming in the sea right now . . .

Princess Diana But I'm not normal!

Guillermo Yes, you are. I know you.

Princess Diana   You don't know me at all.

Guillermo   People say horrible things about you.

Princess Diana   You shouldn't care what people say about me.

Guillermo   Everything is so easy for you, isn't it?

Princess Diana   Nothing is easy for me.

Guillermo   You killed our brother!

The **Princess** *slaps* **Guillermo**. **Guillermo** *runs off.*

Enrique   Is that true, Mummy?

Princess Diana   No . . . I mean, yes. I didn't kill him. He wasn't alive. He hadn't been born yet. I didn't want to have a baby.

Enrique   It's okay, Mummy. I understand. And I love you. I will always be with you. When I grow up, I want to be like you. I want to be as brave and good as you.

Princess Diana   You don't know what you're saying, love. I don't want you to be like me. I want you to be happy.

Enrique   I'm happy when I'm with you. Mummy, what's snow like?

Princess Diana   It's beautiful. I'll take you there.

Enrique   Is that where we're going to live? In a place where it snows?

Princess Diana   Yes.

Enrique   I never want to be away from you again.

Princess Diana   We'll always be together, my love, I promise.

Enrique   I'll look for help right now. I won't let anything bad happen to you. We'll escape. Don't worry. I'll come back tomorrow.

Princess Diana   Thank you, Enrique.

Enrique   Take this, Mummy. It was Tom's. I thought, since he was your friend, you'd like to have something of his.

He hands his mother a wig. Long and smooth like a river of blood. **Enrique** *leaves. The* **Princess** *puts on the wig and looks at herself in the mirror for a moment.*

Narrator   The Princess had never had many friends, but Tom was one of the few. The last time they spoke, he had been crying in the kitchen, and she had tried to console him. 'Someday, I'll be happy,' Tom had said. But some promises are never meant to be kept.

A sudden noise at the window startles the **Princess**. *She freezes. She pulls back the curtain; a hand appears reaching through. Behind it, the strained face of a* **Journalist** *appears, stuck awkwardly between the bars after climbing up to the tower.*

Journalist   Good afternoon, Your Royal Highness. Lovely weather, isn't it? Care to answer a few questions?

Princess Diana   How did you get up here?

Journalist (*pulls out a dictaphone*)   Are the rumours true that you're being kept here against your will?

Princess Diana   Yes.

Journalist   Why did they lock you up here?

Princess Diana   Because I had an abortion.

Journalist   How did you do it?

Princess Diana   I did it myself.

Journalist   How?

Princess Diana   With some pills and some knitting needles.

Journalist   Did it hurt?

Princess Diana   Of course it hurt.

Journalist   Was this your first one?

Princess Diana   Yes.

Journalist   Whose was it?

Princess Diana   I don't know.

Journalist   How can you not know?

Princess Diana   I don't know whose it was.

Journalist   Did you cheat on the Prince?

Princess Diana   Yes.

Journalist   With whom?

Princess Diana   With many men.

Journalist   Did you have many lovers?

Princess Diana   Yes. And you?

Journalist   What about me?

Princess Diana   Have you ever had a lover?

Journalist   No, never. Never in my life. How could you even ask me that? So, you cheated on the Prince?

Princess Diana   Yes. But he cheated on me too.

Journalist   With whom?

Princess Diana   With his old girlfriend.

Journalist   How do you know?

Princess Diana   Women know these things. He was distracted. Angry all the time. We were unhappy for years. I started vomiting and cutting myself, and he stopped noticing me.

Journalist   Are you bulimic, Princess?

Princess Diana   Yes, but it'll pass soon.

Journalist   What would you say to the bulimic people who will read this interview?

Princess Diana   Nothing.

Journalist   Nothing at all?

Princess Diana   What could I possibly say?

Journalist   And to the people who cut themselves?

Princess Diana   Nothing either.

Journalist   And now, do you have any lovers?

Princess Diana   No.

Journalist   Are you alone?

Princess Diana   Yes.

Journalist   Have you had many disappointing relationships?

Princess Diana   You could say so.

Journalist   What advice would you give to women who've had their hearts broken?

Princess Diana   To get a dog.

Journalist   Have you ever been with a woman?

Princess Diana   No, but I would like to try.

Journalist   Anyone in particular?

Princess Diana   No, I haven't really thought about it.

Journalist   Why do you vomit, Princess?

Princess Diana   It makes me feel better.

Journalist   Is it true that you smoke?

Princess Diana   Yes.

Journalist   How many cigarettes a day?

Princess Diana   I don't know. Fifteen . . . maybe twenty.

Journalist But no one has ever seen you smoking.

Princess Diana I'm forced to smoke in secret.

Journalist Are you depressed, Princess?

Princess Diana Yes.

Journalist Why?

Princess Diana Because life is shit.

Journalist You said shit.

Princess Diana Yes.

Journalist Do you swear?

Princess Diana Sometimes.

Journalist When?

Princess Diana On special occasions.

Journalist Have you ever tried to kill yourself?

Princess Diana Yes.

Journalist How many times?

Princess Diana Four.

Journalist How?

Princess Diana That's personal.

Journalist Why haven't you managed to die?

Princess Diana Because I've always changed my mind.

Journalist Because of your children?

Princess Diana No.

Journalist Don't you love your children?

Princess Diana I love them.

Journalist Would you like to have more children?

Princess Diana No.

Journalist Why not?

Princess Diana Because life is shit.

Journalist You said shit again.

Princess Diana Yes.

Journalist Are you happy to die, Princess?

Princess Diana No.

Journalist How does it feel to know they're going to cut off your head?

Princess Diana They're going to cut off my head?

Journalist Yes, didn't you know?

Princess Diana No ...

Journalist How does that make you feel?

Princess Diana I don't know ...

Journalist Do you want to cry?

Princess Diana No ...

Journalist Why not?

Princess Diana I don't cry.

Journalist But they're going to kill you.

Princess Diana Yes.

Journalist What do you think it will be like?

Princess Diana Easy, I have a slender neck.

Journalist What can you say to all the women who are sentenced to death?

Princess Diana Nothing.

Journalist And to women who have had an abortion?

Princess Diana Do not feel guilty.

Journalist Do you feel guilty?

Princess Diana No.

Journalist I don't believe you.

Princess Diana That's your problem.

Journalist May I take a photograph of you?

Princess Diana Of course.

Journalist Can you sit on the bed?

Princess Diana Yes.

Journalist Put on that plaintive, sad face, Princess.

Princess Diana What plaintive, sad face?

Journalist That face you always have.

Princess Diana I don't know what face that is.

Journalist   That face.

Princess Diana   That's just my face.

*The **Journalist** pulls out a large camera with an oversized flash and snaps a photo.*

Journalist   Princess?

Princess Diana   Yes.

Journalist   Could you help me? I'm stuck.

Princess Diana   Do you have a cigarette?

Journalist   Yes. Here you go.

He hands over a cigarette. **Princess Diana** *helps her out of the bars.*

Journalist   Thank you, Princess.

Princess Diana   When is this interview coming out?

Journalist   Tomorrow.

Princess Diana   Brilliant.

Journalist   How far along were you, Princess?

Princess Diana   What do you mean?

Journalist   In your pregnancy.

Princess Diana   Four months.

Journalist   And what was it going to be?

Princess Diana   Good night.

Journalist   Answer me, Princess!

*The **Princess** closes the window and pulls the curtains shut. Then she walks towards her bed, lies down and closes her eyes.*

Scene Four: The Princess gets many visitors

*The same bedroom, now in utter disarray, as if a mob had stormed through, chasing the **Princess** and beating her like a stray dog. **Brunilda** is sobbing uncontrollably, while **Dorotea** pats her back in a futile attempt to console her.*

Brunilda   I cannot believe how treacherous the Princess is. She's an embarrassment, a disgrace! No shame whatsoever. When I read that interview, I nearly died. I swear, my heart stopped for thirty full seconds.

Dorotea   Calm down, Brunilda. This won't go unanswered.

Brunilda   What a pathetic woman. Honestly, I pity her . . .

Dorotea   Everyone's laughing at the royal family on the television.

Brunilda   What does she think she's doing?

Dorotea   What kind of example is she setting for her poor children?

Brunilda   Those poor, innocent creatures. They're the ones who suffer the most. How can she be so selfish?

Dorotea   And why did she admit to being bulimic?

Brunilda   Those things are private. A woman can be bulimic, but within the privacy of her home.

Dorotea   They sent the guards after her.

Brunilda   She deserves it . . . She's a murderer.

Dorotea   I heard she bit them and nearly gouged one of their eyes out with a candlestick.

Brunilda   That woman is a beast. When have you ever seen a princess who knows how to fight? They don't fight, that's what the princes are for.

Dorotea   They finally caught her anyway.

Brunilda   I'm deeply offended by her statements. Not all women are like her. I'm decent. I'm Catholic.

Dorotea   I'm ashamed to be a woman.

Brunilda   I can't stand to look at her. I don't want to see her face. Listen to me, Dorotea, I swear on my sainted mother's name, I will never speak to that woman again for as long as I live. Do you hear me? Never.

Princess Diana *comes out from the bathroom. She's covered in bruises, with dried blood at the corners of her mouth. A cigarette dangles from her mouth.*

Princess Diana   Hello, Brunilda.

Brunilda   Excuse me.

She leaves.

Princess Diana Is this my breakfast? What's that? . . . Oh my God! It's a foetus . . . get it out of here! . . . get it out! . . . I don't want to look at it . . .

Dorotea Don't be dramatic, Princess. It's just a dog's foetus.

The **Princess** *grabs the plate and smashes it against the wall.*

Princess Diana Who did this?

Dorotea How could you have given that interview, Princess?

Princess Diana What's wrong with it?

Dorotea Now you'll have to retract it.

Princess Diana I won't retract a word.

Dorotea If you don't, the guards will come again . . .

Princess Diana I don't care.

Dorotea I heard they pulled out one of your teeth.

Princess Diana They can rip all my teeth out, I don't care.

Dorotea I don't understand you, Princess.

Princess Diana When are you bringing me the phone?

Dorotea Tonight.

Princess Diana Alright.

Dorotea Can my son bring it?

Princess Diana What?

Dorotea Can my son bring it?

Princess Diana Your son?

Dorotea Yes.

Princess Diana Why your son?

Dorotea He wants to meet you.

Princess Diana They won't let him in.

Dorotea He works here. He's a guard at the castle.

Princess Diana And why does he want to meet me?

Dorotea Just because.

Princess Diana What do you mean, 'just because'?

Dorotea Just because.

Princess Diana What do I have to do?

Dorotea Be nice.

Princess Diana Be nice?

Dorotea Yes.

Princess Diana How nice?

Dorotea Nice.

Princess Diana What does he want?

Dorotea Nothing. Just to meet you.

Princess Diana Just to meet me?

Dorotea He'll be here at midnight. Don't do anything bad to him.

Princess Diana Why would I do something bad to him?

Dorotea I don't know.

Princess Diana What's going on?

Dorotea Retract what you said in the interview, Princess. Otherwise, things could go very badly for you.

Princess Diana What are you talking about?

Dorotea You know exactly what I mean.

Princess Diana When are they going to do it?

Dorotea Do what?

Princess Diana When are they going to kill me?

Dorotea I can't tell you.

Princess Diana Do they already know when it'll happen?

Dorotea I'm not saying another word.

Princess Diana I'm begging you . . . I'll give you anything you want.

Dorotea Alright.

Princess Diana What do you want?

Dorotea I want to hit you.

Princess Diana What?

Dorotea I want to hit you.

Princess Diana Why?

Dorotea *slaps the* **Princess** *hard across the face.*

Princess Diana Why did you do that?

Dorotea   Tomorrow your head will roll, Princess.

Princess Diana   Tomorrow?

Dorotea   Yes.

Princess Diana   At what time?

Dorotea *slaps her again.*

Dorotea   At sundown.

Princess Diana   Where are they going to do it?

Dorotea *slaps her one more time.*

Dorotea   I don't know.

Princess Diana   What?

Dorotea   I don't know where it's going to happen.

Brunilda *enters, dragging the* **Journalist** *by the arm.*

Journalist   Hello, Princess.

Princess Diana   Hello . . . What is that woman doing here, Brunilda? Brunilda? Brunilda? I'm talking to you.

Brunilda   I have nothing to say to you, Princess. Not now, not ever.

Journalist   I've come to interview you again, Princess.

Princess Diana   Why?

Journalist   Is it true that everything you told me last night was a lie?

Princess Diana   No.

Brunilda   Tell the truth, you lying Princess.

Princess Diana   Everything I said is the truth.

Journalist   You have bulimia. Your husband cheated on you. You cheated on him. You cut yourself. You were pregnant but didn't know who the father was. You aborted with pills and knitting needles. You haemorrhaged. They locked you in this tower. And tomorrow they're going to cut off your head?

Princess Diana   Yes!

Brunilda   Liar! Tell the truth, or I'll call the guards.

Princess Diana   Call them, I don't care.

Dorotea   Don't be a fool, Princess.

Brunilda   All this vomiting has made this woman stupid, don't listen to her. Write down that during their marriage everything was always perfect and that she's a very balanced woman . . . and that the abortion was actually a miscarriage, and that the

Prince was the father, and if the Princess dies any day soon, it'll be from natural causes . . .

Journalist I'm sorry, but I need to hear it from her.

Brunilda Write what I'm telling you, you lezzer!

Journalist I'm not a lezzer.

Dorotea Calm down, Brunilda.

Princess Diana The guards came into my room last night, beat me, pulled out a tooth and touched me. Write that down.

Journalist Where did they touch you, Princess?

Princess Diana Those things are private.

Journalist What would you say to the women who have been touched?

Princess Diana To hunt down the men who touched them and kill them.

Brunilda Princess!

Dorotea I'm having a stroke, Brunilda . . . My eyes are blurring . . . I'm going to faint.

Brunilda Take it back, Princess!

Princess Diana No.

Journalist What message do you want to give to the world, Princess?

Princess Diana That life is shit!

Brunilda *slaps the* **Princess** *so hard she falls to the floor.* **Dorotea** *collapses, unconscious.*

Journalist You said 'shit' again.

Brunilda This interview is over.

Journalist Is there nothing else you want to add, Princess?

Brunilda Don't you dare publish this, or I'll kill you.

Journalist Princess? Princess, how does it feel to be beaten by a maid?

Brunilda Walk faster, you lesbian.

She shoves the **Journalist** *out and drags* **Dorotea**, *still unconscious, across the floor. The* **Princess** *slowly rises and sits at the dressing table, gazing at her reflection for a moment.*

Narrator A long time ago, when the Princess was just a child, her mother struck her so hard she fell to the floor. That was the first time the Princess felt shame. A shame so heavy it made her dream of becoming someone else. Someone who would never feel such bitter disgrace. But the years passed, and she remained herself. The same person, with the same gaze and the same unrelenting shame.

Suddenly, **Enrique** *appears from the closet, clutching a bouquet of blue flowers. He is covered in dirt.*

Enrique   Mummy.

Princess Diana   My love.

Enrique   What happened to you?

Princess Diana   Nothing . . . Why are you so filthy?

Enrique   I went to find that family you are friends with, Fatima's family, the ones who came to the castle a couple of weeks ago, do you remember? I thought maybe they could help us. But when I got there, they were very sad. They said they couldn't come.

Princess Diana   Why not?

Enrique   Poor Fatima died a couple of days ago.

Princess Diana   Oh my God!

Enrique   She drowned in the sea. They never found her body. She was so small and fragile, the sea must have smashed her against the rocks . . .

Princess Diana   How awful.

Enrique   Can I tell you a secret?

Princess Diana   Yes.

Enrique   One day, Fatima and I held hands.

Princess Diana   Really?

Enrique   Yes. No one saw us. They always told me not to talk to girls who weren't royalty, but Fatima was so beautiful. She reached for my hand, and I gave it to her. We just looked at each other. That's all. I just wanted you to know.

Princess Diana   I'm so sorry, my love.

Enrique   Don't be sad, Mummy. I'm alright. Here, I picked these for you. They're blue, like your eyes.

Princess Diana   They're lovely. Thank you. Where is Guillermo?

Enrique   He hasn't left his room. He's very sad.

Princess Diana   Tell him I love him.

Enrique   We love you very much.

Princess Diana   I love you too, both of you, my love.

Enrique   Mummy?

Princess Diana   Yes?

Enrique   What will happen if you can't escape?

Princess Diana   I will escape, Enrique.

Enrique   I don't want you to die.

Princess Diana   I won't die, my love.

Enrique   Mummy? Why couldn't you have our brother?

Princess Diana   Because I had nothing left to give him.

Enrique   Why not?

Princess Diana   Because everything is falling apart.

Enrique   That's so sad . . .

Princess Diana   Burn down the castle.

Enrique   What?

Princess Diana   If I can't escape, burn down the castle. Set it on fire. Take your brother by the hand and run. Run far away from here.

Enrique   Alright, Mummy. I'd do anything for you.

Princess Diana   Thank you, my love. I don't know what I would do without you, Enrique.

Enrique   I'll come back tomorrow.

Princess Diana   Be careful.

Enrique   Here, I stole these sleeping pills from one of the maids.

Princess Diana   Thank you.

Enrique   Mummy?

Princess Diana   Yes?

Enrique   Look, I cut my leg.

Princess Diana   Why did you do that, Enrique?

Enrique   I want to be like you.

Princess Diana   Promise me you'll never do anything like that again.

Enrique   But . . .

Princess Diana   Here, if you want to feel close to me, take this. It's my favourite necklace. My mother gave it to me when I was very young. Carry it with you wherever you go, like a lucky charm.

Enrique   Thank you, Mummy.

Princess Diana   But you must promise never to cut yourself again. Never.

Enrique Alright, Mummy. I promise.

He exits. The **Princess** *swallows two of the pills* **Enrique** *had given her. Suddenly, the door creaks open, and she freezes. A guard enters. Without hesitation, he strikes her, throwing her to the floor. Then, he rapes her. The* **Princess***'s face remains nearly expressionless, hollow. When he finishes, he stands, adjusts his uniform and silently watches her. After a long moment, the* **Princess** *rises slowly, walks to the mirror and gazes at her reflection. With trembling hands, she fixes her hair and tidies her appearance. The guard approaches and hands her a phone; an old, bulky mobile. Without a word, she takes it and dials a number.*

Princess Diana Hello, Dad? It's me, Diana. I need your help . . . Hello?

She dials again.

Hello? Clara, it's me, Diana. I need your help . . . Hello?

She dials once more.

Hello? Hi, it's me, Diana . . . your sister, Diana . . . Hello? Hello?

The guard re-enters, snatches the phone and leaves. The **Princess** *collapses back to the floor. She stares blankly into the distance.*

Narrator The Princess had never felt so utterly alone in her entire life. She tried to cry, but no tears came. She had spent her whole life swallowing her pain, locking it deep within her chest. But now, her heart was weak, she could feel it. It beat slowly, almost silently, as if ashamed to let the world know that blood still flowed through such a sorrowful, broken body.

Suddenly, **Tom***, a travesti, and* **Fatima***, a girl, emerge from beneath the bed.*

Tom Get off the floor, Princess. You look like a poor little stray dog.

Princess Diana Tom . . . Fatima . . .

Fatima Princess, your eyes look so sad.

Tom Come, darling, sit here. I'll do your make-up.

The **Princess** *sits at the vanity, and* **Tom** *begins applying make-up.*

Princess Diana It's so good to see you both . . .

Tom My poor Princess.

Fatima Despite everything, you still look beautiful.

Tom When was the last time we saw each other?

Princess Diana It feels like a lifetime ago.

Fatima This room reeks of wet dog, Princess. You should open the windows.

Princess Diana I can't open the windows.

Tom You have to escape, darling. Run far away.

Princess Diana I'm being held prisoner.

Fatima Escape.

Princess Diana I can't.

Fatima We brought you something, a little axe to chop down the door.

Princess Diana An axe?

Fatima Yes.

Princess Diana Thank you.

Fatima You're welcome, Princess. I'd do anything for you.

Tom Look at you . . . stunning, as always.

Fatima You really do, like an angel.

Tom Remember when we dressed up in disguises and went dancing?

Princess Diana You dressed me as a man, and no one recognized me.

Tom We danced all night, drank far too much and ended up crying in the street, remember? We collapsed on the pavement, and then you started vomiting.

Princess Diana Then we laughed. That was the only time I ever vomited without crying.

Tom We were so happy that night. We should do it again.

Princess Diana When?

Tom I don't know. When you get out of here.

Princess Diana What if I never do?

Fatima You'll escape, Princess, that's why we brought the axe.

Tom Grab it firmly, darling, and hack down the door.

Fatima For now, hide it under your pillow.

Tom Do you have a cigarette?

Princess Diana Yes, take one.

Fatima Can I smoke too? I've done it loads of times before.

Princess Diana Really?

Fatima Yes, I'm a married woman.

Princess Diana What are you talking about? You're only eleven.

Fatima I was married off a few days ago to a much older man. That's why I threw myself into the sea.

Tom My goodness.

Princess Diana Here, have a cigarette.

Tom   Princess, if you could live anywhere in the world, where would it be?

Princess Diana   Somewhere it always snows.

Fatima   Snow? Why snow?

Princess Diana   I want to live in a place where it's always winter. I hate summer. Everything bad has happened to me in the summer. Being born, getting married, giving birth.

Tom   You didn't enjoy giving birth? I've always wondered what it feels like.

Princess Diana   For me, it was horrific. I had a haemorrhage with Guillermo. I pushed for hours, but he clung to me like he didn't want to leave. When he finally came out, they placed him on my chest. We just stared at each other, screaming and crying. We couldn't stop. Everyone thought I was overwhelmed with joy, but I wasn't. I was actually sad. I'd never felt such deep sadness.

Fatima   I was pregnant too. That's why I threw myself into the sea.

Tom   You said it was because you were married off.

Fatima   And because I was pregnant. There were many reasons to jump into the sea.

Tom   It breaks my heart.

Princess Diana   Is this real?

Fatima   Of course, it's real, Princess.

Tom   Look, Princess, it's snowing.

Snow begins to fall inside the room.

Princess Diana   How beautiful. It makes me want to cry.

Fatima   Then cry, Princess.

Princess Diana   I can't.

Fatima   Why not?

Princess Diana   I don't know why.

Tom   We should all cry together.

Fatima   I want to cry too.

Princess Diana   I'm going to run away.

Fatima   Yes, Princess. Start over.

Tom   Do whatever you want, Princess.

Princess Diana   Stay with me tonight. I can't bear this loneliness.

Tom   Close your eyes, darling.

Fatima   Tomorrow, first thing in the morning, chop down the door with the axe.

Princess Diana (*closing her eyes*)   Good night.

Tom   What would you have named her?

Princess Diana   Who?

Tom   Your daughter.

Princess Diana   Diana . . . I was going to name her after me . . .

Fatima   Good night, Princess.

Tom   Sweet dreams, Diana.

Tom *and* **Fatima** *exit. Snow falls gently onto the* **Princess**'s *bed.*

Princess Diana (*still with her eyes closed*)   Diana . . . Diana . . . My daughter . . .

Scene Five: The last chance

The same room. **Brunilda** *and* **Dorotea** *are tidying up.* **Dorotea** *wears a crown and several pieces of jewellery, her movements exaggerated and ostentatious.*

Brunilda   She's losing her mind. This morning, she woke up screaming like a lunatic. When I checked on her, she was vomiting everywhere. It was a complete spectacle.

Dorotea   She said she was looking for an axe.

Brunilda   An axe? Where would she even find one? She's lost her mind.

Dorotea   Is the Jester coming?

Brunilda   He's outside. I didn't want him to come. He won't be well received here, and he's an artist. He doesn't deserve to suffer such humiliation. But the law is the law. If a member of the royal family is sentenced to death, they must spend their final night with the the High Jester of the Realm.

Dorotea   Maybe it'll cheer her up. She could use a good laugh.

Brunilda   She doesn't deserve it. A child murderer like her should spend her last night rotting in the dungeon, alone with the rats.

The **Princess** *enters. She looks gaunt and frail, her steps slow.*

Dorotea   How did you sleep, Princess?

Princess Diana   Did you find the axe?

Brunilda   No, Princess. You must have dreamt it.

Princess Diana   I was so sure that . . .

Brunilda (*handing her a tray*)   Here's your breakfast, Princess.

Princess Diana   What is this? A decomposed human foot?

Brunilda   Oh, Princess, you always have something to complain about.

The **Princess** *picks up the foot floating in the milk and begins to eat it.*

Brunilda   What are you doing?

Princess Diana   I'm hungry.

Brunilda   How could you even think of eating that? You're completely mad.

Someone knocks at the door.

Dorotea   Princess, someone is here to see you.

Princess Diana   I don't want to see anyone.

Brunilda *opens the door. The* **Jester** *enters with exaggerated clumsiness, falling as a joke. He gets up, stumbles into the closet and accidentally knocks over a vase. He* *tries to set things back in order, but everything keeps falling.* **Brunilda** *and* **Dorotea** *burst into laughter, but the* **Princess** *remains unmoved.*

Brunilda   Welcome the High Jester of the Realm, Princess.

Jester   Greetings, Your Royal Highness. How have you been? I am the Jester.

The **Jester** *extends his hand. The* **Princess** *reluctantly takes it. His fake hand detaches, leaving her holding it. The maids howl with laughter.*

Jester   Princess, I've come to lend you a hand. Word has it you've been feeling down. Is that true? Share your sorrows, and I'll lighten your load. I'm known for being very grounded.

The **Jester** *attempts to sit in a chair but misses and crashes to the floor.*

Dorotea (*laughing uncontrollably*)   Ooohh, for heaven's sake!

Brunilda (*laughing*)   Come on, Princess, tell him how you feel.

The **Princess** *appears on the verge of tears, her composure unravelling.*

Jester   Want me to sing you a song?

Princess Diana   No.

Jester   How about a joke?

Dorotea   Yes please!

Jester   What did the microwave say to the Princess?

Brunilda   What?

Jester   Nothing, because microwaves don't talk.

The maids burst into laughter.

Jester   Don't worry, Princess. I'm not leaving this room without getting a smile from you. Oh, Princess, what's that behind your ear?

The maids giggle. The **Jester** *dramatically produces a drawing of a smiley face from behind the* **Princess**'s *ear. The maids burst into louder laughter.*

Brunilda   Mr Jester, could you show us a magic trick?

Jester   I'm afraid I can't do magic today. I have a stomach ache . . . It must've been something I ate.

Dorotea   What did you eat, Mr Jester?

Jester   I don't know . . . what could it have been?

The **Jester** *begins to pull out a seemingly endless string of multi-coloured handkerchiefs from his mouth. The maids gasp and clap in amazement.*

Brunilda   Look, Princess.

Dorotea   Where are they all coming from?

Jester   Would you like me to sing a song?

Brunilda   Princess, wouldn't you like to hear a song?

Princess Diana   No. Leave.

Dorotea   Oh, sing a song! Please!

Jester   Well, since you insist so much. I will sing you a song.

The maids continue to laugh non-stop.

Jester
Life is a carnival, a dazzling parade,
Just act like a person who's properly made.
Let happiness always remain your goal,
Keep your wits sharp and stick to your role!

The maids clap wildly, laughing and cheering.

Dorotea   He's an artist.

Brunilda   Clap, Princess.

*The **Jester** takes a deep bow, and his wig falls off. As he tries to replace it, it keeps slipping, further delighting the maids. **Guillermo** enters, holding a framed portrait of the **Princess**.*

Guillermo   Mother . . .

Princess Diana   Guillermo . . .

Brunilda   How did you get in here?

Guillermo   Mother . . . I was looking at this picture of you in my room. And you were right. I saw your eyes, they looked so sad . . . The day this photo was taken, you spent all day locked in the bathroom. I thought you were sick, but you were just sad. And I want you to be happy, Mother . . . forgive me . . . forgive me for everything I said.

Princess Diana   I love you, Guillermo.

Guillermo   I love you too, Mother.

Jester   Who is this delightful little boy? I adore children . . .

Guillermo   My name is Guillermo.

Jester (*pretending to mishear*)   Did you say Thermo? Are you always this hot?

Guillermo   My name is Guillermo.

Jester   Nintendo? You want a Nintendo? Alright, you spoiled little rascal, but remind me, what's your name again? Sorry, my ears are absolutely filthy.

*The **Jester** produces a giant plunger and pretends to clean his ears, then pulls out an enormous ball of fake dirt and tosses it toward the maids. They laugh hysterically.*

Princess Diana Get this clown out of my room!

Jester Clown? Clown? I'm not a clown, I'm the High Jester of the Realm.

Dorotea Show some respect, Princess.

Jester Little boy. Do you know where pirates love to sail?

Guillermo No.

Princess Diana Leave, please.

Jester ARRRRGH-entina!

The maids collapse in laughter.

Jester Shall I dance for you?

Princess Diana Get out!

Brunilda Yes, please.

*The **Jester** begins a clumsy, exaggerated dance, knocking over objects as the maids howl.*

Princess Diana Everyone, leave, please. I want to be alone.

Jester Okay, I'm leaving.

*The **Jester** pretends to leave but dramatically walks into the door, falling flat. The maids laugh even harder.*

Jester Oops! Forgot to open the door!

Dorotea Could you do another trick, Mr Jester?

Jester I don't know if I can . . . My stomach aches . . . something I ate didn't agree with me.

Dorotea What did you eat, Mr Jester?

Jester I don't know . . . What could it have been?

*The **Jester** acts as though he's about to pull something from his mouth, but the **Princess** grabs a perfume bottle and hurls it at his head, knocking him to the floor.*

Princess Diana Everybody leave!

Dorotea Princess, what have you done?

Brunilda You're a savage!

Dorotea Mr Jester, are you alright?

Brunilda He's not responding, you've killed him . . .

*The **Jester** slowly gets up, clutching one eye dramatically.*

Jester Oh, my eye . . . my poor eye!

Dorotea   Are you alright?

Princess Diana   Please, just leave my room. Now!

Jester (*producing a fake eye and holding it up theatrically*)   The Princess has taken my eye!

The maids laugh uncontrollably as **Enrique** *enters, wearing one of the* **Princess's** *dresses.*

Enrique   Look, Mummy . . . I drew a picture of how our brother might have looked. I made it for you . . . He'll protect us. He'll help us escape.

Brunilda   And you, where'd you come from?

Dorotea   And why are you wearing a dress?

Princess Diana   It was going to be a girl, Enrique . . . She would've been a girl.

Enrique   Really? I'll have to fix the drawing, then.

Jester   Who is this little maiden?

Enrique   My name is Enrique.

Jester   Enriquetta?

Enrique   Enrique.

Jester   Enriquetta suits you better.

The maids explode with laughter.

Princess Diana   Get out of my room!

Enrique   My name is Enrique. And this dress belongs to my mummy.

Brunilda   Take it off this instant.

Jester   Why are you wearing your mummy's dress?

Princess Diana   Enrique, don't listen to him.

Enrique   Because I love her, and I want to be like her.

Jester   And does your boyfriend like the dress?

The maids laugh.

Enrique   I don't have a boyfriend . . . This is my mum's favourite dress.

Jester   Why don't you have a boyfriend? Haven't you got your period yet?

The laughter from the maids grows uncontrollable.

Princess Diana   Get out of my room!

Jester   Alright, alright, we'll go.

*The **Jester** pretends to leave but walks into the wall, falling dramatically. The maids howl with laughter.*

Jester   Oops, my mistake! I thought the wall was the door. I don't know what's wrong with me . . . It's like I've lost my mind.

*The **Jester** dons glasses with cartoonish, googly eyes. The maids laugh harder.*

Jester   Little maiden, tell me, what dress will you wear to your mother's funeral?

Princess Diana   Get out of my room!

Enrique   I'm not a maiden.

Jester   Dance little girl! Dance!

Enrique   I'm not a girl, I'm my mother!

Brunilda   Laugh, Princess, don't be so bitter.

The maids break into hysterical laughter.

Princess Diana   I don't want to laugh! Go to hell, all of you! Die for all I care. Just leave me alone. You're the ones who should be locked up! You're all idiots! Why would I have brought my poor daughter into this disgusting, wretched world full of sick people like you? Forgive me, boys. I should never have had you either. None of us should have been born. We should have all been aborted. Especially you, you fucking clown!

What I wouldn't give to leave, to escape far away from this miserable, suffocating castle. We're drowning in filth and despair. Let me out, or kill me right now! I can't stand the sight of your faces any longer. Just get out! Go! Leave me in peace. I don't want to see any of you ever again!

Jester   Alright, Princess, we'll go. It was never my intention to make you feel so . . . bad in your final moments.

*The **Jester** pretends to exit but stumbles into the closet and collapses. The maids try to stifle their laughter.*

Jester   Sorry, I made a mistake, I'm as dumb as a dog.

*He dons a dog mask, sending the maids into another wave of laughter. Enraged, the **Princess** storms over, grabs him by the arms and throws him against the window. The wooden bars break, and the **Jester** plummets to the ground. A loud thud echoes.*

Brunilda   She's gone mad!

Dorotea   Dear God! The Jester!

Princesa Diana   The bars broke . . . Boys . . . let's climb out of the window, help me make a rope with the sheets . . .

Dorotea   Don't you dare, Princess.

Brunilda   Call the guards.

Princess Diana   Quickly, boys.

Guillermo *and* **Enrique** *begin tearing the bed sheets to make a rope. Suddenly, the* **Journalist** *appears at the broken window.*

Dorotea   Guards! Guards! Help!

Journalist   Hello, Your Royal Highness.

Dorotea   What are you doing here?

Brunilda   Princess, stop this madness, or you'll regret it.

Princess Diana   Oh, really? What will you do? Sentence me to death again?

Journalist   What's happening, Princess? I saw the Jester fall from your window.

Princess Diana   I pushed him.

Brunilda   Shut up, Princess!

Journalist   Did you push him?

Brunilda   Don't you dare publish that!

Princess Diana   Yes.

Journalist   And now? What are you doing?

Princess Diana   I'm escaping.

Dorotea   No, you're not.

Journalist   How are you planning to escape?

Princess Diana   Through the window.

Brunilda   Boys! Don't help her!

Journalist   And what about the guards outside?

Princess Diana   I'll kill them all . . . Come on, hurry, boys!

Dorotea   Guards!

Brunilda   You're not going anywhere, Princess. You'll pay for what you've done. You murdered a royal child. God wants you dead, Princess. It's God who won't let you escape . . . .

Journalist   Princess, may I take your photo?

Princess Diana   No . . .

Brunilda   Go away, you dyke.

Dorotea   Guards! Help! She's lost her mind!

Journalist   Could you move closer to Guillermo? Enrique, give me a sad face.

Enrique   A sad face?

Journalist (*taking many photos*)   Perfect. Guillermo, look at your mother please . . . lovely.

Brunilda   Guards!

Journalist   Princess, can you move your hair in front of your face? . . . Let us see the vomit.

Princess Diana   Quickly . . .

Dorotea   I'll help you down . . . if you hand over your princess titles, or add me to your will.

A guard bursts into the room.

Brunilda   She shoved the Jester out the window and now she's trying to escape. She's completely deranged!

Journalist (*taking a photo*)   Princess, look this way.

*The guard grabs the **Princess** and blindfolds her.*

Enrique   Let her go!

Guillermo   Unhand her! I'm your future king!

Journalist   Princess, what's your final message for women condemned to the scaffold?

*The guard forces the **Princess** to her knees. The **Journalist** positions their camera for a final shot.*

Princess Diana   Boys, look away. Don't cry for my death. Don't look at my head lying on the ground. Close my eyes. Don't let my flesh and blood keep witnessing this vile world anymore. Don't let anyone leave flowers on my grave. Throw me into a mass pit, let me bake under the sun and let the birds feast on me by the morning. Let no hypocrites or those who despise me come to my funeral. Let only those who love me attend: the sick, the outcasts, those who have no place, those who don't exist in this bitter country.

We don't exist. I was born not existing in this shitty world where only men exist. They rule the world and crush us like flies. Even we are men disguised as women.

Women don't exist. They never did. They are a myth, a legend, just something someone once said existed.

We are men who bleed and give birth to other men.

Leave me in the garden next to the lilies and let the dogs devour me. Let everyone see my insides and my blood spilling across the floor.

Isn't that what you wanted? To disarm me, to dismantle me, to make me disappear?

Turn me to dust. Turn me to flour. Turn me into bread and give me to the poor. Grind my bones into glass and let the misogynists choke on me. Let the patriarchs, the rulers of this universe, bleed out and die. Let them stop killing women, stop raping their daughters, stop exploiting their friends, stop manipulating their sisters, stop murdering their princesses, stop humiliating their mothers.

Let women burn the galaxy, let them exist again. Let them kiss each other, be young, and never crash beneath the bridges in their cars. Let their hearts no longer burst from their mouths, left splattered on some desolate street.

The guard raises his sword and swiftly beheads the **Princess**. *Her head rolls forward. The* **Journalist** *snaps the final photograph.*

Scene Six: The end

The same bedroom. **Enrique** *lies on the bed, still wearing his mother's dress. The broken window allows the curtains to flutter in the wind.* **Tom** *and* **Fatima** *sit on the edge of the bed.*

Fatima Enrique, wake up.

Tom Prince . . .

Enrique What are you doing here?

Fatima Your mother sent us.

Enrique My mum is dead . . .

Tom Who is the woman in that drawing?

Enrique That's my sister.

Fatima She would've been so beautiful.

Tom She would've had the Princess's eyes.

Enrique I wish I could see her . . .

Tom Would you like to see your mother one last time?

Enrique Yes . . .

Fatima Come with us.

Enrique I want to stay here for a moment.

Tom Poor Prince.

Fatima Don't let grief take you.

Tom Your mother is here . . .

Enrique Am I dreaming?

Fatima No, it's real.

Enrique Where is she?

Tom There, by the door.

Enrique I can't see her.

Fatima She's right there. Now, she's sitting on the bed.

Enrique I can't see her . . . I can't . . .

Tom She's stroking your hair.

Fatima Do you feel it?

Enrique No, I don't feel anything.

Tom   She's telling you she loves you . . .

Enrique   I can't hear her . . . Mummy?

Fatima   She's leaving . . . she's going . . .

Enrique   No . . . no, I need to see her one last time . . .

Fatima   Don't go, Princess . . .

Tom   You can't see her, love.

Enrique   Why not?

Fatima   Can you hear her?

Enrique   No . . .

Fatima   Burn the castle.

Tom   And go far away . . .

Fatima   Far away . . . to the snow . . .

Enrique   Don't let her go! I want to see her . . . tell her to stay with me . . . tell her I don't know how to go on without her . . .

Fatima   She's gone . . .

Tom   Sleep now, love . . .

Fatima   Sweet dreams, Enrique . . .

Enrique (*lying down and closing his eyes*)   No . . . don't go . . .

He lies back down, his eyes slowly closing. **Guillermo** *enters, also dressed in one of the* **Princess**'s *gowns. He approaches* **Enrique** *and shakes him awake.*

Guillermo   Enrique . . . Enrique . . . wake up . . .

Enrique   What's wrong?

Guillermo   We have to go. They're waiting for us.

Enrique   You're wearing a dress too. She would've loved that.

Guillermo   Come on, Enrique.

Enrique   I need to stay here for a moment . . . just a moment longer . . .

Guillermo   Are you crying?

Enrique   No, I don't cry.

Guillermo   I'll be waiting for you.

Enrique   Brother.

Guillermo   Yes?

Enrique I love you.

Guillermo And I love you, Enrique.

He exits.

Narrator That summer afternoon, Enrique set the castle aflame. But he did not flee, as his mother had begged. His sorrow was too great, his heart too heavy to carry him far. Instead, he returned to the Princess's bed, where shadows and dreams still lingered. He closed his eyes so deeply, so completely, that he never opened them again.

The End.

She

Susana Torres Molina

Translated by Gilda Bona

An Odyssey into the Unknown

By Gilda Bona

Author Susana Torres Molina and I are friends and fellow theater colleagues in Buenos Aires, Argentina. Recently, Susana called to ask me if I could translate her play *She* for the upcoming anthology. I said yes, not only because I'm fond of her but essentially because I like the text. A lot. And I thought it would be a gratifying experience. In the end, it proved to be something more significant; it was a challenging, cogitative task.

I had read the text some time ago, and I remembered the overall dramatic action and its characters, the emotions and thoughts it stirred in me, but not the specific development and dénouement of each scene. I chose not to re-read it before beginning the translation work, with the deliberate purpose of diving into it the same way I set out to do my own writing (clueless, or with only a slight idea of what's to come), aiming to venture into the emerging universe of the play with rapt attention as if driving up a spiral road on the edge of a deadly abyss. The motivation behind my approach was two-pronged: to bear the uncertainty of an immediate destination and, as a resonance of this, become deeply engaged in whatever arises during the trip: a leap into the void without a net. As a journeyer into new horizons, on her own, immune to tour guides pointing at conventional sightseeing. Rendering *She* was like that: an odyssey into the unknown. I was familiar with the landscape as a reader. Now I stepped into the fantasy of reliving the emotions and frame of mind of the author as she brought to life Marley and Iriondo.

The two male characters of the play are masterfully delineated: their pettiness in prioritizing their own needs before the person they say to profess fervent passion for awakens both disdain and compassion, together with a rich tapestry of emotions and reflections inherent to human behavior. "Deep inside we are so juvenile. What is it that makes her so powerful?" says Iriondo. This line reinforces the strategy used by the author and is worth noting: in a masculine context, the female character's absence permeates the sauna where the action unfolds. Both try to win the metaphorical arm-wrestling match by claiming to possess the true version of her. They repeat her supposed words, attempting to convince each other that it is he whom she has chosen. Ironically, one of them refers to her as "our chosen one," a phrase that recalls a recurrent chauvinist tango refrain: "she is mine." Paradoxically, the female character's absence is omnipresent, granting it a profound political condition of the undervalued and ignored.

After a long and painstaking journey of seeking the appropriate words, expressions and idioms to faithfully recreate the author's world with all its nuances, I arrived at the destination. I leaned back in my seat and meditated on this play and how it exposes the universal and apparently eternal theme: the misguided notion that love and possession are synonymous and how unrequited lust can assault another's will.

* * *

Susana Torres Molina is an Argentinian playwright, theater director, drama teacher, and author of more than thirty-five theatrical plays. Some of her awards include: First Prize Fondo Nacional de las Artes contest (2005), Trinidad Guevara Award (2006 and 2020), Florencio Sánchez Award (2008), Municipal Prize (2012), Konex Award (2014), and First National Prize (2019). She has directed most of her plays, as well as plays by other authors and musical shows for singers. She has served as a judge on numerous playwriting contests. Her texts have been translated into several languages and have been performed in the USA, England, Mexico, Brazil, Peru, Uruguay, and the Czech Republic, among others.

Gilda Bona is an Argentinian writer, playwright, theater director, and drama teacher. Her publications include *Memoria en la fragua* (Baltasara Editora, 2014), a collection of short stories based on testimonies from family members and acquaintances of the disappeared during Argentina's military dictatorship, compiled by the Biographical Archive of Grandmothers of Plaza de Mayo; *Mundos Celestiales* (Editorial Eudeba, 2016), a collection of her plays; and *Una oscuridad de jungla* (Editorial Brumana, 2023), three plays that explore the world of Latinos in New York. Some of her awards include: La Escritura de las Diferencias (2014), International Prize for Women's Playwriting (2014), Monologues of the Plague Award (2020), Argentores Award for Best Author of the year (2021), and Municipal Prize (2022). She has also been shortlisted for the awards Trinidad Guevara, ACE, María Guerrero, and Teatro del Mundo.

National Premiere

She, at Payró Theater (Buenos Aires, Argentina), January 2005, directed by Susana Torres Molina.

International Productions

She, at Federal District (Mexico), 2009–2010, directed by David Jiménez.

She, at The Red House Arts Center (Syracuse NY, USA), 2010, directed by Milton Loayza.

She, at Montevideo (Uruguay), 2010, directed by Patricia Yosi.

She, at Terezín (Czech Republic), 2010, directed by Tma Group.

She, at Porto Alegre Em Cena Festival (Brazil), 2011.

She, at Current Contemporary Latin America Playwrighting Cycle (Madrid, Spain), 2018, coordinated by Guillermo Heras.

She, at 750 AM radio broadcast production, 2020, directed by Susana Torres Molina and performed by Patricio Contreras and Luis Machín.

The text was published in the following editions:

Argentina Female Playwrights, La Abeja Publishing Co. 2003.

New Argentine Theater, compilation by Jorge Dubatti, Interzona Publishing Co. 2003.

Contemporary Anthology of Female Argentinian Writers, Biblos Publishing Co. 2004.

Teatro Vivo Publishing Co. 2005.

Seven Plays by Argentine Playwright Susana Torres Molina, translated by María Claudia André and Bárbara Younoszai, The Edwin Mellen Press Publishing Co. 2026.

Additional recognition includes:

First Prize winner in the Theater Play Contest Fondo Nacional de las Artes (2001).

Trinidad Guevara Award. Category Best Author. Granted by the Government of Buenos Aires City (2006).

Shortlisted for Best National Author at the María Guerrero and Florencio Sánchez Awards (2006).

Shortlisted for Best Off-Theater Show. Clarín Awards (2006).

Selected to represent the City of Buenos Aires at The National Theater Festival (2006).

Characters

Iriondo
Marley

The two men sit in a sauna with towels wrapped around their waists, their upper bodies naked and covered in sweat. There are some benches onstage. The air is thick with steam.

Scene One

Iriondo This is awful!

Marley It's meant to be pleasant.

Iriondo Taking care of your appearance is never enjoyable.

Marley Why are you here, then?

Iriondo . . .

Marley Is it by request?

Iriondo How so?

Marley If someone asked you to work on your looks.

Iriondo No.

Marley No, of course not.

Iriondo Why the: "No, of course not"?

Marley No reason.

Iriondo It didn't seem that way to me. Speak . . . I'm intrigued.

Marley Nonsense. I was just wondering . . . Is she young?

Iriondo Oh, that was it.

Marley Youth is demanding.

Iriondo And contagious.

Marley You think so, huh?

Iriondo Don't you know?

Marley Why should I know?

Iriondo I don't know . . . I just assumed that . . .

Marley What?

Iriondo Never mind.

Marley No, now I want to know, tell me.

Iriondo I imagined that with such a well-groomed appearance . . . Why should a man take so much care of himself if not to conquer? And a man your age . . . What is it he wishes to conquer?

Marley You're wrong. You speak as if we were all . . .

Iriondo I apologize, there are exceptions, of course. You're right. I'm not here for my own benefit. No, this is more like a sacrifice. Torture. (*Laughing.*) The last gasps of a drowning man. No, there is no conquest involved here.

Marley I'd never seen you before.

Iriondo I'd never been here before. A man trying to win back a woman becomes ridiculous. (*Restrained laugh.*) Look at me: I've tried to lose weight, keep my hair from falling out, I even thought about dyeing my grey hair, and doing two hundred push-ups a day. But deep inside I know, with certainty, that everything is useless. That any desire, if it exists, comes from somewhere else. What's expected is another thing. But I don't know what. Sometimes there's no solid ground, everything . . . seems like paper.

Scene Two

Iriondo She went on a trip . . . on vacation, with her husband.

Marley Honestly, I'm not interested.

Iriondo For a month. To the beach.

Marley It's not that long.

Iriondo No. I miss her. I can't sleep.

Marley There are pills. I take a couple before bedtime.

Iriondo When I'm lying awake, I have crying fits and outbursts of anger.

Marley Excuse me but I think it's too intimate.

Iriondo I break things. The first thing I run into I smash it against the wall. Alarm clocks, telephones, lamps. It feels good. It brings relief.

Marley You should see someone.

Iriondo Who?

Marley Someone who can help you.

Iriondo I come to places like these to be able to doze for a while. It's the only way.

Marley It's getting late. Until we meet again. (*Leaving.*)

Iriondo You know who I'm talking about.

Marley (*stops*) Me?

Iriondo Yes. I've seen both of you together several times.

Marley You've seen me with whom several times?

Iriondo Her red hair is like a blaze of fire. Difficult to go unnoticed. And her height . . . Now that I see you standing, she might even be taller than you. (*Amused.*) I guess that's why she stopped wearing high heels. Out of pure consideration.

Marley Are you . . . her husband?

Iriondo No. Her lover. Just like you. Another one.

Marley *begins to laugh, a slow, spasmodic chuckle that conveys a deeper bitterness.*
Iriondo *joins in. A crescendo of sound that ultimately fades away, leaving only silence.*

Scene Three

Marley Have you been following me?

Iriondo Just for a couple of months.

Marley Why?

Iriondo Why? It's more than obvious.

Marley I mean . . . Why now?

Iriondo I found a poem in her purse. I don't mean it's okay to snoop around, but sometimes it's necessary.

Marley And?

Iriondo Her husband can barely sign his name. I must admit that the poem wasn't that bad. (*Amused. Ironic.*) Overly sweet, but with some glimmer of originality: "Trapped in your net letting myself be swept up by the tide of our embrace . . ." etc., etc., etc. It is yours, isn't it? Well, you never know . . . It was signed: "Your unquenchable explorer." Or something similar.

Marley . . .

Iriondo I burnt it. It went up in flames like toilet paper.

Marley What do you want?

Iriondo To know. To know a little bit more. I also feel cheated.

Marley How long?

Iriondo Does it matter?

Marley Yes. It does! How long?

Iriondo For quite a while.

Scene Four

Marley I was suspicious too.

Iriondo Share it with me, like I did.

Marley No. I don't think so.

Iriondo We might laugh even more.

Marley I doubt it.

Iriondo Listen, we probably won't see each other ever again. This is a unique opportunity to get to know more about our *chosen one*.

Marley I don't trust you.

Iriondo I don't trust you either, of course. But it's not an issue of trust. We are confirming the facts. Nothing more.

Marley . . .

Iriondo You have your version. I have mine. Don't you feel curious to see how Frankenstein is coming together?

Marley Don't call her that!

Iriondo Why not? Passion has something monstruous about it. Share it, share it.

Marley *hesitates.* **Iriondo** *encourages him to speak with a nod and a stare.*

Marley One afternoon . . . she seemed to be in a great hurry, too nervous. She told me that her husband was waiting for her in his studio, that he'd been acting . . . strange, lately: that we'd have to take some time off for a while. When she was leaving, something in her goodbye kiss, in her face, just before entering the elevator, made me pick up the phone as soon as I closed the door. I called the studio, asking for him. They told me he was on a trip, that he would be away the whole week.

Iriondo Let me remember . . . September of last year?

Marley It's possible.

Iriondo Yes, I gave her an ultimatum.

Marley You?

Iriondo What's the surprise? I knew about her husband's trip, so I didn't understand why we saw each other so little. Until then I wasn't suspicious. I hadn't realized that lying was part of her very breath. And what would you've done if he'd answered?

Marley Hang up, I guess. But I was sure that her anxiety, her excitement, weren't because of him . . . It didn't fit with such a long relationship. Do you know what I mean?

Iriondo   Perfectly. Routine brings many things, but never excitement. And were you calm? Didn't you try to find out more?

Marley   No.

Iriondo   No?

Marley   My wife . . . (*Interrupts himself.*)

Iriondo   Don't worry. I also know her. Don't forget that I followed you. And one thing leads to another.

Marley   Bastard!

Iriondo   Your wife must think the same about you. When I saw her, she was pregnant. Did she already deliver? A girl? A boy? I don't have children. We always thought it would happen someday but no. Something didn't work out. Maybe it was for the best.

Marley   Are you married?

Iriondo   Of course, what did you think?

Marley   I don't know . . . I have three children.

Iriondo   Congratulations!

Marley   My wife is someone very special. I care about her. I care much about her.

Iriondo   Again, congratulations. But let's be honest, here, in this place, we're not talking about affection. We're talking about something else. We're talking about passion! About hunger! About thirst! Aren't we? I also feel something very special . . . for my wife, so special that sometimes, I don't know what it is.

Scene Five

Marley It's very disturbing, it's aggressive to learn that one's been watched.

Iriondo It wasn't you I was following. What do I care about your life? I was following her. I needed to know how far she would go.

Marley And? Did you find out how far?

Iriondo See? You also want to know. But of course, without doing the dirty work. No, I won't tell you. It's enough. I'm leaving.

Marley Wait, wait.

Iriondo I'm not telling you! Go do your own dirty work.

Marley On Sundays . . . when she says she goes to the countryside with her husband . . . do you see her? Do you meet? (**Iriondo** *laughs.*) Answer me!

Iriondo (*amused*) Sometimes.

Marley And the evening she . . . has dinner with her friends.

Iriondo Thursday. Yes. She does have dinner. I assure you. Sabere, Sabore! And what's your day?

Marley Monday.

Iriondo Ah! Sure! Acting classes, right? And we all know about those late-night people. Bohemians. Yes, I remember when she asked me if she wasn't too old to start acting. That art of lying with the truth. I told her she's not. On the contrary, age adds experience. And with experience, one lies better. More sincerely. But I never imagined . . . I feel like smashing your face in!

Marley And I feel like running you over with my car. Put it in reverse and run you over again and again!

Iriondo You're becoming more and more disgusting.

Marley We agree, once more.

Iriondo I try to guess: what could you have awakened in her? What kind of interest?

Marley And looking at you it's just pathetic! Quite sad!

Iriondo Careful!

Marley What bothers me the most is to admit that I don't know her as well as I thought I did. Because . . . what's the point?

Iriondo Yes! What's the point?

Marley Your presence here is clear proof that I have no idea.

Iriondo About what? Her bad habits?

Marley Stop it!

Iriondo What blows my mind about her is that she always shoots for the moon. This thing of not having boundaries . . . rather, of being lured by excess. To double down. She is an extraordinary lover. Do you agree?

Marley That's enough. Shut up.

Iriondo What's the matter with you? Do you think that perversion is exclusively yours? Or that deceit exists but only for others? Or . . . that danger means a proof of love? Something like "I am taking risks. I'm all yours." No! No! No! You're wrong! You're delirious! You poor fool!

Marley *jumps on* **Iriondo**. *They wrestle. Fall to the ground. As the lights slowly fade to semidarkness, their silhouettes are visible, engaged in a brief but intense struggle. Then, silence.*

Scene Six

They are sitting. **Iriondo** *has an injury on the side of his mouth.* **Marley** *has wounds on his neck and around his left eye. Long and awkward pause.*

Iriondo (*breathing heavily*)   Where did you copy it from? The poem.

Marley (*breathing heavily*)   It's mine, you moron!

Iriondo   I've read it somewhere. You probably took it from some cultural magazine. Do you know what I do for a living? I am an editor.

Marley   So what?

Iriondo   I have a proposal for you.

Marley   Let me guess . . . You want me to leave her? To step aside for the three of you to be happy? (*Laughs.*)

Iriondo   Your mind is appallingly simplistic. My proposal was that we kill him.

Marley   Who? Her husband?

Iriondo   Yes.

Marley   . . .

Iriondo   And we'll share her between us.

Marley   . . .

Iriondo   But now the two of us would control her. On our terms. According to our needs.

Marley   Have you lost your mind?

Iriondo   It must be the lack of sleep. But it's a good idea.

Marley   You're a repulsive being!

Iriondo   So are you. I wouldn't dare to suggest something like that to a friend. It's only suitable for butchers.

Marley   You speak about killing . . . as if to press *delete*.

Iriondo   Do you suffer? Do you suffer for her?

Marley   What do you care?

Iriondo   Do you think it's reasonable to suffer for love?

Marley   To me, nothing about love is reasonable. But what are we talking about? I've had enough. (*He walks towards the door.*)

Iriondo   We don't use protection when we . . . have sex. I wonder if you . . .

Marley   Excuse me?

Iriondo   "Don't put it on, I want you so much." (*Ironically.*) It seems she says it to everyone.

Marley   Everyone! What does it mean?

Iriondo   That we don't know . . . That we don't know anything. For instance, right now, do we really have any idea where she is? Would you swear she is with her husband? She could be with her husband and a new lover. I just can't imagine her life without that adrenaline rush. Did she get in touch with you?

Marley   . . .

Iriondo   Has she called you?

Marley   . . .

Iriondo   She calls me every morning and tells me about her boredom. I don't believe anything she says. She tries too hard to seem dull. You understand, don't you?

Marley   Every morning?

Iriondo   Yes, it's an old habit, wherever she might be.

Marley   How long has it . . .

Iriondo   Years, years . . . years of sorrow.

Marley   Then, why are you so determined to keep going?

Iriondo   Who's determined, you idiot! It's inevitable! It's an addiction! Something that cannot be controlled. My body only responds to her desire. Do you know what that's like?! Do you know what it means?! No, I don't think so. That animal passion makes me forgive her everything. Everything! Even the fact that she got involved with an idiot like you! (*Comes closer to the back wall and bangs his forehead against it several times.*)

Marley   Calm down. She told me . . .

Iriondo (*mocking him*)   She told me, she told me, she told me. (*Violent.*) Please! Do me a favor! (*Continues hitting himself against the wall.*)

Scene Seven

Iriondo *is sitting. Holds the edge of a towel to his forehead. His face shows pain.*

Iriondo   What did . . . she . . . What did she tell you?

Marley   . . .

Iriondo   Let's see, let me guess . . . (*Caustic.*) With a gaze radiant with emotion, her voice cracked as she whispered: "You are my one and only love."

Marley   That's enough!

Iriondo   Why blame me if she is always saying the same thing!

Marley   What is it you want me to believe? That she doesn't stop . . .

Iriondo (*interrupts*)   I wouldn't say she is a total nymphomaniac, but the description is quite close.

Marley   Stop bugging me! I know her . . . (*Rectifying.*) Well . . . kind of . . . She can't pretend so convincingly.

Iriondo   She does it so convincingly that she succeeds. Just listen to yourself: "No, it can't be. I know her. Well, kind of . . ." On Monday, doesn't she go to acting classes? She's a fast learner. She picks up things quickly and has good teachers.

Marley   And why does she take risks? Why doesn't she take care of herself with you, with me, and let's suppose with all the others?

Iriondo   That's a good question to ask her. As far as I'm concerned, I'm not particularly interested in staying alive. (*Aggressive.*) And you . . . a married man, a macho breeder who, out of sheer convenience and vanity, chooses to believe a whore.

Marley *comes closer to* **Iriondo**, *who stands up.* **Marley** *puts his hand on* **Iriondo's** *chest and pushes him several times.* **Iriondo** *lets it happen without reacting.*

Marley   Don't you call her that! Don't you dare to call her that again! In a matter of minutes, you've managed to turn everything into a sewer!

Iriondo   You're right. I'm sorry. My nerves are on edge. I'm going through withdrawal. There are times I wish to throw myself against a wall. Damn her! I hate her! I abhor her! (*He flops onto his seat. Bends forwards. His hands holding his head.*) I want her! I want her! I want her . . . so much! So much!

Scene Eight

Marley *walks around looking uneasy.* **Iriondo** *remains seated, eyes closed.*

Marley   She . . .

Iriondo   What?

Marley   No, nothing.

Iriondo   What? What . . .? I'm waiting! What?

Marley   Your relationship . . . is it passionate?

Iriondo   Fire! I melt in her arms, and she melts in mine. When we are done loving each other—physically, I mean—I smother her with kisses, her face, every inch of her body, again and again. It's inevitable. In those moments I wish I could raise an altar for her. I'm overwhelmed with happiness!

Marley   How . . . how can it be?

Iriondo   What? (*Ironic.*) Do you feel the same?

Marley   After each orgasm she clings to my body eagerly. Her eyes filled with tears. She begs me to stay with her forever. I feel her entire body trembling with emotion. Surrendered to my desire. In moments like those I know I could do anything . . . I could kill her, tear her in two. And our embrace is so passionate . . . She sometimes asks me for things that . . .

Iriondo (*interrupts*)   Don't go on! Don't go on, it's unbearable! Why don't you leave? Go. Go! Enough! We have shared too many secrets, don't you think?

Marley   Yes, you're right.

Both remain motionless.

Scene Nine

Marley   And her husband?

Iriondo   I forbade her to bring him up. It turns me off. Totally.

Marley   She's told me a few things about him.

Iriondo   She has to get it off her chest with someone.

Marley   Quite a typical story.

Iriondo   Did I ask you for details?

Marley   I thought you were interested in putting together . . .

Iriondo   You still can't say Frankenstein? (*Laughs.*) All right, go ahead! It's not a big deal for me to cool off in this moment. Besides, from the spark in your eye I can tell you're rejoicing at the idea of bringing to light certain *things*. Things that, most likely, I'll not like at all. At all! But be careful, don't overstep the boundaries. I can heat up again at once. And I'm increasingly less aware of my own boundaries.

Marley   With that introduction, I don't feel like talking anymore.

Iriondo   What's wrong with you? Do you think this is an ordinary conversation? Two guys having a drink, talking about holes? I bleed! Understand? I have a wound . . . And I'm bleeding!

Marley   In fact . . .

Iriondo   What?

Marley   It's quite a common story.

Iriondo   You already said it: *"A typical story."*—What else?

Marley   He abandoned her, he neglected her for a long time while trying to make it at what he does.

Iriondo (*bursts out laughing*)   *"Trying to make it at what he does."*—Poor guy!

Marley *gradually starts laughing too.*

Marley   When he finally made it, there was distance between them.

Iriondo (*interrupts*)   Unbridgeable. Distances must be unbridgeable to exist. And what did she tell you? Why does she stay with him?

Marley   He threatens her. He told her that if she leaves him, he'll kill her. Or himself. He has told her that many times. That he can't bear the thought of living without her.

Iriondo   That makes two of us. And . . .?

Marley   And, what?

Iriondo   Would you tolerate it?

Marley I . . . I have children. It's a different story.

Iriondo Of course, family always comes first. (*Aggressive.*) What a hypocritical worm! I could swear we are three and four and five! A bloodbath! And all . . . for the flesh and its urges. (*Pause.*) We're so juvenile. What is it? What is it that makes her so powerful? Have you ever thought about that?

Marley No.

Iriondo No? (*Bitingly sarcastic.*) No thoughts. No emotions. No actions. A happy man.

Marley Actually . . .

Iriondo Yes . . .? What?

Marley . . .

Iriondo Come on, open up! Spill your guts out just like I'm doing with you. Can't you see I'm serving them up on a platter? Eat! Eat!

Marley Many times after an encounter . . . when we part, I sigh, relieved that it might be the last time I see her. That carefree feeling, that lightness, lasts for hours, sometimes even a couple of days. And, suddenly, I don't know how, or what triggers it, her presence starts creeping into my mind slowly, gradually. It consumes everything. Her image, the memory of specific moments, becomes an obsession. The same movie plays over and over. Everything else fades away. I struggle to break free, but it's useless. I'm no longer present for others. I'm gone. The waiting begins. My mind on hold . . . waiting for the signal. Like a lap dog.

Iriondo Trained to satisfy the monster's voracity, that can never be satisfied. It needs a pack of lap dogs.

Marley Shut up! I'm sick of you! Your comments disgust me! And I assure you I won't pave the way for you. Besides . . .

Iriondo Yes?

Marley Never mind.

Iriondo No? You have never thought about running away? Leaving everything behind and beginning anew?

Marley . . .

Iriondo We discussed it many times. I was hesitant. The prospect of a daily routine suffocating passion frightened me. And without desire . . .? No more altars or offerings. The desert. No escape. Today I regret my hesitation, but it's too late.

Marley Doesn't she want to?

Iriondo Losing a chance like that makes it tough to discern what you really want later.

Marley Maybe it's too late, because now she's . . . talking about it with me.

Iriondo   What?

Marley   Us . . . leaving.

Iriondo   Are you looking for a fistful of knuckles?

Marley   Yes, I am! And what? You miserable wretch! Sicko! Weak-minded fool!

They exchange blows, dodging each other until **Iriondo** *lands a solid punch on* **Marley***'s face. Wincing in pain,* **Marley** *clutches his nose and sits down, stumbling.* **Iriondo** *stands in front of him.*

Iriondo   Is it true what you've just said?

Marley (*aching*)   No.

Iriondo   Better that way. So . . . have you considered the idea?

Scene Ten

Iriondo It's simple. Either we kill him, or he kills her. Sooner or later, he'll find out, just like I did. He might even kill her and her current lover. I won't deny that the option adds excitement to the situation.

Marley Why do you suddenly trust her? Maybe she's exaggerating and her husband just wants to hold on to her at all costs.

Iriondo Most of the time, repeated threats come true. I've read it. But it doesn't matter. I already knew I couldn't count on you. (*He bursts into uncontrollable sobbing.*)

Marley What's wrong with you now?

Iriondo . . .

Marley Look at yourself! You're pathetic!

Iriondo . . .

Marley That's enough! Cut it out!

Iriondo (*between sobs*)   Maimed . . . I feel maimed.

Marley Don't you think that's too much?

Iriondo No! It isn't! Unless holding her in your arms is the same as holding a magazine. And judging by your stupid expression it probably is. Oh, God, why, why did she choose you! You're worthless!

Marley Not this again! "No one loves her like I do, no one hurts like I do." You make me sick!

Iriondo *stops sobbing.*

Iriondo Do you think fidelity is feasible?

Marley It's a possibility.

Iriondo I wonder if she feels she is faithful to each of us.

Marley . . .

Iriondo She is happy. She doesn't seem to feel either guilt nor remorse. How strange, huh? Since I met her, I fantasize about getting into her head, seeing how it works, find out how she jumps from one body to another with such ease . . . such levity.

Marley Did he hire you to follow me?

Iriondo Who?

Marley Her husband.

Iriondo That's just stupid! Look at me: do I look like a hired guy? Do you want her? I'm not referring to *her* . . . not to her but the mother of your children.

Marley   Don't drag my wife into this! My wife has nothing to do with this, she isn't part of this plot.

Iriondo   Mediocre petit bourgeois! (*He mimics him mockingly.*) "Don't you mess with my wife. The cuckolded has nothing to do, nothing to do with all this."

Marley   Damned fool! (*Comes closer, looking threatening.*)

Iriondo (*backs off*)   Listen, your wife and the kind of relationship you two have is of no interest to me. Not in the slightest. Besides, you don't need to be a genius to guess . . . What I'm trying to figure out is . . . Can you take a step back? You're not letting me think clearly. (**Marley** *takes a few steps back.*) What I'm interested in finding out is why does desire sometimes remain alive? Or why does it sometimes die?

Marley   That question always pops up when desire is in its death throes. Neither before nor after.

Iriondo (*claps, amused*)   That's the most interesting thing you have said so far! Well, it feels good after having waited for a thought every now and then. Perhaps she discovered in you the art of patience. And that made her . . .

Marley (*interrupts*)   I'm tired of this game. Goodbye. (*He makes a move as if to leave, but only takes a few steps forward, unsure of where to go.*)

Iriondo   She is not doing well.

Marley   She is OK. Much as we dislike it, she's spending the summer by the seaside with her husband.

Iriondo   No, she is not fine. Not fine at all.

Marley   Why do you say that?

Iriondo   . . .

Marley   Stop playing hide-and-seek! If you have something to say, say it, if not, shut up!

Iriondo   Two days ago she called me crying. He'd threatened her again. But this time, he hit her. And when he had to leave the hotel, he left her tied up, hands and feet to the bed. Later, he said he was sorry. He'd never done anything like that before. She was terrified. What worries me most is that she didn't call me yesterday, and she hasn't called me today either.

Marley   And why didn't you say anything before?

Iriondo   I didn't trust you. I still don't but . . .

Marley   Being aware of the danger you kept on playing, going round and round! You nasty coward! Why don't you just say everything at once? (*With suppressed violence.*) I hope nothing bad happens to her because . . .

Iriondo (*defiant*)   What?

Marley I'll kill you! I'll kill you both! I'll kill you and him!

Iriondo Don't be ridiculous. Look at yourself in the mirror.

Marley I swear it.

Iriondo Oh, really? You swear? You swear on her?

Marley Of course, I do!

Iriondo You love her.

Marley Madly! And she loves me! Get it?

Iriondo She doesn't.

Marley She does! She's going to leave her husband. She can't stand the situation anymore. The distance. The distance between her and me! Do you understand?! She's leaving everything for me, and I believe her. Did you hear me?! I believe her!

Iriondo She might leave him, but she's not leaving me.

Marley I can promise you she will. Any community between us is over.

Iriondo You . . . you deceived me. At first you seemed indifferent, and I wondered if I hadn't made a mistake following you for months.

Marley I don't trust you either. Don't expect honesty.

Iriondo I felt you were being honest when you said you love her madly.

Marley Think whatever you like. You should call the hotel.

Iriondo I'm not sure where they are. She is the one who calls me . . . and not from her cell phone.

Marley But we can try to find her.

Iriondo Then what?

Marley See how she's doing. If she needs anything.

Iriondo Will you rescue her?

Marley I don't know, but I need to know she's safe. What's wrong with you now?! Weren't you banging your head against the wall? Weren't you crying uncontrollably? Didn't you feel maimed? And now that she's at risk . . .

Iriondo She's confused.

Marley She's in danger!

Iriondo If she told you what she did, she is very confused.

Marley Again, the bait . . . You like to play, huh? If you know something, say it once and for all! (*Pushes him furiously.*)

Iriondo I don't think you'll like it, but it's better if you find out sooner rather than later.

Marley   No more beating around the bush, you clown!

Iriondo   Before leaving, she told me the same . . . that she would leave everything behind for me.

Marley   That's a lie! You're lying! You can't stand being pushed aside! Defeated! You make things up! You rave! Since you started talking you haven't stopped lying and turning all this into filth. Don't speak anymore, you're miserable! It's over!

Iriondo   Yes, it's over. I know it. For years she's called me every day. It was her lucky charm. "So, everything goes well." She believes in these things. Nothing would have prevented her from . . .

Marley   What are you saying? (*Collapses.*)

Scene Eleven

Iriondo (*studying* **Marley** *for a few seconds*)   How many does it take to make desire work . . .? At first, when I followed you, I was desperate with jealousy, I suffered a lot, I had nausea just imagining what the two of you might be doing. But after seeing you several times, I started to notice that nothing extraordinary was happening between you and her, that both of you were always the same, you didn't do silly things, you didn't run hand in hand through the streets, laughing in the rain, like in the movies: nor did people stopped to stare at you—people are sensitive and curious about each other's happiness—but no, there was nothing remarkable that could make me feel the harrowing poison of envy. I've seen you almost indifferent to each other, serious, preoccupied, gazing down at the ground, quiet. As the two of you became more familiar and predictable, I started to feel excited, yes, turned on by watching you, and so I kept on going, but now for my own pleasure. (*Provocateur.*) You two had unknowingly become my greatest source of arousal. That's when my relationship with her reached new heights. My sexual vitality!

Marley *lunges at him. They wrestle. They tumble to the ground. They brawl.* **Iriondo** *manages to grab* **Marley** *by the neck and squeezes it.* **Marley** *frantically tries to break free, desperate to breathe. Just as he is about to suffocate* **Iriondo** *lets go.*

Iriondo   Did you have an erection? Or did it just seem to me that you did? Either way, it's a well-known fact in hanged men. A purely physiological phenomenon.

Marley (*rubbing his neck*)   You almost . . . strangled me.

Iriondo   Yes. I don't know why I didn't.

Marley   You won't get her back this way.

Iriondo   No.

Marley   She loves me.

Iriondo   . . .

Marley   I'm going to leave my wife.

Iriondo   . . .

Marley   We've been planning this for months.

Iriondo   Shhh! Be quiet. That's more than enough. (*Pause.*) I am her husband.

Marley   . . .

Iriondo   I truly don't know why I didn't kill you.

Marley   But then . . . where is she? She, where is she? And . . . what was all that about her husband hitting her? (*He approaches* **Iriondo** *and starts shaking him.* **Iriondo** *lets him.*) Answer me! Have you hurt her? Where is she? (*Slaps him repeatedly.*) Where is she?! Speak! Where is she!

Iriondo *suddenly reacts, pushing* **Marley** *away.*

Iriondo We returned yesterday. From the beach. She is at our house packing her things. She is leaving.

Marley Where to?

Iriondo With you, I believe. You two were planning to run off together, weren't you?

Marley That is why you put on this charade.

Iriondo I needed to be sure that I had done the right thing.

Marley I didn't trust you . . .

Iriondo But you confessed many things. All I needed to know. And more. Much more than I wanted to hear.

Marley You've lost. That's it. Leave her alone.

Iriondo Yes, that's the idea. Would you understand if I told you that I wanted to know the truth and to be mistaken at the same time? I did everything I could. Yes. Everything . . .

Marley The others? Are they even real?

Iriondo I have already told you, now it's your turn to do the dirty work. (*Laughing.*)

Marley What's wrong with you?

Iriondo (*with a bitter smile*)   Fidelity . . . I pity you.

Marley Have you seen your face? It's the image of perfect misery.

Iriondo I can imagine you chasing after her, controlling her every move, listening behind doors.

Marley Not me, I won't do that.

Iriondo Those things are not thought through. They are done. They are primal urges. Uncontrollable. The fear of being excluded leads to unimaginable places . . . Shameful ones. I don't want to remember . . .

Marley Do you still love her?

Iriondo Madly. The worst part of it is . . . the feeling of being impregnated. That's what hurts the most. That everything gives signs of the same thing. And reveals time after time again what I want to forget. Her skin on my skin. Her gaze upon mine. My sex buried in hers. I who am no longer just myself. She dwells in me. I am taken, filled with her. Life becomes a horrific coexistence! It's like her name is tattooed on every cell. On every nerve ending. It's . . . devastating. Unbearable.

Marley Yes, I know what you're talking about. I'd better leave now.

Iriondo Yes, that would be for the best.

Marley Don't you even think about following us.

Iriondo No. I give you my word.

Marley And leave her alone. I wouldn't want to have to . . .

Iriondo What?

Marley To have to get rid of you.

Iriondo Would you do that?

Marley Yes.

Iriondo You love her. You truly love her.

Marley Yes! Yes! How many times do I have to say it!

Iriondo Apparently many. It does me good to hear it.

Marley What are you saying?

Iriondo Everything falls into place. It makes sense.

Marley She told me, 'He's crazy. He's totally out of his mind.'

Iriondo Hopeless.

Marley Goodbye. (*Heads towards the exit.*)

Iriondo I hit her. I'd never done that before. (**Marley** *halts in his tracks.*) In the face, on her body. She let me. She didn't resist. She didn't utter a word. It seemed she enjoyed the blows, as if daring me to reveal how far I could go. I became enraged. More. Even more. My arm moved mechanically. Back and forth. Frantic. Out of control. There was only one scream.

Marley What are you saying?

Iriondo You are not going to find her. *He* . . . killed her.

Marley . . .

Iriondo She was packing her bags. Taking her most intimate things out of the bathroom. I saw the empty spaces in the drawers, the empty hangers . . . the house was turning into paper . . . Tearing itself apart. No place to lean on. Nothing solid. I stopped her before she reached the door. Now it's your turn to do the dirty work. You swore. I made you swear on her. You said: "If something bad happens to her, I'll kill him." Well . . . I have told you several times: life without her . . . I do not want it.

Iriondo *and* **Marley** *are motionless. Facing each other. Staring at each other. Their fists clenched. Faces and bodies at maximum tension. Their breathing becomes deeper and more agitated. Lights slowly fade to black. In the darkness, only their amplified breathing is heard. Then, total silence.*

Nezahualcóyotl Dreams in Mictlan York

Xavier Villanova

Translated by Roberto Cavazos

Where Dreams Die Alone

By Roberto Cavazos

As a Mexican who once sought his fortune away from his homeland, only to be hastened away from his adopted nation by a wave of resurgent animosity toward "undesirable" foreigners, I feel a considerable degree of sympathy for Ronald and Juan, the desperately lonely and inescapably "othered" Dreamers and protagonists of Xavier Villanova's *Nezahualcóyotl Dreams in Mictlan York*.

As a translator, on the other hand, the challenge of faithfully translating Xavier's work came with an added wrinkle: Certain lines of dialogue had been lifted by the playwright directly from an article he had read in *The New York Times*: "The Lonely Death of George Bell" by N.R. Kleinfeld. Having not been aware of this before, I was translating into English (in my own words) sentences that had originally been written in English by Mr Kleinfeld (using different words) before Xavier translated them into Spanish for the purposes of his play. Thankfully, I had the advantage of being personally acquainted with the playwright and he was able to point out the relevant passages, as well as sending me the original article, which I recommend to you, dear reader, as a fascinating companion piece to this play.

The plight of Dreamers in the USA is well-known, at least at a surface level: people who came to the country as children, growing up and shaping their lives and relationships around an identity that is neither here nor there, impossible to place due to a lack of proper documentation needed to consider themselves American and without a genuine cultural connection to Mexico, the country they left in search of the American Dream.

These Dreamers often find themselves stuck in the most undesirable jobs, those no "proper" American would want to do. These jobs are antisocial by their very nature, and the work Ronald and Juan do for the Queens County Police Precinct, Public Administrator and Forensic Investigation Department is no exception, plunging their hands elbows-deep into the debris of the poor, unfortunate beings who shuffled off this mortal coil with no one left to mourn their passing, no discernible connection to another living soul.

This job would be considered a cruel and unusual punishment under any circumstance, but exponentially so for two men who are in perpetual search for a connection, a friend, a lover, a community. Wading through the remains of so many solitary deaths, they may as well be charting a path toward their own inevitable demise, their bodies eventually to be found in an advanced state of decomposition, a state their own psyches have inhabited for far longer than the time they presumably have left to find someone to share at least an aspect of their lives with. It is clear why they must do this job in pairs, for the inescapable solitude in which their subjects perished is a disease, a highly contagious one at that, and the only vaccine available is companionship.

Xavier's play, though initially feeling like it may be set in a heightened version of our own world, is painfully prescient at a time when the precious commodities our forebears took for granted (touch, laughter, complicity) have become rare, despite us being more interconnected as a global society than at any other point in history. We are currently in the midst of an emotional famine, sifting through the ashes of a once-thriving human race looking for crumbs of affection, helplessly watching empathy evaporate before our eyes as wealth and resources are hoarded by those who never learned (or cared to learn) how to love, meaning they have never known love themselves and are now left to chase the waning adrenaline rush derived from acts of callousness and cruelty.

Even the solitary "proper" American of the piece, Rose, has fallen prey to the loneliness pandemic experienced by the characters and audience of this play, oscillating between the cold detachment and cruelty she shows her subordinates and the clingy neediness of someone who cannot even forge a meaningful connection with her pets, with whom many people (myself included) are still able to find the unconditional love that has become such a rarity among human beings. In her emotional flailing, Rose reminds us that proper documentation or the right passport won't save us from potentially sharing the same fate as the unseen, the undesired, the Dreamers of this world.

We are all exposed.

We are all at risk.

We are all vulnerable.

In the end, all that will be left of any of us is our detritus: photos, record collections, takeaway menus, moth-eaten jumpers. Our only hope is to be remembered, mourned by someone who cared for us. This care need not come in the shape of love; even the warm smile of the barista from whom we buy our large almond-milk latte with extra caramel (and who would likely lament our passing if they were to learn of it) might console someone who hasn't felt the physical touch of another person since that one time they shook hands with a new acquaintance whose name they immediately forgot five months ago.

Like Juan, we may have to take solace from a small act of kindness done for someone who may or may not know it even took place.

Like Rose, we may run repeatedly toward and away from those who offer aspects of what we seek.

Like Ronald, we may die as utterly alone as we lived.

This is why we need art like Xavier's play. We need to relearn empathy. We need to remember those we have forgotten. We need to help each other belong, lest we drift even further apart.

* * *

Xavier Villanova is a Mexican playwright, screenwriter, stage director, translator, actor. His plays have been read and staged globally, including the US, UK, Colombia, Venezuela, and Spain. He is the author-in-residence at the prestigious International Writing Program at the University of Iowa, and the winner of multiple national awards and recipient of creative grants. As professor, he has taught playwriting, drama, and theater history at several universities in Mexico. He is the founder of Movimiento Íntimo, a renowned theater movement for site-specific spaces and households, co-director of the theater company ABSIDE, and co-creator and host of TheatrePodcast: Question Teatral.

Roberto Cavazos is a Mexican actor, director, and translator. He trained at E15 Acting School in London. Roberto is formerly Head of Translation & Surtitling at CASA Latin

American Theatre Festival (2012–2015), during which he translated over fifteen plays into English, including works by Arístides Vargas and Alejandro Ricaño. He has also had translations commissioned by the Royal Court Theatre and Theatre Uncut. His translations of British and American plays into Spanish include *Lungs* by Duncan Macmillan, *Cuttin' It* by Charlene James (commissioned by British Council México), *The Motherfucker with the Hat* by Stephen Adly Guirgis, *Orphans* by Dennis Kelly, and *Rotterdam* by Jon Brittain.

"Allow Eurydice to recover
that thread which from her destiny hath snatched.
what once before was offered now is owed,
all debts must sooner or later be paid.
Thus now we come upon our last refuge,
his infinite empire shall be our seat."

Ovid,
The Metamorphoses

Characters

Juan Uribe
Fifty-two, male. Born in Mexico. Dreamer.[1]

Ronald Romero
Fifty-seven, male. Born in Mexico. Dreamer.

Rose E. Oakwood
Thirty-three, female. American of Irish descent.

---

1 Dreamers are undocumented immigrants who arrived in the United States as children, lived and attended school there, and identify as American. Most of them have no legal status, and thus have to apply for Deferred Action for Childhood Arrivals (DACA), sometimes not getting that protection status, ending up as low-paid labor or doing jobs that most people would rather avoid.

Rose E. Oakwood Another one.

Juan Uribe His body was found in the living room.

Ronald Romero The police found him all crumpled up on the mottled carpet.

Juan Uribe Sniffing a fetid odor, a neighbor called 911. The apartment was in north-central Queens, in a building on 79th Street.

Rose E. Oakwood What qualifies someone for the job? People willing to go into these disgusting apartments.

Ronald Romero I'm fifty-seven, divorced, try to live each day as if it were my last . . . One of the scant few gifts God gave me is knowing how to park.

Juan Uribe Facing that many deaths is tough. I fear someday it will be me splayed on the floor in one of these apartments.

Ronald Romero You never know when you're going to die.

Juan Uribe I turned fifty-two in May, also divorced, no children; it's why I try to make a new friend every day: the young man handing out brochures, the waitress at the bar, the man who hit your car this morning . . . They could all be your friends. If you say a motivational phrase to a stranger, he'll turn and smile. In that moment, you just made a friend. It's incredible. For example, you're in the supermarket, uncertain what milk to buy, there's whole, semi-skimmed, lactose-free . . . Is lactose-free milk still milk? So, you're deciding between soy, almond, coconut, pasteurized, ultra-pasteurized, premium, light, 0%, extra nutrients, anyway; you're standing in front of shelves of multicolored cartons that don't taste the same, nor do they yield the same benefits, and just then, a man says to you: get out of the way, will ya? The aisle doesn't belong to you. Then you realize you're blocking the way with your cart, and of course you could answer, excuse me, friend, where's the fire, but what I say is: "With every sunrise, let us cherish each moment" or "Be kind and the world shall smile upon you" . . . Some of them look at me as if to say get lost, moron, but most people down arms and bam, I made a friend who'll smile at me whenever I run into him, someone who, given the delicate news of my passing, might feel sorry and go to my funeral.

Ronald Romero You're an asshole, Juan.

Juan Uribe I may be an asshole, but when I die, I won't be a lonely asshole; someone will learn of my death before the sun sets. I will not die alone.

Ronald Romero People who show up at funerals without ever really having known the deceased, what they're thinking is: gimme, gimme, gimme, gimme; but in life it was all, *I'm busy, I'll see you later, what does this guy want? Why won't he leave me alone?*

Juan Uribe Pass me the VapoRub?

Ronald Romero So annoying.

Juan Uribe For my nose.

Ronald Romero Screw your nose.

Juan Uribe   Do you know why they put us together?

Ronald Romero   Because it takes two people to do this crappy job.

Juan Uribe   You love it.

Ronald Romero   Yeah, sure, in fact, whenever anyone asked me as a kid: what do you want to be when you grow up, Ronnie? I'd answer: I'm going to spend my life sifting through the belongings of decomposing people.

Juan Uribe   It isn't exactly anybody's dream job, but someone has to do it. (*Pause.*) Aren't you curious what strange habits they had, what team they rooted for, what fetishes they were hiding? Who they loved or who loved them, if anyone did love them? Come on, everyone fantasizes about nosing around in someone else's house without the fear of getting caught.

Ronald Romero   Not me.

Juan Uribe   Okay, but you still haven't answered my question.

Ronald Romero   To justify the budget, I guess.

Juan Uribe   Are you saying you could do the job on your own?

Ronald Romero   And without having to smear VapoRub on my nose every ten seconds.

Juan Uribe   I think it's so we can keep each other company.

Ronald Romero   Sure, Queens County is deeply concerned with ensuring the nature of our job doesn't depress us.

Pause.

Juan Uribe   Is that a Vermeer hanging on the wall?

Rose E. Oakwood   They work in pairs because . . .

Ronald Romero   How do you know it's a . . . what did you call it?

Juan Uribe   Vermeer.

Ronald Romero   That.

Juan Uribe   I love the Met.

Ronald Romero   Everyone loves the Mets, so what?

Juan Uribe   The Metropolitan Museum of Art.

Ronald Romero   Why?

Juan Uribe   Free entry, well, not free, they suggest you make a twenty-five dollar donation, but you can leave a dollar or a nickel, whatever you have in your pocket, and there you have it, instant culture.

Ronald Romero   And you can tell the painter from the painting?

Juan Uribe Can't you?

Ronald Romero No.

Rose E. Oakwood Investigators work in pairs, to discourage theft.

Juan Uribe Take it.

Ronald Romero Are you sure? I don't even know who he is.

Juan Uribe Exactly. (*Pause.*) Did I tell you about the lady who died standing up?

Ronald Romero You're kidding, right?

Juan Uribe Your loss.

Ronald Romero No it isn't; I was there, not you, I told you, remember?

Rose E. Oakwood A woman, Leila Feldman, Feldsman, Friedman, Feldespat . . . I don't remember. Leila . . . Feldskin. That's it, Feldskin, seventy-one years old, died alone, standing up. We know she died standing up because the police found her standing up.

Juan Uribe I've always wondered if it was the agents that stood her up like that.

Ronald Romero Are you serious?

Juan Uribe I'm just saying.

Rose E. Oakwood She didn't know anyone, there was no family or friends to claim her and who knows how many days she was standing there. There's no record of it in the file, there's also no physical explanation to shed light on how she could have stayed in that position after death or how gravity didn't claim her. "Holding on to the bars" said the report, clinging, I'd say, to life. (*Pause.*) It was up to us, well, them, Ronald Romero and Raymond García, his old partner, to dive into her belongings to find some clue as to who might give her a funeral or claim her belongings. Raymond resigned that day . . . In his letter of resignation, if one can even call it a letter, were a couple of sentences. "I want to die in my bed. I do not wish to be found looking out the window, waiting for something to come save me, perhaps love." Love? No one was about to fall in love with Raymond.

Ronald Romero Twenty dollars.

Juan Uribe Mine!

Ronald Romero You're letting me have the famous painting and you want the twenty dollars?

Juan Uribe I could use the twenty now, you still have to sell the painting, and that's not going to be easy, you could get caught. Where's someone with your salary going to get a painting like that? You're going to have to hang it up at home or sell it on the black market . . . It's a risk. What are the odds it's an original? I bet it's a copy.

Ronald Romero I'll bet you that twenty it's an original.

Juan Uribe We have no way of proving it.

Ronald Romero You're right. (*Pause.*) Check the fridge.

Juan Uribe It's blocked.

Ronald Romero Brilliant deduction, Einstein. Clear a path.

Juan Uribe Why are people like this?

Ronald Romero Dead?

Juan Uribe Hoarders.

Ronald Romero They can't imagine someone's going to have to make an inventory of all their shit.

Juan Uribe Or they want to punish the world.

Ronald Romero Enough chit chat; the fridge.

Juan Uribe Do you think he'll have some serviceable beer?

Ronald Romero Doesn't matter. Grab the post-its, notes, grocery list, anything he wrote down.

Juan Uribe You can be so neurotic sometimes . . .

Ronald Romero So?

Juan Uribe Three overdue gas bills and a grocery list . . . Groceries: sea salt, garlic, carrots, TV guide . . . Sea salt? Pretty gourmet for someone who lived like this, wouldn't you say? Or maybe some woman would come and cook for him?

Ronald Romero Here?

Juan Uribe A lonely woman.

Rose E. Oakwood Being Chief of Police in a man's world . . .

Ronald Romero In this dump?

Rose E. Oakwood Heading a division no one cares about . . .

Juan Uribe Not everyone has somewhere to go.

Rose E. Oakwood Can be lonely.

Ronald Romero Anything else?

Rose E. Oakwood Cooking isn't my strong suit. I buy frozen. You lose some nutrients, but it's better than fast food.

Juan Uribe Seven magnets from the same pizza place . . . Velo's Pizza. The logo is a green velociraptor, like Yoshi. Who wants to eat at a dinosaur pizzeria? Did you know Yoshi was a velociraptor? The dinosaur Mario rode . . . Mario Bros. Where were you in the eighties? Anyway . . . I mean, what kind of advertising is that? Are they saying their recipe is prehistoric? That they use dinosaur meat? That your pizza is free of charge if it arrives before a meteor hits? What are they saying, Ron? Ronnie? (*Pause.*) Do you know the place? Do you like it? What's the matter?

Ronald Romero My sister used to go there with her husband before she moved to Los Angeles and we lost touch.

Juan Uribe The transparent fat guy who swore he was a golfer?

Ronald Romero Basketball player.

Juan Uribe Same difference.

Ronald Romero A white guy playing golf is normal; a fat white guy playing golf, even more so; a practically transparent obese white guy who says he plays basketball practically to a professional standard, and that he'd be playing in the NBA if he hadn't hurt his knee, that's . . . Yeah, him.

Juan Uribe Well, our John Doe was a big fan of this dinosaur pizza place . . . Oh, I get it. The logo is saying if you eat at this pizza place you become like a tyrannosaur.

Ronald Romero Bloodthirsty?

Juan Uribe Huge, like your brother-in-law.

Pause.

Ronald Romero Hand me the magnet.

Juan Uribe Triple pepperoni, please.

Ronald Romero And mushrooms and extra cheese. I don't understand why you like them so packed.

Juan Uribe Force of habit.

Ronald Romero Hand me the phone.

Juan Uribe Don't be a cheapskate, use your cell phone.

Ronald Romero You haven't found the phone?

Juan Uribe Must be somewhere in the disaster area.

Ronald Romero Try by the window.

Juan Uribe Which one?

Ronald Romero Telephones go next to windows. That way you can answer it and ignore the person you're talking to to look at the sunset or at the lady fighting for her life carrying five bags of groceries.

Rose E. Oakwood I do very little grocery shopping.

Juan Uribe Use my cell.

Rose E. Oakwood I order it over the phone.

Ronald Romero It has to be from his landline.

Rose E. Oakwood So I don't have to go out.

Juan Uribe Must be that Garfield one, right?

Rose E. Oakwood And because the delivery boy is . . . nice.

Ronald Romero Thought that was a toy.

Juan Uribe It's a vintage, TYCO Garfield phone, Ron! Seriously, did you skip the eighties?

Ronald Romero Some of us were busy living life.

Rose E. Oakwood I've never said anything to him. It wouldn't be appropriate.

Juan Uribe If you say so. Take the receiver.

Ronald Romero See how you can be useful?

Juan Uribe You don't have to be like that, you know?

Ronald Romero I miss García.

Juan Uribe What did Raymond have that I don't?

Ronald Romero He worked in silence.

Juan Uribe Just the kind of friend you'd would want to liven up Thanksgiving.

Pause.

Ronald Romero Didn't you say you could make friends with anybody?

Juan Uribe If they talk.

Ronald Romero You said all they had to do was smile.

Juan Uribe You're right. García must be some guy.

Pause.

Ronald Romero Yeah. (*Pause. Dials. Waits.*) How you doing? I'm calling from number 23 on 79th . . . You have my number, right? Yeah. That's the one. This is his son. (*Pause.*) Good. Isaac? He's resting. Could you send me a pepperoni pizza with mushrooms and extra cheese? Cash. Yeah. Twenty-dollar bill. Thanks.

Juan Uribe Not with my twenty.

Ronald Romero Thanks. Later.

Juan Uribe So?

Ronald Romero On its way.

Juan Uribe Isaac?

Ronald Romero The pizza.

Juan Uribe His name was Isaac?

Ronald Romero Isaac Ezban.

Juan Uribe My father's name was Isaac.

Ronald Romero   You said his name was Iván, that it rhymed with your name and everything.

Juan Uribe   They're similar.

Ronald Romero   Uh huh.

Juan Uribe   What was your father's name?

Pause.

What was your mother's?

Pause.

Rose E. Oakwood   The county has assigned a psychologist to evaluate the employees under my supervision every three months. The evaluations are quick. According to regulations, the psychologist should come to the station, but he just sends the forms and I ask the questions; when the employees answer, I return them for analysis and the psychologist sends a satisfactory report to headquarters. It's a bureaucratic process, simple, effective. They make sure the job isn't getting to them. They're basic questions. (*Pause.*) How are you feeling?

Juan Uribe   Motivated.

Rose E. Oakwood   Are you sleeping?

Ronald Romero   Yes.

Rose E. Oakwood   Exercise?

Juan Uribe   Every other day in the gym at the station, they have good equipment, have you used it?

Rose E. Oakwood   Do you eat?

Ronald Romero   Yes.

Rose E. Oakwood   Distractions?

Juan Uribe   I watched Finding Nory the other day. I enjoyed it.

Rose E. Oakwood   Dory.

Juan Uribe   I didn't understand the plot, it reminded me of the first one, Finding Emo.

Rose E. Oakwood   Nemo.

Juan Uribe   What?

Rose E. Oakwood   Nemo, like the captain.

Juan Uribe   You're right.

Rose E. Oakwood   Go on.

Juan Uribe   I thought . . . It's odd that a fish would go looking for its family. (*Pause.*) I used to have a shoal. They told me in the store they were brothers. I think they were. They looked alike. They didn't swim together, actually, they each stayed on their own side. (*Pause.*) I usually go to the movies on my own. It's better, you can focus on the plot. If I'd gone with someone else, I wouldn't have noticed how odd it is that a fish would go looking for its family . . . When you go with someone you worry about them having a good time. (*Pause.*) I sometimes watch TV at home. I have Netflix, I recommend it.

Ronald Romero   No.

Rose E. Oakwood   No hobbies?

Ronald Romero   You never know when you're gonna die.

Rose E. Oakwood   All the more reason.

Ronald Romero   I don't leave anything undone, not even the bed. I don't want to leave any debts; that closes any window on distractions. I focus on my to-do list, leaving everything paid, clean, tidy . . . I update photo albums, check my CV, calendar, laptop . . . I make sure there are no details that might complicate my death certification . . . Once a day I call a different person from my phone book to see how they are, I'm going from A to Z. I make sure to remain present in people's minds. The people you neglect become ghosts, names that lose meaning . . . I wouldn't like to become that for anyone . . . A complication. Oh, and I do the dishes.

Rose E. Oakwood   Vacations?

Juan Uribe   I'm thinking of going to the Mexican Caribbean in August next year. I've been saving up. I don't have anyone to go with . . . But I read that it's cheaper to go as a couple, and it's all-inclusive, food, drink, mezcal, Mexican tequila. I have brochures.

Ronald Romero   Juan told me last week he's planning on going to the Mayan Riviera. He mentioned that it's best to go as a couple; he knows I'm single, but he said it to make conversation. He does that, finds excuses to talk. I miss my ex-wife. Especially on vacation. She used to take care of those kinds of things. (*Pause.*) If I . . . paid for the tickets, would you like to go with me? As friends, of course.

Rose E. Oakwood   That wouldn't be . . . I'm sorry. We're done. I have to hand in the questions to the psychology department. (*Pause.*) I won't be including the last thing you said.

Ronald Romero   Of course not.

Rose E. Oakwood   No.

Ronald Romero   Of course.

Rose E. Oakwood   That's it.

Juan Uribe   That's it?

Rose E. Oakwood   Anything to add?

Juan Uribe   Aren't you going to ask me how I feel about going into other people's homes where there's rotten fruit, flies, old newspapers, frozen pizza boxes, mixed up garbage, stacks of beer bottles, dirty sheets, unidentified substances on the carpet . . .? Sometimes I want to vomit. That's why I carry VapoRub. These are uninhabitable spaces, really. Don't you want to know if this is harming us?

Rose E. Oakwood We asked you how you were feeling, you said: motivated.

Juan Uribe I am. No doubt. I love my job. I . . .

Rose E. Oakwood Would you like me to write down that this negatively affects you? That going into these insalubrious spaces has a detrimental effect on your mental, physical or emotional wellbeing?

Juan Uribe I need the job.

Rose E. Oakwood That isn't what I asked you.

Juan Uribe Of course. (*Pause.*) Please, leave it as it is.

Rose E. Oakwood Out of the question. I cannot omit your answers. That's the point of these evaluations. To record. (*Pause.*) I'll add a suggestion for a more in-depth evaluation.

Juan Uribe Thank you. I'm sorry. I love working here. Please write that down, too.

Rose E. Oakwood Don't worry. That'll be all.

Juan Uribe Yes. Thank you.

Rose E. Oakwood My last vacation was somewhere nice. It didn't look like the postcard, but it was enough. Yeah. I like it when places are nice.

Ronald Romero The Riviera is . . . nice. I mean, I understand that you and I can't . . . but in case you wanted to go with someone else or . . . It's a nice place.

Rose E. Oakwood I don't doubt it.

Pause.

Juan Uribe Did you see the calendar?

Ronald Romero The one in the bathroom?

Juan Uribe Yeah.

Ronald Romero Any relevant information? It has dates marked in red, but no notes. Did I miss something?

Juan Uribe It's from 1977.

Ronald Romero The one on the wall?

Juan Uribe Who puts a calendar in the bathroom?

Ronald Romero You don't want to forget when the last time was you shat blood. Think about it, you're sick, you take medicine, you have side effects. I'd have a calendar in the bathroom.

Juan Uribe From 1977?

Ronald Romero   You're right.

Juan Uribe   Who was Isaac Ezban?

Ronald Romero   We're about to find out.

Pause.

Juan Uribe   I need to step outside for some air.

Ronald Romero   We haven't found anything yet.

Rose E. Oakwood   They have to put their hands in the shit. All the way in, with gloves on, sink their arms in up to their elbows or their shoulders or their necks if they have to and . . . They always have to. Because the lives of the people no one claims are found scattered under furniture, inside packed drawers, written in the dust, wrinkled like sticky plastic wrapping. They are looking for any vestige of identity. A will, an address book, a computer, a cell phone, pictures of relatives. (*Pause.*) Who is the woman in the picture?

Ronald Romero   Wait. Did you see that picture? (*Pause.*) On the shelf. Under the stuffed bear head.

Juan Uribe   I need a cigarette.

Ronald Romero   Can I have one?

Rose E. Oakwood   Romantic interests are what can tell us the most about a person. (*Pause.*) Who is the woman in the picture?

Ronald Romero   I can't imagine any woman setting foot in this apartment.

Juan Uribe   You already said that.

Rose E. Oakwood   Who is . . .

Juan Uribe   They could make love amongst the garbage.

Rose E. Oakwood   The woman . . .

Juan Uribe   Some people like that kind of thing.

Rose E. Oakwood   . . . in the picture?

Ronald Romero   I'm going to pretend you didn't say that.

Juan Uribe   Don't tell me you and your ex-wife never did anything "dirty."

Ronald Romero   I'm gonna ignore that comment, too.

Juan Uribe   Olga and I did all kinds of stuff in motels, never garbage or anything like that, but . . . One time she urinated in my mouth. I've never told anyone . . . We did it in the shower. It was a warm liquid, it wasn't bitter, it felt like water . . . It was . . . A romantic way of telling her: I love anything that comes out of you. Understand? (*Pause.*) She didn't like it, or maybe she did in the heat of the moment, but we never did it again.

Rose E. Oakwood Hoarding is a mental disorder that causes people to behave incoherently. They buy things just for the sake of having them.

Ronald Romero I'm going inside. I'll check the shelves and between the books.

Juan Uribe Aren't you gonna finish your cigarette?

Ronald Romero No.

Rose E. Oakwood Hoarders are aware of their disorder, but they can't help feeling like something's missing, like they need to fill a void.

Juan Uribe There's lots of things we never did again, actually.

Rose E. Oakwood I've never been married. I have a dog and two cats. The dog, Kirmen; the calico cat, Chuck, and the black cat is called Black. I'd named him Winston but he never answered. Cats respond with a look, you call them and they let you know they heard you. The cat understands his name is Chuck even though he doesn't come so I can stroke him. Winston never once responded to Winston. He doesn't respond to Black either, but he prefers that name. The most profound relationship I have in the world . . . is with Black, my cat, it's not that I don't love Kirmen or Chuck, it's just that . . . in this shit-filled world, it's impossible not to have a favorite . . . Do I have a favorite out of Ronald and Juan? It would be unprofessional of me to say; or even ask myself, but . . .

Ronald Romero Juan! Get in here.

Juan Uribe Coming.

Ronald Romero Who's the woman in the picture? Some romantic interest?

Juan Uribe I don't know.

Rose E. Oakwood Who am I to my cat?

Ronald Romero Let's look around and see if she turns up anywhere else.

Juan Uribe I'll check the bedroom. (*Goes to the bedroom.*)

Rose E. Oakwood Does he love me or am I merely his feeder?

Juan Uribe (*returns to the living room*) It's worse. There's a mattress on the floor and piles of magazines and boxes of Chinese food and endless rivers of ants going in and out forming paths and . . . Styrofoam cups for instant noodles full of cigarette butts . . . It's your turn to do the bedroom.

Ronald Romero You do the bedroom. I'll do the living room.

Juan Uribe You say you can do this job without applying VapoRub every ten seconds, that means you don't retch, that you can do the fetid work while I gather the . . . the other, the . . . the information, the . . . that . . . It's fucking disgusting, Ron. Please, you take the bedroom.

Ronald Romero I'll take the living room.

Juan Uribe Are you always like this? (*Pause.*) You don't have to be like this.

Ronald Romero   García was like this with me. It's my turn.

Juan Uribe   Of course.

Pause.

Rose E. Oakwood   There was another cat who used to live in my house, well, at first it was a she, then I discovered it was a he. He had testicles . . . He ran away. His name was Agatha. Then Coconut. (*Pause.*) Then nothing.

Juan Uribe   How could he live like this? Where did he sleep?

Rose E. Oakwood   He ran away . . . Or rather . . .

Juan Uribe   Maybe he didn't sleep. (*Pause.*) Nosferatu!

Rose E. Oakwood   He didn't come back because cats aren't inside animals. They use the house, but they belong outside.

Ronald Romero   Look. Two dozen packages of unused bed sheets, eight brand-new boxes of Christmas lights. Can you imagine Christmas in this apartment?

Juan Uribe   Who would come?

Rose E. Oakwood   I like Christmas and Thanksgiving. Two days a year. My birthday, too. Three days a year. They're holidays, official holidays, except my birthday, but they're holidays because they're for everyone; they let us know when the fun begins and ends. For example, tomorrow is Saturday, it's Saturday for everyone. Everyone chooses how they spend their Saturday, but there's a consensus that it's a day of rest. To me, that means that I mustn't think of anything work-related between 12 a.m. and 12 a.m. Twenty-four hours off.

Ronald Romero   Listen to this: Parachuting certificate. First jump, 1963.

Juan Uribe   Can you imagine him flying?

Ronald Romero   To me Isaac is everyone until we shape him. Time to put the puzzle together.

Juan Uribe   He has a riding crop hanging on the wall.

Ronald Romero   I don't want to hear it.

Juan Uribe   Hear what?

Ronald Romero   Whatever it is you want to tell me about your ex and a whip.

Juan Uribe   She was never into that. Handcuffs yes, but that was it, or come to think of it . . .

Ronald Romero   I said I didn't want to hear it.

Rose E. Oakwood   The woman in the picture could be his mother or sister.

Juan Uribe   I'm gonna call Rose.

Ronald Romero   What for?

Juan Uribe   She might have some information about Mr. Ezban . . . Maybe someone called the station to claim him. Maybe she . . .

Ronald Romero   You're worried about your evaluation.

Juan Uribe   I shouldn't have said the last part.

Ronald Romero   No.

Juan Uribe   Do you think they'll transfer me to another unit or fire me?

Ronald Romero   If you call her in the middle of the day to ask a stupid question, probably. Do your job. Don't talk so much. Finish what you start. There you go. That way they won't have grounds to fire you.

Juan Uribe   I told them I was motivated.

Ronald Romero   Too much.

Pause.

Juan Uribe   Three copies of *Top Gun. Braveheart* on VHS and DVD. Remember that movie? When Bruce Willis yelled . . .

Rose E. Oakwood   Cats are free thinkers.

Juan Uribe, Ronald Romero & Rose E. Oakwood   Freedom!

Ronald Romero   I like *Gladiator*.

Juan Uribe   There wouldn't be a *Gladiator* without *Braveheart*, just like there wouldn't be a *Braveheart* without *Ben-Hur*. They're the same movie.

Ronald Romero   I haven't been to the movies in a long time.

Juan Uribe   There's a book here. A single, solitary book on the night stand. A rusty metal cooler for a night stand?

Ronald Romero   What book?

Juan Uribe   *One Hundred Years of Solitude*, by García Márquez.

Ronald Romero   Check if there's an inscription.

Pause.

Juan Uribe   You're not gonna believe this.

Pause.

Rose E. Oakwood (*reading aloud from a book*)   "Rose, I know you're my boss. I'm clear on that and I want to apologize for the other day. I don't want you to think I was trying anything. I was being polite. You asked about vacations and my wife used to plan our vacations. That's all. I thought about how nice vacations are. I was making conversation. I like talking to you. Professionally. You seem capable. You're very organized at the job you do. Last year during the station Christmas party I thought no one can run this office better than you. Anyway. Please accept this book as a token of apology for my remark about the Riviera. I ask that you take this inscription as an affectionate and professional apology. I hope I'm not being inappropriate. Sincerely. Ronald R." (*Pause.*) *The Lord of the Rings*, by John Ronald R. Tolkien. Part one . . .

Ronald Romero   What?

Juan Uribe   It's dedicated to Isaac. It says: "I rarely say it, but I hope you know how much it means to me to have you as a friend. You matter to me." Signed: Miriam (Puffy) Logan.

Ronald Romero   Puffy?

Juan Uribe   Puffy.

Ronald Romero   She should have said it more often.

Juan Uribe   I guess. (*Pause.*) So the woman in the picture is Puffy?

Ronald Romero   We don't know.

Juan Uribe   Could be her.

Ronald Romero   Open the book and shake it.

Pause.

Juan Uribe   Nothing.

Ronald Romero   We're going to have to search the records for Miriam Logan. There's probably more than one.

Juan Uribe   Not all from Red Bank, New Jersey.

Ronald Romero   How do you know she's from there?

Juan Uribe   I shook the book.

Ronald Romero   You said there was nothing in it.

Juan Uribe   I didn't want you to be right. (*Pause.*) That's why you sent me to the bedroom, isn't it? Because you're the expert.

Rose E. Oakwood   I didn't watch *The Lord of the Rings* movies. Each of them was three hours long. Who can spare all that time?

Ronald Romero   So there was a postcard, a letter in the book. What does it say?

Juan Uribe   I used to be a waiter.

Ronald Romero   Isaac Ezban was a parachutist and a waiter?

Juan Uribe   No. I was a waiter.

Ronald Romero   When?

Juan Uribe   My whole life. I quit last year. Before I joined the station. Actually, they quit me. The owner said he couldn't have a fifty-two-year-old waiter. That I'd spent too much time waiting tables, that I'd done my time, that the restaurant needed younger, more able-bodied people, that I should to prosper. I asked him: Why don't you give me a raise or promote me to manager? We have a manager, he said. A thirty-year-old manager, the perfect age for a manager. I didn't want to stop working. I wanted things to stay as they were.

Pause.

Ronald Romero   Which restaurant? Do I know it?

Juan Uribe   Doesn't matter. I don't work there anymore, I'm not going to give them free publicity.

Pause.

Ronald Romero   What does the postcard say?

Juan Uribe   "I called on Sunday, around two, no one answered. I'll call again." Elsie Logan, Red Bank, New Jersey.

Ronald Romero   Call Rose and tell her we have information, don't ask about your evaluation. Call and give her the information about Miss Logan from Red Bank. Only that. If she mentions anything about your evaluation, nod and say thank you. Doesn't matter what she says. You nod and say thank you. Understood?

Juan Uribe   Yes.

Ronald Romero   Or would you rather I call?

Juan Uribe   Let me do it.

Ronald Romero   Nod and say thank you.

Juan Uribe   Aye aye, captain.

Pause.

Rose E. Oakwood   Do you think we should fire him?

Pause.

Juan Uribe   I have new information regarding the Isaac Ezban case . . .

Pause.

Ronald Romero   He needs the job.

Juan Uribe   . . . he had an acquaintance,

Rose E. Oakwood   That isn't what I asked.

Juan Uribe   . . . we think it might be the woman in the picture.

Ronald Romero   He's noisy, unruly, lacks discipline, but he's a good partner . . . He's constantly putting VapoRub on his nose, I think he has some kind of allergy, I don't know if it's dust or . . .

Rose E. Oakwood   Or if it's a mental thing.

Pause.

Juan Uribe   This woman, who might presumably be the one in the picture, sent him a postcard, in that postcard she . . .

Ronald Romero   Exactly.

Rose E. Oakwood   Could you do this job on your own?

Pause.

Ronald Romero   Without stealing?

Rose E. Oakwood   You're saying that so we won't fire Juan.

Ronald Romero   It's awfully tempting.

Rose E. Oakwood   You've grown fond of him.

Juan Uribe   . . . she says she loves him, that she should say it more often, she . . .

Ronald Romero   It's hard not to grow fond of people in this line of work.

Rose E. Oakwood   Have you told him?

Ronald Romero   What?

Rose E. Oakwood   That you love him.

Ronald Romero   No.

Rose E. Oakwood   I understand. (*Pause.*) He filed a report on the postcard the two of you found in the apartment, well, he called and left a message on the answering machine, would you like to hear the end?

Ronald Romero   Why the end?

Rose E. Oakwood   It might be of interest to you.

Ronald Romero   I was there when we found the postcard, the lady is from Red Bank, New Jersey, they called her Puffy and her name is Miriam Logan.

Rose E. Oakwood   But you weren't there when Juan made the call, were you?

Ronald Romero   No.

Juan Uribe   Could you give me a second? I'm going to . . . I want to file the report in private.

Ronald Romero   You inform, you nod and . . .

Juan Uribe   And say thank you if she says anything, got it.

Rose E. Oakwood   So, would you like to hear the end?

Ronald Romero   Does it concern me?

Rose E. Oakwood   I'll play the end for you.

Juan Uribe   . . . That's all the information we have on Miss Puffy Logan . . . I would have liked to deliver personally, but I assumed that if you checked the records after listening to my message, the case would move along faster, besides . . . There's something that can't wait. Ronald told me not to say anything. Ronald is always telling me what to do, he's a good partner, he's experienced, actually, he said he could do this job without me and, to be honest, I believe him. I don't want you to think I'm giving you more material to use against me, I know I'm being evaluated, and about that, I want to say that Ronald is . . . He's a capable guy, he's mean to me, but I know he's doing it to teach me; this job would make anyone mean; dealing with the dead day in and day out, the smell, the broken objects, the yellowed books . . . Who wouldn't turn mean? Ronald is, well, he's doing a stupendous job, and you know that, the point is . . . The point is that, before you fire me, I would like you to know that you have an exemplary agent in Ronald, hard-hearted, but exemplary . . . You're keeping the better man. I'll save you the trouble of firing me, I quit. I'd rather save myself the disappointment of being replaced or having to sit in front of a supervisor who would politely encourage me to retire . . . Thank you for the opportunity, Miss Oakwood.

Rose E. Oakwood   End of recording.

Ronald Romero   Hard-hearted.

Rose E. Oakwood   An exemplary agent.

Ronald Romero   I'm mean to him?

Rose E. Oakwood   Perhaps you were too strict with him.

Ronald Romero   I'm firm, but I don't think I'm mean to him.

Rose E. Oakwood   Do you think we should fire him?

Juan Uribe   I'd rather save myself the disappointment of being replaced or having to sit in front of a supervisor who would politely encourage me to retire . . .

Ronald Romero   Didn't he just quit?

Rose E. Oakwood   As a precautionary measure; he's protecting himself, but we can call him this instant, actually, I thought that you, that you could call him and tell him that we, that you want him to stay, that you can't do the job on your own, that you need him . . . to stop you from stealing. Of course, that is if you think we shouldn't accept his resignation.

Ronald Romero   Can I think about it?

Rose E. Oakwood   Didn't you just say a moment ago that he's a good partner?

Ronald Romero   Do you think I'm harsh?

Juan Uribe   Are you always like this?

Rose E. Oakwood   You're polite to me. (*Pause.*) Sometimes . . . too polite.

Ronald Romero   I'm sorry. I'll call him.

Rose E. Oakwood   Perfect. Let me know how it turns out. In the meantime I'll have them look into a Miriam from Red Bank, New Jersey.

Juan Uribe   Hey, Ronnie. Have you heard? Yeah. Don't worry about it, it was my decision. I wasn't going to give them the satisfaction of . . . Really? (*Pause.*) I don't think it was very professional of them to show you what I said, but . . . I understand. I didn't mean to get you into trouble, I was . . . I also told them they had the best agent. Really, Ron? Thanks, but I already got my old job back waiting tables. The thirty-year-old manager was in a crisis, a couple of teenagers quit and he gave me a job while he finds more staff. Thanks for calling anyway.

Rose E. Oakwood   No answer. We have a number for Miriam, but even though we keep calling it, there's no answer. We don't know if she's alive: there's no record of any credit card purchases, the address we have was vacated over six months ago and there's no known address she might have moved to . . . There is no trace of Miss Logan. How does someone become nothing?

Ronald Romero   He said no.

Rose E. Oakwood   And you let him go?

Ronald Romero   He said no.

Pause.

Juan Uribe   Good afternoon, welcome to Velo's Pizza, what's it going to be? We have the Acrocanthosaurus pizza, with triple pepperoni, anchovies, fresh mushrooms, red onion, and cabbage slices; the Tyrannosaurus Rex, which comes with a Chicago-style base, a selection of house meats, four cheeses, and a stuffed crust; the Velo's Raptor, light and aerodynamic to hunt down your appetite, designed with fine artisanal dough, with goat cheese, arugula, prosciutto, balsamic oil, and cherry tomato; we also have vegetarian pizzas like the Brontosaurus, the Diplodocus, the Stegosaurus, and the Ankylosaurus . . . That last one comes with steamed spinach, carrots, cabbage, lettuce, and . . . and . . . and . . . I'm sorry, they changed the menu while I was away . . . Oh, and sliced baby potatoes. So, are you ready to order?

Ronald Romero   You didn't tell me you worked here.

Rose E. Oakwood   It was in his references.

Juan Uribe   Would you like a minute to think it over?

Ronald Romero   Does us eating here make you uncomfortable?

Juan Uribe   Our selection of beverages includes Coke, Fanta, Sprite, Paleozoic drinks, Sabertooth milkshakes, beers, and a selection of juices. Would you like to see the drinks menu?

Rose E. Oakwood   I'll have a sparkling water.

Ronald Romero   One Acrocanthosaurus pizza with triple pepperoni, fresh mushrooms, and everything else.

Juan Uribe   Right away. (*Pause.*) Would the gentleman like something to drink?

Ronald Romero   You don't have to be like this, Juan.

Juan Uribe   We have Coke, Fanta, Sprite, Paleozoic drinks, Sabertooth milkshakes, beer, and a selection of juices.

Rose E. Oakwood   He'll have a beer.

Juan Uribe   I'll be right back with your drinks.

Ronald Romero   Thanks. (*Pause.*) Did you know he'd be here?

Rose E. Oakwood   We need him back, you need him back, the station needs him back, nobody wants to do this job, and he wasn't going to go back to the station of his own accord.

Ronald Romero   Is that why you wanted to have dinner with me here?

Rose E. Oakwood   He's your partner, you have to ask him to come back.

Ronald Romero   I thought you wanted to spend some time alone, I mean, in a professional capacity, it's cool, but that you wanted to talk about the case, about Isaac, that . . . You could have warned me this was why we were coming, seeing him waiting tables makes me uncomfortable.

Rose E. Oakwood   He said you were harsh, I imagine you treated him like an apprentice.

Ronald Romero   He was an apprentice.

Rose E. Oakwood   I don't see what's so humiliating about him serving us, it's a dignified job, worse pay, but less disgusting than the one you do every day.

Ronald Romero   Thanks for the encouragement.

Rose E. Oakwood   You don't do that job because you love it, we know that.

Ronald Romero   No.

Juan Uribe   Beer for the gentleman, sparkling water for the lady, I'll be right back with your pizza.

Ronald Romero   Juan . . .

Juan Uribe   Can I get you anything else?

Ronald Romero   Sit down.

Juan Uribe   Unfortunately, we're not allowed to sit with customers, but is there anything I can help you with? Shall I call the manager? Has my service been lacking in some way? Was it unsatisfactory? Do I not seem motivated, smiling? I'll happily fetch the manager so you can give him my performance review.

Ronald Romero   I understand, I overstepped, I treated you like an idiot; You're not an idiot. I behaved like an idiot and, well, Rose would like . . .

Rose E. Oakwood   Leave me out of it, boys; in fact, if you'll excuse me, I'm off to the ladies'.

Juan Uribe At the back, up the stairs and on your left; opposite the prehistoric play area.

Rose E. Oakwood Thank you.

Ronald Romero Will you forgive me?

Juan Uribe We're all out of onion rings for the moment, but I can send you and order of Pterodactyl fries and we apologize for any oversight on my part as your waiter this evening.

Ronald Romero Juan . . .

Juan Uribe I'll bring those fries right over. On the house, don't you worry.

Ronald Romero . . . Thanks.

Pause.

Rose E. Oakwood He turned us down.

Ronald Romero Yes.

Rose E. Oakwood I considered asking García to come back.

Ronald Romero But?

Rose E. Oakwood He'll turn us down.

Ronald Romero So . . .?

Rose E. Oakwood You'll have to work alone. (*Pause.*) Without stealing anything.

Ronald Romero I'm going to miss Juan.

Rose E. Oakwood Don't you worry. We'll soon find a replacement, there must be more undocumented Mexicans around, right?

Ronald Romero I hope so.

Rose E. Oakwood Unless doing this job is negatively affecting you, if entering these unwholesome places of your own accord has some harmful effect on your mental, physical, or emotional health.

Ronald Romero If I answer in the affirmative you'd be left with no one. You'd be forced to carry out a more in-depth evaluation of my person and you'd have to fire me, too.

Rose E. Oakwood We didn't fire Juan, we weren't going to fire Juan, you made sure of that. We were simply evaluating him as part of a bureaucratic process. If anyone complains to the administration or is showing signs of suffering some form of psychological, emotional, or physical affliction due to the work they are doing, it is our job to evaluate it, make note of it, put it on record that our employees matter to us, but . . . We weren't thinking of firing him. We're in no condition to fire anyone. In actual fact, the evaluation is a formality.

Ronald Romero   But you . . . You made him nervous. He felt pressured by what you said.

Rose E. Oakwood   Admit it, your partner didn't quit because of our evaluation, he quit so he wouldn't have to spend another day with you. I'm sorry to tell you this, agent, but you have a hard heart, and if you carry on like this, you're going to end up like Mr. Ezban.

Ronald Romero   I don't think it's very professional of you to say so.

Rose E. Oakwood   But you find it appropriate to give me a copy of *The Lord of the Rings* with a suggestive inscription?

Pause.

Ronald Romero   I don't want to die alone.

Pause.

Rose E. Oakwood   Kiss me, Ronald.

Ronald Romero   Are you being serious?

Rose E. Oakwood   I won't ask a second time.

Ronald Romero   Whatever you say.

Pause.

Juan Uribe   I hope I'm not interrupting. Here's the check. We hope the food was to your liking and we leave you with a dinosaur joke to bring the evening to a close: Who was the King of Hip Hop during the Late Cretaceous?

Rose E. Oakwood   The veloci-RAP-tor?

Juan Uribe   You're a regular customer, please allow your companion to answer the next one: Which dinosaur always has a cold?

Ronald Romero   Please don't think that Miss Oakwood and I . . . This happened tonight and we . . . We want you to come back.

Juan Uribe   The Tricera . . . coughs.

Rose E. Oakwood   It's time to go.

Ronald Romero   I don't know what you saw, but I assure you it was just a kiss.

Juan Uribe   We know it's Triceratops, but . . . The joke wouldn't work if we said tops instead of coughs, right? Because it has a cold.

Ronald Romero   Hope to see you soon, friend.

Juan Uribe   Friend?

Ronald Romero   Yeah.

Juan Uribe   You never called me friend.

Ronald Romero We'd been working together a year, I wasn't feeling it.

Juan Uribe You say that now because you don't want to work alone.

Ronald Romero I need someone to stop me stealing paintings or money or whatever it is we find.

Juan Uribe You know that's not me.

Rose E. Oakwood I shouldn't be hearing this conversation.

Juan Uribe You didn't know we kept things? Please, everyone keeps things; a righteous man may fall seven times and rise again.

Rose E. Oakwood Ronald?

Ronald Romero I'd prefer not to answer that question.

Rose E. Oakwood I'll see you outside.

Ronald Romero Wait. Tell him. I think he needs to hear it from you.

Rose E. Oakwood That we weren't going to fire him? No, Juan, we weren't going to fire you.

Juan Uribe What about the evaluation?

Rose E. Oakwood It was just that, an evaluation.

Juan Uribe Glad to hear it.

Rose E. Oakwood Wonderful, we'll see you Monday at building number 23 on 79th Street in Queens, bring your gloves.

Juan Uribe No offense, but . . . I've got tables to wait on on Monday, actually, I've got tables to wait on right now, so . . .

Ronald Romero You're not coming back.

Juan Uribe I didn't take this job because I enjoy it, but if you mean it, we can still be friends.

Ronald Romero Of course.

Juan Uribe Good night, friends . . . Oh, and congratulations on your relationship. I'm glad you found each other.

Ronald Romero Relationship?

Rose E. Oakwood Good night.

Pause.

Juan Uribe Of course I'm not coming back. Who would want to go into these disgusting apartments when he can clean the tables of spoiled children who leave half-eaten pizzas and snot all over the backs of their chairs? I love being a waiter. Serving people. It's a dignified, American job.

Pause.

Ronald Romero Look what I found. / What? / This hat. / Wanna keep it? / Isaac was a Mets fan. / So? / So things are changing. / How? / No one likes a loser. / What do you mean? / For the first time in history there are more Mets fans than Yankees fans, you know why? Because the Mets are winning, and in a city like New York, we like to root for a winning team. / If you say so. / The Mets have been to the World Series twice in the last few years while the Yankees haven't made it since 2009. And what does that tell us about Isaac? That despite living in a dump and being practically alone, he dreamed of winning. / How do you know he used to be a Yankees fan? How do you know he wasn't a Mets fan when they were losing? / He liked Neil Diamond. / Uh huh. / And Donna Summer. / Uh huh. / Neil Diamond and Donna Summer are winners. / Now I see what you're getting at. / What? / That we miss Juan. You should call him. / Yeah, that's not a bad idea.

Pause.

Rose E. Oakwood I'm glad you agreed to come.

Juan Uribe I did it for you.

Rose E. Oakwood Ronald confessed about the painting.

Juan Uribe The copy?

Rose E. Oakwood "The Concert," 1664, Johannes Vermeer.

Juan Uribe What?

Rose E. Oakwood It was stolen in 1990 from the Gardner Museum in Boston.

Juan Uribe Mr. Ezban's painting?

Rose E. Oakwood Its value is estimated at two hundred million dollars.

Juan Uribe And I'm busting my balls for nine dollars an hour.

Rose E. Oakwood The minimum wage went up to fifteen since you left the station.

Juan Uribe And what are you going to do?

Rose E. Oakwood Ronald gave it to me so we can return it to the Gardner.

Juan Uribe I have a contact in the black market. (*Pause.*) If you want . . .

Rose E. Oakwood The art black market?

Juan Uribe What else?

Rose E. Oakwood How did you get it?

Juan Uribe An arms dealer in the alley behind the pizza place. I met him years ago the first time I took out the trash. He aimed a .45 at me and told me I had two choices: One, keep quiet and get a 30 percent tip whenever he came to the restaurant or get 100 percent of a bullet in the head. I think the first option, though a lower percentage, was the more fruitful. (*Pause.*) What do you think?

Rose E. Oakwood   And how do you know he also traffics in art?

Juan Uribe   He's a regular American entrepreneur. He's been moving up in the world. First it was weapons, then cocaine, then heroin, then anthropological pieces, and finally classical and contemporary art.

Rose E. Oakwood   I don't plan on returning the painting to Boston.

Juan Uribe   So you want the contact?

Rose E. Oakwood   No.

Juan Uribe   Why did you call me?

Rose E. Oakwood   Ronald gave me the painting because . . . He wanted to give me grounds to fire him. He can't do this job alone. (*Pause.*) He's taken to putting VapoRub on his nose and vomiting on the job. He realizes that spending so many hours in insalubrious places has taken a terrible toll on his physical, mental, and emotional health and . . . He's started talking to himself.

Juan Uribe   Hard-hearted Ronald is talking to himself?

Rose E. Oakwood   He told me about it himself.

Juan Uribe   So . . .

Rose E. Oakwood   Are you willing to come back?

Juan Uribe   Not for a million dollars.

Rose E. Oakwood   How about two hundred million?

Juan Uribe   You're joking.

Rose E. Oakwood   You can have it, it's right here, under my desk. It's been here ever since Ronald brought it. (*Pause.*) We could go to prison if I give it to my superiors. Do you know how the painting disappeared?

Juan Uribe   No.

Rose E. Oakwood   A couple of thieves dressed as police officers stole it. (*Pause.*) Now imagine it gets returned by the Queens County police precinct. A lot of people think the police are corrupt, that we bail each other out, that we couldn't care less about the public, that we only look after our own interests and . . . The painting has been missing for twenty-seven years. No one is going to believe we found it in Mr. Ezban's house.

Juan Uribe   If you were to give it to me, I would sell it to my contact, and if I get two hundred million bucks, or a hundred, or fifty or ten million . . . You understand I would have no reason to come back here.

Rose E. Oakwood   I understand, but you're not going to sell it.

Juan Uribe   What makes you so sure?

Rose E. Oakwood   Ronald said . . .

Juan Uribe   Excuse me. (*Pause.*) Hello? Hi. Yeah, a little busy.

Ronald Romero   If you're waiting tables I can call back later.

Juan Uribe   I'm at the station.

Ronald Romero   With Rose.

Juan Uribe   Exactly.

Ronald Romero   What do you think?

Juan Uribe   That I'm going to be rich.

Ronald Romero   Are you going to sell the painting?

Juan Uribe   Or hand it in to the authorities, I expect there will be a generous reward, maybe do something worthwhile with my life, maybe it'll ensure I'm remembered. The man who found and returned Vermeer's "The Concert." The international community will be grateful, maybe they'll take me to see his paintings in the Netherlands, maybe I'll meet his descendants, or . . . I don't know, I think I finally have an opportunity on my hands.

Ronald Romero   I'm happy for you, Juan.

Juan Uribe   You still think I talk too much, don't you?

Ronald Romero   What we need is an eighties nostalgic talking out of his ass amidst the debris.

Juan Uribe   You'll find someone.

Ronald Romero   I owe you twenty dollars.

Juan Uribe   Keep it.

Ronald Romero   So you're not coming back?

Juan Uribe   No, Ron.

Ronald Romero   But the painting is supposed to be part of the deal, you get it, you keep it, you sell it, you return it, whatever, but you come back to work.

Juan Uribe   You can't make me.

Ronald Romero   Then no painting.

Juan Uribe   I have it in my hands, Ron. (*Pause.*) I don't think Rose wants anything to do with this. (*Pause.*) You shouldn't have given it up if you didn't want to get rid of it.

Ronald Romero   Say hi to Rose from me.

Juan Uribe   My pleasure. (*Pause.*) He says hi.

Rose E. Oakwood   Say hi back.

Juan Uribe   She says hi back. (*Pause.*) Ron? (*Pause.*) He hung up.

Rose E. Oakwood If you do decide to return the painting, I ask that you leave out the part where you found it while under the employment of Queens County. Leave me completely out of it. Say you found it in the garbage behind the pizza place or whatever. Anything but the truth.

Juan Uribe Thank you.

Rose E. Oakwood It's been a pleasure having you under my command. (*Pause.*) Can I tell you something? (*Pause.*) You're the better agent of the two.

Juan Uribe You don't have to say that. We both know it's not true.

Rose E. Oakwood I don't have to say it, but I want to.

Juan Uribe Okay. Thank you. Take care of Ron. He doesn't sound so good.

Rose E. Oakwood We'll do our best.

Juan Uribe Take care, Rose. Anytime you drop by the pizza place tell them you know me, they'll give you a discount.

Rose E. Oakwood You mean you'll take the painting and won't come back to work with us, but you will work at the pizza place?

Juan Uribe It's my home.

Rose E. Oakwood What do they offer you that we don't?

Juan Uribe Compassion.

Rose E. Oakwood I admire you.

Juan Uribe Why did you kiss Ron?

Rose E. Oakwood He gave me a book. He's lonely. I think . . . out of compassion.

Juan Uribe May I kiss you?

Rose E. Oakwood No.

Juan Uribe Take care, Rose. I would have liked to take you to the Riviera.

Rose E. Oakwood I don't think any of us are going to the Riviera, or, well, maybe you will after you return the painting.

Juan Uribe Yeah, maybe.

Rose E. Oakwood Mr. Uribe . . . Before you go . . .

Juan Uribe Yes?

Rose E. Oakwood . . . Nothing.

He's gone. The best agent we've had walked out the door carrying a painting valued at two hundred million dollars. I should have kissed him.

Pause.

Ronald Romero   We finally found a filing cabinet in Ezban's home. In it, cards signed by an Alan Rickman, addressed to "Big Isaac" and signed "your friend, Al." Tax returns, $14,207 pension and $21,311 social security. Bank statements . . .

Rose E. Oakwood   Queens County Police Precinct, Public Administrator and Forensic Investigation Department, how can I help you?

Ronald Romero   Could you check an account number?

Rose E. Oakwood   Uh huh.

Ronald Romero   86120400437118

Rose E. Oakwood   Give me a second. (*Pause.*) It's in Isaac's name. $357 thousand dollars.

Ronald Romero   Unbelievable, he had a stuffed bear's head, an original painting valued at two hundred million dollars, and a bank account with three hundred and fifty-seven thousand dollars in it? Who was this guy? A wise guy? A crook? Why did he live like he lived?

Rose E. Oakwood   The painting is a fake.

Ronald Romero   What?

Rose E. Oakwood   It's a knock-off.

Ronald Romero   What about the curator's confirmation?

Rose E. Oakwood   I lied.

Ronald Romero   Why?

Rose E. Oakwood   We wanted Juan to stay, right? You said he wouldn't sell the painting, that he wouldn't return it, either, that he was a fan of this painter, right? I thought he'd take it home, that he'd be happy just looking at it, that he'd feel special, that it'd help him come to work with a spring in his step . . . I never thought he'd do the right thing.

Ronald Romero   What's going to happen when he tries to return it?

Rose E. Oakwood   He's going to be very disappointed.

Ronald Romero   We should tell him before he . . .

Rose E. Oakwood   You tell him, if you want. I doubt he's returned it. I would spend at least one night with the painting. If I were him, I would hang it up in my living room, admire it, knowing I have it all to myself. I would eat dinner in front of it. I'd talk to it for a bit. ". . . You must have seen so much history," I'd say, "so many owners, so many adventures, only to end up in the home of a run-of-the-mill agent." I'd stay up late staring at the painting, and the next morning, I would return it knowing it had been mine for a day.

Ronald Romero   I also found a will from 1982. Isaac split everything evenly between three men and a woman. These are the names: Frank Murzi, Albert Schober, Martin Westbrook, and Miriam Logan.

Rose E. Oakwood Are you listening to me?

Ronald Romero Are you?

Rose E. Oakwood No.

Ronald Romero Frank Murzi, Albert Schober, Martin Westbrook, and Miriam Logan, Isaac Ezban's heirs.

Rose E. Oakwood I'll check. If we find them and they answer, I'll let you know.

Ronald Romero I hung it up in my house. (*Pause.*) The painting. Before I gave it to you. Before you told me it was valuable. (*Pause.*) Why'd you have to lie to me too?

Rose E. Oakwood Only the painting and I can be false, no one else. (*Pause.*) I didn't want you to ruin everything if you spoke to Juan.

Ronald Romero Thanks, I guess.

Rose E. Oakwood I shouldn't have kissed you.

Ronald Romero You're right.

Rose E. Oakwood Pretend it never happened.

Ronald Romero Okay.

Rose E. Oakwood Good day, Ronald. (*Pause.*) What's so good about it?

Juan Uribe Are you serious? Why didn't you tell me before? I just quit my job at the pizza place. I just finished telling the manager everything I've always wanted to say to a superior but never dared to. I even said some things that were meant for Rose and others that were meant for you, but he had to take them. Oh well, righteous men stumbling and all that. I told him he was going to end up like me, old, useless, and doing a job only Mexican immigrants want to do; up to his elbows in other people's shit; that he might be managing a pizza place today, but tomorrow he'll be a living corpse, dragging himself out of bed only to wander out into an extinct world pretending to be full of happiness, but has been rotting for eons. I told him he didn't deserve to be in charge, but that it's better that way, because the most important jobs are given to unqualified people to make up for their lack of intelligence, it's the justice of this world. I told him it's a shame he's an ignorant kid with no idea who Johannes Vermeer was, but not to worry, that he should read tomorrow's paper, because he's gonna find out. I told him life had finally rewarded the weak. I told him . . . Are you sure it's a fake?

Ronald Romero It's what Rose said, and it makes sense, Juan.

Juan Uribe I suppose it was naive of me to think a painting of such caliber would turn up in a hoarder's apartment . . . But I wanted to believe it, you know? I wanted to believe something good could happen in my life.

Ronald Romero So . . . You're unemployed.

Juan Uribe I have no intention of going back to that cockroachs' nest.

Ronald Romero We found a bank account and a will. Apparently Rose tried to contact the beneficiaries. They weren't relatives or close friends. They were coworkers from a moving company Isaac worked for over forty years ago, and now they're going to inherit a quarter of 357 thousand dollars each, well, if they answer the phone.

Juan Uribe Do you think they deserve it?

Ronald Romero I'd like to think so.

Juan Uribe And us?

Ronald Romero What?

Juan Uribe Do we deserve the hand we were dealt?

Ronald Romero Maybe the next case won't be as disgusting, maybe we'll get the nice residence of a forgotten old lady in a terracotta brick house east of Brooklyn. Not everything in this world is shit, Juan.

Juan Uribe Fine. (*Pause.*) See you tomorrow.

Ronald Romero You don't know how happy I am to hear that, Juan.

Juan Uribe On one condition.

Ronald Romero Whatever you say.

Juan Uribe You treat me as an equal.

Ronald Romero As a friend, Juan, as a friend.

Juan Uribe See you tomorrow.

Rose E. Oakwood We were finally able to track down Miriam "Puffy" Logan. She's dead. A neighbor found her. She lived alone in a trailer. Heart attack. Her arteries were clogged. Fat. 127 kilograms. She didn't fit through the door. They had to cut her into pieces to get her out. She was cremated. No one is worth a piece of land nowadays, it's preferable that we disintegrate into dust that causes allergies in the living, rather than be recycled and end up as organic matter in artisanal compost. (*Pause.*) Apparently, Miriam was engaged to Isaac, but her mother wanted her to sign a prenup so . . . Mr. Ezban terminated the engagement. Men. (*Pause.*) A quarter of Mr. Ezban's estate wound up in the hands of Miriam's nephew. His name is Marianno Capozzi, he drives a bus at Disney World. We spoke for hours. Best conversation I've had in weeks. He's thirty-five, lives with his mother, and thanks God every day for having the best job in the world: every day he transports hundreds of people, from their hotels, to the happiest place on Earth; and through the bus's PA, he tells them the story of a man who dreamed of creating an amusement park that people of all nationalities would visit, Koreans, Japanese, Spaniards, Mexicans, Hungarians, Palestinians, Iraqis, Macedonians, Israelis, Chinese, Venezuelans, Argentinians, Australians, Nigerians . . . A place where, regardless of skin color or religion, they could hold hands and be equal, united by the magic of the illusion. Distractions are important. I enjoyed listening to him. He ignited something inside of me. Like an early birthday present.

While he was talking, I looked through the brochures Ronald left in my office. The Mayan Riviera. Epiphany. I went online. I followed an impulse. I bought two tickets. I have no one to go with, but . . . Perhaps Juan would like to join me. I don't know if it is the happiest place on Earth, but the pictures look promising. Perhaps we could try that Mexican tequila, drink margaritas in a hammock or forget our troubles in the sun. Not that I have troubles, in fact, it might be nice to have some for a change.

Ronald Romero   Welcome aboard, captain.

Juan Uribe   Thank you, Ron.

Ronald Romero   You owe me twenty dollars.

Juan Uribe   Is that how you want to start the day off?

Ronald Romero   I'm kidding, friend, in fact . . . I brought you a present.

Juan Uribe   What is it?

Ronald Romero   I had some money saved up . . . I wanted to go to the Mayan Riviera, it sounded good when you told me about it, so . . . I'd mentioned something about it to Rose before the kiss, something about planning a vacation together, because, well, she always seemed attractive to me, ever since the station Christmas party and . . . That business in the restaurant was a one-time thing, but then things got weird between us. I thought the weirdness would fade away, that she and I would have something, something serious, that it was just a matter of time, you know? So I took a risk and bought tickets to an all-inclusive hotel on the Mayan Riviera. I spent a fair amount of money.

Juan Uribe   When are you going?

Ronald Romero   The day I was going to surprise her, she . . . She told me she wished she hadn't kissed me.

Pause.

Juan Uribe   I'm sorry, friend.

Ronald Romero   Not as sorry as I am.

Juan Uribe   And you're telling me this because . . .?

Ronald Romero   I want you to go in my place. I spent a few more dollars and changed the name. Take a week off before you come back to work. I want someone to enjoy this deal.

Juan Uribe   I don't have anyone to go with.

Ronald Romero   I thought we could go together, you know, as friends, but then I thought it might be weird, I mean, I don't want you to think I'm that kind of guy, not that there's anything wrong with it, I just don't want any more misunderstandings or for Rose to think that of me. So here you go: One reservation for two at the Mayakoba. It's sensational, the rooms look out over the lagoon, they're on the mangrove and I don't even want to tell you about the view. Find someone to go with and say hi to the ocean for me, will you?

Juan Uribe   Thank you, Ron.

Ronald Romero   It's my way of saying sorry.

Juan Uribe   Consider it water under the bridge. What's done is done.

Ronald Romero   Okay. You better go pack. The tickets are for tomorrow.

Juan Uribe   You expect me to find someone to go with before tomorrow?

Ronald Romero   I thought you could do what you said, bump into a stranger at the supermarket who has an inexplicable smile and blue eyes, someone you feel you could have something special with and say: "With every morning, let's cherish the new dawn, want to go to the Mayan Riviera with me tomorrow?"

Juan Uribe   I didn't realize you actually listened to me.

Ronald Romero   I listen, I don't always know what to say, but I listen. (*Pause.*) Have a good trip. Find love. I'll be waiting for you when you come back to carry on digging up the forgotten graves of New Yorker pharaohs.

Juan Uribe   I'll do my best.

Ronald Romero   There goes a great man.

Pause.

Rose E. Oakwood   Hello, Ron, Good afternoon. Was Juan at work today?

Ronald Romero   He showed up at Mrs. Marwan's apartment on time, but I sent him home.

Rose E. Oakwood   Who told you to do such a thing?

Ronald Romero   He deserves a vacation before coming back. I'll take on the extra work load, another week won't do me any harm and since he won't be coming to work you can either not pay him for those days or take it out of my salary. That way you won't have to explain why you're paying a man who isn't showing up to work.

Rose E. Oakwood   And what will he do at home alone for a week? He'll get terribly depressed, the man needs to be kept busy.

Ronald Romero   I sent him to the Mayan Riviera, I gave him my tickets. I thought if you and I weren't going, someone had to make use of that deal. Actually, he's probably found a willing travel partner by now. Maybe a waitress at Velo's Pizza or a cashier or . . . Who knows. I don't think he'll find it very hard to find someone who wants to go with him.

Rose E. Oakwood   You had tickets for us?

Ronald Romero   And now Juan has them.

Rose E. Oakwood   Our best man is running off to Mexico with some lucky young lady.

Ronald Romero   No one better than him, that's for sure.

Rose E. Oakwood   And is there a reason why he's not answering his cell phone? I've been calling him all morning.

Ronald Romero   I don't know. Anything urgent?

Rose E. Oakwood   I just wanted to welcome him back, that's all. Thank you, Ronald.

Ronald Romero   You're welcome, Rose.

Rose E. Oakwood   Oh, Ron . . . What are you doing the week of the 14th to the 20th of September?

Ronald Romero   Working I guess, why?

Pause.

Rose E. Oakwood   No reason. I like that week. It's my birthday week.

Ronald Romero   Of course! I forgot, I'm sorry. I'll make sure to send you a cake.

Pause.

Rose E. Oakwood   Don't go to all that trouble. A card will suffice.

Ronald Romero   I'll do that. Good afternoon, Rose.

Juan Uribe   Ron! I'm glad you're still here.

Ronald Romero   I get off at 6, where else would I be?

Juan Uribe   I wanted to give you this. At the end of the day, I told you to take it to begin with, right?

Ronald Romero   Really?

Juan Uribe   It isn't worth two hundred million, maybe thirty dollars at most, but I'd like you to hang it up in your living room.

Ronald Romero   That's very kind of you, Juan. Thank you. (*Pause.*) Anything else?

Juan Uribe   Yes. I found someone to go with.

Ronald Romero   Is she young, does she have red hair like a sunset and coral lips?

Juan Uribe   My mother.

Ronald Romero   Seriously? Wouldn't you prefer a complete stranger to urinate on you in the shower?

Juan Uribe   My mother turned eighty-one this summer, I think she's going to die soon. I'd like her to see the ocean one last time. She's the only person I have left and I have her holed up in a home. The worst crimes you can commit are always the most ordinary . . . Some days she doesn't recognize me or remember me or prefers not to give me the pleasure of her saying my name, I don't know if it's Alzheimer's or resentment, but it doesn't matter. The ocean breeze will help heal the fracture.

Ronald Romero   You're a good son, Juan. (*Pause.*) Thanks for the painting. (*Pause.*) My mother died in a home in Washington Heights. The last time I went to visit her they were cleaning out her room. They hadn't notified me because they couldn't find my number. (*Pause.*) Oh, Rose wanted to talk to you.

Juan Uribe   What about?

Ronald Romero   She wanted to welcome you back personally.

Juan Uribe   That's nice of her. If she calls again, tell her I lost my cell phone, but I'll stop by her office when I get back from the Riviera.

Ronald Romero   I'll let her know.

Juan Uribe   Oh, and Ron . . . "Be kind and the world will smile back at you."

Ronald Romero   I'll keep that in mind, Juan, I'll keep that in mind.

Juan Uribe   See you, Ronny.

Pause.

Ronald Romero   It's nice, this little painting.

Rose E. Oakwood   I guess I can resell my tickets on the internet.

Ronald Romero   Shame it's a knock-off.

Rose E. Oakwood   I can't believe Ronald had tickets too.

Ronald Romero   What makes one painting worth two hundred million dollars and an identical one worth thirty? Does time add value? Is it the name of the artist? Then it isn't the beauty of the painting, but the knowing it's "real" . . . But what is real? Or who? Real things are either locked up in a museum or in the hands of a thief. I wish people would stand in line to see other people instead of looking at dry paint on a canvas. The world would be a better place.

Rose E. Oakwood   It's so easy to get rid of belongings nowadays. All it takes is a click and any stranger can keep what were once your obsessions. Like Isaac. A life accumulated in an apartment, whose valuable content was auctioned off in half an hour and the rest thrown in the trash without the slightest bit of wonder or remorse. All that's left of his life are stains on the carpet.

Ronald Romero   Who was Yaara Marwan? Maybe she had a hard heart. Maybe she gifted a vacation to her work colleague before being left alone, maybe she never had the nerve to tell people she loved them. They say time flies when you're having fun, they don't know it flies by even faster when you disconnect. Who was Mrs. Marwan? She was everyone until I shape her. Time to put the puzzle together. (*Pause.*) Although there may not be much time for putting together, like Isaac, we found someone to distribute his belongings to, we found out about his failed marriage, about him having been a parachutist, about the company he worked for, but . . . Nothing that leaves a mark. No one is going to mention him at Thanksgiving dinner and say: "That Isaac was a scoundrel!" Or "Remember the time grandad fell down the stairs?" Or "Now who's gonna fart in public at the most inappropriate times?" No one is going to laugh at the expense of the deceased to ease the pain of their passing. We'll remember him, as a case, but we'll remember him . . . But we aren't alive, or dead yet, either.

(*Pause.*) I would have liked to have been alive. Made love to a noisy woman, dared to be dirty, sunk into sin and emerged drenched in experience, gone to bed at four and woken up at twelve, stopped planning everything, even my trips to the bathroom, been restless, mischievous, lazy, or terrible, been somebody to somebody, betrayed the trust of a loved one, used and been used, left and been left, been . . . I would have liked for someone to at least have had the decency to tell me to go to hell every once in a while. (*Pause.*) I, Ronald Romero, who am nothing to no one, ask the sink: What is the point of existence? Nothing on this Earth is forever, just here for a little while. Even jade can break, even gold breaks, even the feathers of a quetzal can tear. No forever on this Earth, just here for a little while. We'll have to go, we have to perish. We'll walk home like this, like paint slowly fading, like a flower drying up, we'll go like ghosts, here on Earth, and tired of walking, we'll have to sleep, alone and so on, on this Earth. (*Pause.*) When I was a boy, I dreamed of being a clown. My father told me the world hates clowns, that their wives hate them the most, that no one makes a living painting their mouths and blowing up balloons. I would have liked to have invented laughter, at the end of the tunnel and with the bathroom light turned on, I, Ronald Romero, ask: Are we men or are we clowns?

Rose E. Oakwood   Another one. (*Pause.*) The body was found in the living room.

Ronald Romero   The police found him crumpled up on a mottled carpet holding a bottle of sleeping pills.

Rose E. Oakwood   Sniffing a fetid odor, a neighbor called 911. The apartment was in 103 Monroe Street in Brooklyn.

Ronald Romero   What does it take to do this job? People who are willing to go into these disgusting apartments.

Rose E. Oakwood   He was fifty-seven, divorced, tried to live every day as if it were his last . . . One of the few gifts God gave him was knowing how to park. He didn't own a car.

Ronald Romero   They found me clinging onto the bars, onto life, Juan would say.

Rose E. Oakwood   The Vermeer painting hanging on the wall. The only clean, intact thing in the apartment. The rest, an organized disaster. Ketchup stains on the wall, wine spilled on the carpet, shattered bottles, bedsheets soaked in urine, clothes spilling out of drawers, broken windows, plates with soy sauce on them, defrosted meat on the floor, folders and papers, garbage cans full of tissues . . . A chaotic scene that no one would consider to be the result of a life, but rather of an outburst. On the pillow, a book: *The Lord of the Rings*, Part Two. *The Two Towers*.

Ronald Romero   Open the book and shake it.

Rose E. Oakwood   Nothing.

Ronald Romero   There was a postcard in the book, a letter. What does it say?

Rose E. Oakwood   Oh . . . No. There is something. A birthday card. "Happy birthday, Rose, I would have liked to sleep with you. In a professional, organized, and noisy manner. I hope this isn't unprofessional of me. Sincerely, Ronald Romero, P.S.: I dreamt that you were sleeping next to me."

Ronald Romero   I rarely say it, but I hope you know how much it means to me to have you as a friend. I care about you.

Rose E. Oakwood   He should have told me. (*Pause.*) I should have told him the painting was the original. We should have dared to plunge our hands into the shit. All the way in, with gloves on, sink our arms in up to our elbows or our shoulders or our necks if we have to . . . And we always have to.

Juan Uribe   My mother is dead. She died on the Riviera. I was with her. I don't know if she knew we were by the ocean, but I want to believe she knew it was her son holding her hand. She didn't die alone. She didn't die in New York. She died in Mexico, as my father would have wanted. México lindo y querido, si muero lejos de ti, que digan que estoy dormido, y que me traigan aquí,

Ronald Romero   Que digan que estoy dormido,

Juan Uribe, Ronald Romero & Rose E. Oakwood   Freedom!

Rose E. Oakwood   y que me traigan aquí,

Ronald Romero & Juan Uribe   México lindo y qué herido, si muero lejos de ti . . .[2]

Blackout.

---

[2] Translator's note: Following a conversation with the playwright, it was decided that the final lines of the play would be left in Spanish, seeing as they are the words to the famous Mexican song "México Lindo" by composer Chucho Monge. The fact that the characters themselves are Dreamers, Mexican immigrants living in the USA, means leaving the song to be sung in Spanish will give an added dimension to their yearning.

Extraordinary Life

Mariano Tenconi Blanco

Translated by Catherine Boyle

Extraordinary Life and the Poetic Dramatic Invention of the Nation

By Catherine Boyle

'Let's suppose that a country, Argentina for example, were an invented country. That a whole system of books created what we call Argentina. What, then, would the end of the world be, in a country invented by books?'

These words come from the final scene of *Extraordinary Life*, a scene in which two lifelong friends, Aurora Cruz and Blanca Fierro, sit in their bookshop in the southerly Argentine town of Ushuaia, determined not to let the imminent end of the world stop them from reading. The reader may feel that this opening needs a spoiler alert. It's not got one because that final act of the two friends frames and informs the whole play. It is a moment of outrageous glory and decisiveness. It arises from the lived experience of these two brilliant friends, who have, at different points, each asked themselves about the sense of literary metaphors, and their capacity to say anything about their experience of a life that is too real to be experienced through metaphor. Life just is, painfully and miraculously so. For is life not the constant and repeated miracle of existence and the constant and repeated pain of being human, being women, in this world we have created and are destroying?

This play has developed massively since it won the National Prize for Playwriting of the Argentinian National Institute for Theatre in 2017. The play as it is now has developed from the rehearsals and performances with Compañía Teatro Futuro and the performances of Lorena Vega and Valeria Lois, and through its success with audiences in Argentina. As a translator, I have followed it both from afar and in the intimate ways a translator discovers a text. This process has taught me how to be attentive to the poetics of the play and to bring to the new play the possibilities for performance. When translating Mariano Tenconi Blanco's work, that means being alert to the resonances of Argentine literary voices (though not exclusively) in the text, engaging in minute ways with the work of enlivening the voices and written forms that create the potential for performance. As Tenconi Blanco says in conversation with theatre critic Jorge Dubatti (2022, p. 200), these forms include: monologues, with and without interlocutors, or addressed to the public; texts in third person; dialogues; interior monologue; poems; secret diaries; letters; travel journals. As a translator who has been reading Latin American literature for many decades, the different voices feel present to me, and I find in them moments of recognition and delight, and also admiration for the subtlety and, often, humour with which they spring up from the page. The academic in me wants to stop and follow their trails, and I often do as the translator's subterranean work. But more important for the translation of a play to be performed is the translation of the poetics of the play, the specifics of the language, the dramatic and performative coherence that is being created.

In this kaleidoscopic play, that 'proceeds' on the assumption that 'all of Argentine literature is material for a piece of Argentine theatre' (2022, p. 200), the reference that speaks first and foremost to an Argentine audience is undoubtedly the foundational epic gauchesque poem *El gaucho Martín Fierro* by José Hernández (1872), followed by *La vuelta de Martín Fierro* (1879). Fierro and Cruz are the surnames of the protagonists of this long epic of the role of the rural gauchos in the brutal domination of the vast pampas of Argentina. Theirs is a story of friendship, adversity, endurance and agony, written in the form of the oral poetry of the gaucho, and bringing the duelling poetic density and imaginary of the form into the elite literary salons of the country; a devastating counter-narrative to the sanitizing modernizing narrative of the emerging nation-state.

There is no attempt here to map one experience onto the other, but the play calls on the literary knowledge of the audience, evokes recognition, perhaps provokes questions about how a nation is constructed in the individual and collective imaginary. Yet, this new Fierro and Cruz duo also live their lives on the periphery of national history. They are from the southernmost town of Ushuaia, the place of their real lives, of their imagination, of their torment, in the case of Blanca, and of their necessary return, in the case of Aurora. It is the place of their friendship, kept alive across time and space through letters and poetry. The dramatic force of the play is forged by the ways in which this Fierro and Cruz friendship performs the endlessly extraordinary feat of committing to the act of life, regardless of the imminence of the end of the world.

Work cited

Tenconi Blanco, Mariano. 2022. *Mitos y maravillas*. Ed. by Jorge Dubatti. Editorial Losada.

* * *

Mariano Tenconi Blanco is an Argentine writer, playwright and theatre director. He has written and directed *La Fiera (The Beast)*, *La vida extraordinaria (Extraordinary Life)*, *Las Cautivas (The Captive Women)*, *La Mujer Fantasma (The Phantom Woman)*, among others. In 2013 he founded Compañía Teatro Futuro with the musician Ian Shifres and the producer Carolina Castro. He obtained the first prize in the 18º National Playwright Contest of the National Theater Institute (2016), a national playwriting contest that awards contemporary Argentine writing, for his play *Extraordinary Life*. He was distinguished by the Konex Awards as one of the five best playwrights of the decade 2011–2021 and as one of the ten directors of the decade 2014–2024. His plays have been translated into English, German, Italian, French, Portuguese, Catalan, Romanian and Chinese.

Catherine Boyle is Professor of Latin American Cultural Studies at King's College London. She was a co-founder of the *Journal of Latin American Cultural Studies*. She leads the theatre translation and performance project, the Out of the Wings Collective. She is a translator of Spanish and Spanish American theatre and poetry. Her translations have been performed internationally and she has published widely on questions of Latin American theatre, cultural, gender studies and translation. Since 2016, she has been the Director of the Centre for *Language Acts and Worldmaking*), dedicated to regenerating and transforming approaches to teaching and research in Modern Languages.

World Premiere

La vida extraordinaria, at Teatro Nacional Cervantes (Buenos Aires, Argentina), August 2018, directed by Mariano Tenconi Blanco.

Prologue

0.

Nothing. Absolutely nothing. There was no space. There was no time. There was nothing. It's impossible to imagine. But that's the way it is. There was absolutely nothing. It wasn't darkness. It was nothing. And the Universe started in nothing. It was by chance. An instant of glory. Or simply a caprice. A caprice out of nothing. And all of a sudden, a great explosion. An unimaginable explosion that lasted a millionth of a second. And in three minutes the universe was created. It takes longer to cook a boiled egg than it does to make the universe. A universe that has no limits, but is nevertheless finite. We don't understand it, but that's how it is. And then the universe got cold. Also like a hard-boiled egg. And the atom appeared. And then gigantic clouds that formed stars and galaxies appeared. One star was the Sun. And near the Sun, some planets. One of those planets, the planet Earth. To explain the origin of life on Earth is even more difficult. Some think it was water. That the process could have taken millions and millions of years. But that life was chemically destined to be. Others believe it was a small meteorite that brought substances that weren't found on Earth. That life was sowed on Earth by intelligent aliens. And others believe in God. Whatever it was that started life, it is the most extraordinary fact of biology. Perhaps the most extraordinary fact we know. It happened once. Only once. And since that time, it never stopped happening. Genetics. And evolution. And time. Every living being is an amplification. A reversion. A remix. What came after is easier. Or more or less so. Our ancestor is some form of biped monkey. There are thousands of options. *Australopithecus*, *Homo erectus*, *Homo sapiens*. Whatever it was, we are still that monkey. There are more genetic differences between a zebra and a horse than between us and a monkey. One of those monkeys got its hands on a stone. And that was how industry started. Progress. Wars. In short: humanity. So many things had to happen for us to be here. What an enormous series of chances. From the creation of the universe to the quantity of people who had to have sexual relations in an exact moment, or the number of wars, plagues, natural disasters, domestic accidents, military dictatorships, armed robberies, suicide attempts, that a hundred people had to avoid for thousands and thousands of years so that we are here, right now. Life. Life is one and the same. We are related to everything that has lived and everything that lives. To a bacterium. To an insect. To a fruit. To everything. The same genetic thing transmitted from generation to generation for 4,000 million years. To have a life is a miracle. To exist. Every transcendent moment and every insignificant moment. This second is a miracle. This second is a miracle. This second is a miracle. And so on and so on.

Part One

1.

Aurora   I always hated the simulacrum of the self. And yet, here I am. Performing the drama of the self. I had forgotten that snow isn't white and made of cotton wool like my pupils draw it. Snow is frozen water that covers everything with mud. We've only walked about fifty metres, and I'm caked up to the ankles. Also, Juan Carlos is holding my hand and, far from helping, is sliding along like an idiot and so the procession becomes slow and out of sync. It didn't matter how much I told my aunt that I preferred something intimate, she invited the whole of Ushuaia. Your father always owned the town bookshop, Aurora, everyone's going to want to come. But nobody reads in this town, Aunt. Me and my stupid irony. And the whole town, even the Mayor, and Juan Carlos waddling along like a penguin, and me: a sad procession. And well, Blanca Fierro, my lifelong best friend. And her mother too. I walk with a feeling as cold and ugly as the snow in Ushuaia. I don't cry. I'll cry later, for the rest of my life. I walk with a feeling in my chest, here, like a tightening, as if struggling for air. Like when you're a girl and you test how long you can go underwater without breathing. I don't understand this. How can it be that people die? And me? What will I do with the rest of my life without my father? Death is the worst of life. These thoughts are going to make me cry and I want to look strong, so I breathe, I look up, I think of something else. I think that in two days I'll be back in Buenos Aires. The priest talks very well. A friend of the town is leaving us, he says. People come up to me. I'm very sorry. You were always the light of his eyes. How grown up you are. They all know what to do. Perhaps this is what death is: a ready phrase, something practised, trivial. And Blanca comes up to me and looks me in the eye. And I look at her. And she winks at me and it's what my father always did and then all of a sudden, I understand everything and what was always there appears right there, right there. Everything that always was is never going to be again. My childhood. And then I hug her, and I gather my strength, and I don't cry. No catharsis. I'm not a girl anymore. My father is dead forever.

2.

Blanca   The day starts in a commotion as always because my mother wakes me up shouting that it's late Blanca, it's late. She's my mum and I love her very much, but the truth is I must say that sometimes I'm not very tolerant of her. Just have your coffee, it's late, she says, and then I just drink my coffee and I leave the house a bit out of sorts because of all the rush and because I haven't eaten anything. I need to eat something every two or three hours because if I don't, I feel bad and I can't get on with anyone for the rest of the day. And I was just thinking that the truth is I'm not yet ready for my mother to die. No, no. I'm still not ready, no. Maybe when I'm older, like when I'm forty, I don't know, maybe then, yes. That might be it. Or if I have children. Maybe then. But not now. Not now. Even though she drives me mad sometimes and makes me cry, I don't want my mother to die. It's snowing, it's snowing heavily, as if the sky wanted to unload itself because it too is sad. Here everyone loves Aurora's father. He's a very nice man. He was always making new friends. And, well, now he's not going to be able to make any more friends because he's gone, hasn't he? That's so sad. Because it means there's going to be less friendship in the world. I'm sure that when someone dies and people say how sad and a great loss, they mean things like this, something that's lost. Friendship makes the world a better place and then when people like that die, people who made the world better, then suddenly the world is a worse place because they've died. All the same I'm determined not to cry so as to help Aurora who I know prefers not to be crying in front of everyone, she's more about hiding her feelings, keeping her feelings for herself, or for me, she tells me, and she cries, with me she does, but not in front of everyone else, no. As soon as we all start walking, I see her first amongst all the people and there were a lot. She's thin and beautiful like she always is, a bit serious but firm, yes, and wearing a lovely dress I made for her – beautiful, to be truthful, and, well, she's walking beside Juan Carlos, who's a good man but . . . Well, yes, he's good. And we walk on and we get to the church. And the priest speaks and says some prayers and then he says something very wise, it must be that the wisdom of God's taken over him, let's say, the priest who never was very bright, Father Esteban, all of a sudden, he said something nice, he said that Don Osvaldo Cruz has gone, a great friend of the people has gone. Very true, I thought, Don Osvaldo was everybody's friend. And then one by one all the women of the town greet her, all of them customers, I know them all well. My mother's one of the first, as soon as someone dies, she's the first there. All the same, my mother really loves Aurora, and her father too, she always said Aurora's father what a good man, not like the monster you got, she always said that. And all of a sudden there's a type of gap in the crowd and Aurora and I are looking at each other, she looks at me as if she's bereft, on the verge of tears, and I don't know what I can say to her and I'm so clumsy that I feel a sort of tic, a sort of wink, that's what I do, what an idiot, and she hugs me and I hug her and we weep, I, really, I weep. And in her ear very close so that she can hear me I say to her, your dad was very nice and a very good friend, and you're a very good friend so as long as you're a very good friend your father will be alive in you. But she might not have heard me say that.

3.

Aurora We have to leave in half an hour, Juan Carlos tells me. Before we go, I want to see the sea, I say, and when I see that he's looking for his coat a bit confused (Juan Carlos's movements are always confused) I say NO, NO I prefer to go alone. This is mine, I say, I make him complicit. I put on my coat and start walking. By the last two blocks I almost can't move forward; I'm weak, I'm not used to Ushuaia anymore, can't be. I walk on against the wind without knowing why. The wind's cutting through my face, I think. A saying. In fact, the wind isn't cutting my face, it's producing a type of tachycardia; it's like bathing in frozen water. But all of a sudden, also, I smile. The strong wind sort of tickles me, makes me feel alive. Or makes me realize that I belong to nothing more than to this place. Even my father is the wind. And then I close my eyes and I imagine that I'm flying, that my father's taking me for a walk like before, like he always did. But in truth, he's not. Not at all. It's just the wind slapping me in the face and me smiling for no reason. Like almost everything. Just because. Being born just because. Dying just because. And in the middle, everything. And everything the same. I get to the seashore. The blue sea. Blue like nothing else. No shades. Pure blue. Black it's so blue, white, grey. Or just blue. In the wind I can't hear anything, but there's nothing to hear anyway. All of a sudden, it's stopped snowing. To my left, in the distance, I see a black stain. Immediately I think, it'll be oil. Since childhood I've heard that there's oil here, that the Malvinas is all about the oil; who knows. I walk towards it. Towards the oil. Suddenly it's as if I've understood so many wars and so much ambition, because the oil looks like a kind of magical mountain, black and gleaming. I took the pill for my nerves that Juan Carlos gave me, and I ate almost nothing, perhaps I'm hallucinating. I'm a few metres away and to my surprise the first thing I make out are two enormous eyes, the size of my whole body. The eyes are open and expressive, calm. Yet, there's no life in them. I've never seen anything so dead in my life. But, at the same time, I've never seen anything as alive as that dead whale. I understand something. Everything. I don't know what it is. There it is. There am I. We're alive. Always. We're dead. Always. I touch it. I touch the dead whale. I greet it, I offer my condolences, I encourage it, hold on, I say, hello. How much life and how much death there is in everything. I don't mean the cycle of life. I'm not emotionally ready to see this biologically. I'm talking about a mammal as large as five houses dead by the edge of the sea at the end of the world. I mean this whole unfolding life. Its body as enormous as a train, soaked and with its open eyes. As if in all this death there were something that isn't yet dead, something infinite and inexplicable, something that makes us family, this whale and me. All of a sudden, I feel my pain. I cry. With no other connotations. The pure verb. To cry. I cry. I want to hug that noble animal. There's something that I understand now that I couldn't explain. Everything is transitory and, nevertheless, definitive. This whale and I have lived in this country, in this time. And my father too.

4.

Blanca   No, Aurora, no. You look like a drunk penguin. Grace. Style.

Aurora   The odyssey of style.

Blanca   Okay, we're going to practise for when Juan Carlos asks you to dance.

Aurora   No, Blanca, I'm never ever going to be with Juan Carlos.

Blanca   But haven't you seen how much he fancies you? He's in love with you.

Aurora   He's an idiot, Juan Carlos.

Blanca   Good evening, oh, Aurora, would you do me the honour of this dance?

Aurora   No, Juan Carlos, you're an idiot.

Blanca   Dance with Juan Carlos, Aurora, if not, you'll be standing around by yourself all night.

Aurora   I should stay at home reading, instead of going to this stupid dance.

Blanca   You can't just read, you've got to live, Aurora.

Aurora   Okay, I'll dance with you, Juan Carlos.

Blanca   Very good, Aurora. It turns out that you're a great ballroom dancer.

Aurora   Of course, Blanca.

Blanca   We should practise the conversation. Train you how to speak to people, Aurora.

Aurora   Hello, Juan Carlos, what are you reading?

Blanca   No, Aurora, it's me you talk to about books. You've got to seem interesting to Juan Carlos, unattainable, mysterious.

Aurora   Show me. Let's practise. I'm Alberto.

Blanca   Ay, no, I don't know, I don't know.

Aurora   Hello, Blanca darling, you're gorgeous, come with me, let's dance in the workshop the two of us without our clothes.

Blanca   Ay, no, Alberto. Sort yourself out. Dance with me like a gentleman.

Aurora   Blanca, I like you very much.

Blanca   You're an attractive man too, Alberto.

Aurora   Let's have babies, Blanca. You drive me mad, baby.

Blanca   Calm down, Alberto, I know I cause uncontrollable passions, but you must control yourself, do you understand?

Aurora   Kiss me all over, baby.

Blanca Exactly, Aurora, we've still got to practise the kissing.
Kissing.
The kiss.

Aurora Can I kiss you?

Blanca What?

Aurora You've already kissed Alberto. You know how to kiss. Show me. Kiss me.

Blanca You mean us, you kiss me, us?

Aurora Me kiss you. Yes.

Blanca On the mouth?

Aurora Yes.

Blanca Tongues?

Aurora With my tongue, yes.

Blanca No, I mean, yes, you're very pretty, a very pretty girl, yes, but no, I think better not, I don't know, I think not me, do you understand, better not, Aurora, one short one, okay, a quick one maybe, yes.

Aurora I was only kidding, Blanca, how are we going to kiss.

Blanca No, of course, I thought that too.

Aurora You believed me, you thought I meant it.

Blanca I didn't believe you!

Aurora Ay.

Blanca Sorry.

Aurora No, I'm sorry.

Blanca Okay, I'll show you how to kiss.

Aurora Fine, I'm ready.

Blanca Like this.

Aurora Just like this?

Blanca Yes. Come on.

Aurora No, that's not it. I've got enough information, plenty, thank you.

Blanca No, sir. You come here and kiss me, do you hear.

Aurora No.

Blanca Yes, yes.
No, as if you wanted to.
Think about some character in a book that you've liked.
That's it, that's it, good, you're getting it, that's good.

Aurora Thanks, teacher.

Blanca What you need now is more attitude, Aurora. You're never going to get kissed with that Virgin Mary face.

Aurora And you know so much, Virgin Mary, all because of a pathetic kiss with Alberto.

Blanca What do you mean pathetic, you've no idea how Alberto and I kiss. You should see, litres of saliva.

Aurora Disgusting.

Blanca Maybe now on the way to the dance, a prisoner will be on the run, and he'll show us his willy.

Aurora They must be horrible, those purple willies, like a hammered finger down there between their legs.

Blanca Would you suck one?

Aurora Please, you've seen those dogs when their willy comes out, it's disgusting.

Blanca But not a dog's, a man's. A man's willy. Or maybe we have one too.

Aurora Yes!

Blanca Look at Blanca's willy, pink and in the form of a triangle, an amazing, extraordinary willy like a flower.

Aurora Look at Aurora's willy, golden and in the form of a rectangle, a pleasing and extravagant willy, like an ingot of gold.

Blanca Suck my willy, Aurora, come on.

Aurora You suck my willy, Blanca, look, mine is more beautiful.

Blanca Let's suck each other's.

Aurora Awawaw.

Blanca Owowow.
Fight with me, cowardly willy.

Aurora Take that.

Blanca Ay. Take that,

Aurora Ouch. Take that.

Blanca Oh, you won.

Aurora Ehhh.

Blanca How lovely it would be to have a willy and not need those idiots, they're so stupid.

Aurora We don't need anyone.

5.

Blanca Hello. Good evening. Is this working? Hello. Hello. It is an honour for me . . . I'm nervous . . . it is an honour for me to be here and to share poetry with all of you. My name is Blanca Fierro and I'm going to read a poem I wrote called 'Anxiety'.

Anxiety

I put the rabbits in my vagina. Lambs. Goats. I put my bed, my house. I put all my customers' clothes. I put my Singer sewing machine. My Singer in my vagina. While it's working. I put my working Singer. I put my mother in it. Yes. In my vagina. I put all the guys I like. I put all of Ushuaia. The church, the town hall, the square. I put the whole lot. Ushuaia. All of it. I put all the wind, all the snow, everything. All of it in my vagina. I put all of Argentina. I can't stop putting things inside me.

6.

Ushuaia, 2 August

Dear Aurora:

WHAT JOY WHAT JOY MY GOD!

What beautiful news! What happiness! What can I say? I'm beside myself with happiness.

And Juan Carlos? What does Juan Carlos say?

Know something I thought? Sorry if it's sad, but you know, Aurora, YOUR FATHER. He'd go crazy. Crazy. Your father would go crazy, Aurora. I'm going crazy too. I'm going crazy right now. A person like you, but tiny. Like you when you were a little girl. But no. Because really it's another person. Two like you. The world's going to be a better place. If only there were ten like you. Or a hundred. A thousand! Or the whole world!

But it's not here yet, we know that. Seven more months to wait. It worries me. I can't imagine what it's like for you, your heart must be in your mouth. Because it's closer to you, inside you in fact. Let it come out, let it come out. I'm sure that's how you're feeling. But no. Seven more months to go, Aurora. And you've got to enjoy it, in my view. Enjoy this time of being a pregnant woman, because that's what you are, Aurora. I'm not getting on too well with Alberto. It's been so many years now it and it's as if we're going nowhere, no. So, it's difficult . . . Everything is difficult . . . The freezing cold and the sun that goes in at four in the afternoon . . . and Mum isn't very well. It's her stomach. It seems that something isn't working. I hope it's nothing. I'm worried. Anyway, I'm sending you with this letter a handful of poems I wrote. I'm writing well, in all humility. Send me your poems, it's been a long time since I've read your work.

Shall I tell you something else? I think it's going to a boy. I've got a really strong hunch and it beats in my heart. A boy. Like your father.

I love you with all my heart, and the new baby too.

Blanca

7.

Blanca You've no idea, Aurora, how strange the masculine body of a man can be. And I'm not just saying that because of the hair, you know, although Alberto, you've no idea, looks like a fox, thick hair, and coarse to the touch, rough hands, he's strong but of medium height, as if he's compressed, he's firm, wherever you touch him he's really firm, and me the first thing I asked him was to grab my breasts and Alberto grabbed them really hard like when they look for a puncture on a bicycle tyre, like that, he grabbed really hard, I didn't like it, it wasn't like I imagined. Then we kissed, he had that really ugly taste of tobacco, I didn't want to kiss him anymore but I thought better of it, because I want to do it, how much longer am I going to wait, I'm like that, see, anxiety takes hold, ever since I found out that it existed, I don't know, at twelve, I've wanted it to happen once and for all so that I know what it is, you know, and it's been about six years waiting and waiting because no matter how much it was explained to me I couldn't work out what it was really like. So, then I said okay we'd better get on with it, let him put it in me, so I'll find out what this sex stuff is all about, so I took everything off, because he's so clumsy he'd most likely tear my clothes. His prick was long and had a strange shape at the end, and black, or grey, it was grey, and Alberto started to put it in me and he couldn't and he couldn't then at some point I thought ach don't tell me we're not going to do anything, I thought, it pissed me off, then I said let's see, Alberto, that's what I said to him, let's see, Alberto, like saying, see, you're hopeless, because the prick's his not mine, so, I got hold of his prick and I sort of jumped on it, hard, a few times, and all of a sudden it sort of started to go into me, the prick, to go into me, and I started liking it, it hurt me, and I was shouting, and Alberto was breathing more heavily, umm umm, he was going, and I even liked Alberto breathing heavily, and Alberto's prick was inside me and it was as if my organs were turning, and I felt damp inside, like soaked with blood and oil, my oil, funny, and as if my legs were relaxing, and as if inside in my organs there was some type of activity, something happening inside me that the prick must have been causing, the prick in contact with my whole body, and all of a sudden I sort of looked at the ceiling and I felt that the ceiling was opening and the wind was carrying me away flying and I was flying all over Ushuaia on top of Alberto's grey prick, that's how I felt, beautiful, Aurora, you've no idea, and well, the fantasy was cut short because then I see Alberto coming out of me, and he's taking out his tiny prick, half the size it was before, and half red, or reddened, it was my blood, and Alberto looks at me and cleans himself, that's me he says, that's me?, as if he didn't want seconds of dessert, that's me. I was dirty, but I wasn't disgusted, no, the absolute opposite. I felt as if we'd only just begun. As soon as I can, I'm going to try again.

8.

Aurora   In the end nobody chooses to be born but someone else does choose I mean someone chooses whether you are born or not born or lets you be born I don't understand why he's going so quickly because I need to get there but I need to get there in one piece the two of us need to get there in one piece how is it that all of a sudden someone you love and that was with you your whole life goes wherever they go wherever they go wherever they are wherever you are I'd give everything for you to be here, here with me and with him you were always infinite you're everything I am you always gave me everything I'M OKAY YES CALM DOWN WE'LL GET THERE FINE and that street which is it how strange that I've been living in Buenos Aires for years and yet there's always a street that I don't know or maybe this guy's taking me for a ride no no I don't think so if I end up having to give birth in his car it's worse for him because then he has to stop to clean the car and he'll lose hours of fares everyone's always thinking about money and how to survive the thing is it costs so much to be alive how much it costs to live day to day you set off owing money and you wake up in the red and YES, SIR, I'M CALM YOU KEEP CALM why is that man shouting at other men AHA AHA I'm getting nervous and I've got a massive migraine coming on when did these migraines start of course my head's really sore because that's how my head is it never stops my brain never stops there's always some kind of voice in my head speaking to me and also maybe that's why I'm never totally happy because there's always a voice in my head talking to me WHAT A LOVELY PHOTO BEAUTIFUL BIG WELL-BUILT let him be born healthy let him be born healthy let him be okay let everything be okay how lovely the sun it's a sunny day I'm going to tell Juan Manuel you were born on a sunny day I can never get my head around autumn I couldn't stand it I'm not so generous I don't know maybe you say something and then do something else you never know what you might do and I think and I think and I feel as if I'm shut inside my head but what nonsense I'm thinking not only am I not shut in but I have a person shut inside me or rather I have two because I have a person that's talking to me and a real person or three because there will be a person inside my baby that will think things the baby already how incredible that a person grows inside you inexplicable it would be more normal to lay eggs I don't know some other method not walking around with a human being inside you growing and all of a sudden they take it out from inside you as if we were Martians YES I'M FINE THERE'S NO NEED TO RUSH, DO YOU HEAR ME? I'm thinking nonsense or maybe it's fear could it be happiness? could this be the happiness we're all looking for? all of a sudden someone comes out from inside you and that's happiness or maybe not or maybe it is but everything goes on as always only with the happiness outside that is a child of yours that's going to be yours for ever for ever because we're all afraid of being left alone and then all of a sudden there's someone who's going to love you for ever my hands are feeling so cold especially my fingers like if I had to touch something I wouldn't know how to touch it as if my hands were strange to me I hope there's not long to go I can't stand it much more I can't stand it I can only think about the baby ay, it's coming out! I CAN'T HOLD ON, SIR, ARE WE NEARLY THERE YET? it hurts it hurts it hurts I'm so nervous it hurts STOP WHEREVER YOU CAN, YOU WANKER, I CAN'T WAIT

ANY LONGER if only he were here to hold me or she were here and they'd give me a hug and that's the thing that at the end they give you a hug giving birth is the most animal thing a human can do in the world it hurts it hurts and this head that won't stop how scary it all is everything yes.

9.

Aurora   Good evening. My name is Aurora Cruz. I am going to read one of my poems, which is included in my *Anthology of Patagonian Women Poets*, which was published recently. It was written for a very special being, and it's called 'Ulysses'.

Ulysses

I have a dog.
It's called Ulysses.
It wasn't my idea,
My husband brought it home.
He said that my son Juan Manuel asked for it.
'I want a bow wow.'
But I know that it was my husband's idea.
I didn't want to accept it, but in the end I agreed.
And now this dog is indispensable to me.
He looks sort of side-on.
Or smells the air.
His is existence in the raw.
His is a world of plenty.
This dog is my source of energy.
He is electricity,
and I am the lamp that lights up the house.
He helps me through my daily disaster.
Ulysses is my love this year.
He is true purity.
Everything and nothing.
The non-metaphor.
I at times am a bit melodramatic.
He simply lives.
So now I'm standing.
And I say Ulysses.
And he comes running.
We've got time.
We've got time enough.

Included in *Anthology of Patagonian Women Poets*,
compiled by Aurora Cruz

10.

Blanca Mum is as if suspended. She's hanging by a thread. I hover around her with my head full of useless stuff. Yet I love being able to look after her. She's very thin. I've put a little seat in the shower for her and I gently wash her back with a sponge. She never complains about anything. She lets me bathe her gently, wash her hair, dry her. Well, the truth is that she does complain a bit about her food. What I cook for her she eats reluctantly and what they cook for her in the hospital she leaves half-eaten and says, 'it tastes of nothing'. And she's right, I've tried it, and it tastes of nothing. This is sad and maybe it's me that's trying to find the good in all of this and maybe there's no good, there's nothing nice about it. But the thing is that sometimes I feel as if I'm giving her something back, I don't know, something. That now I'm looking after her, bathing her, feeding her. And the circle closes. Life. The wisdom of life. A bit sad but that's the way it is. Life is like that. You have a baby, and you look after it and you know that in the end that baby's going to grow up and you'll be old and that baby will look after you and won't abandon you, no matter what. It's lovely. The loyalty between mother and daughter. My case. And I also think that I'd like to have a daughter. And I'll be sad that Mum won't know her. That'll make me sad. But that's the way life is, the cycle of life. But I can't understand why people have to die. I can't understand it. Because life has its sad moments, of course. But dying? Because everything that you live, learn, the experiences you gather, sentimental things, like loves, friends, all of that, does it all go? How can that be? That it all goes. Dying. I don't understand it. I hope there is a heaven. And then we'll all meet again. Hello. How are you? So, you're here too, hello, hello. Everyone we love, all together. Like an incredible birthday. I hope that's what heaven is like.

11.

Aurora   'There is nothing more beautiful than the plane landing in Ushuaia, my daughter,' her father always said to her. The noise of the plane is deafening. She looks out the window. She thinks: death is the end of the metaphor. She thinks: death can't be expressed through another concept. She thinks: death is death. The only reality. And while she thinks things her son wakes up. Being born is real. As real as dying, at the very least. Or maybe more. And Juan Manuel was born. Juan Manuel is real. Juan Manuel is more real than death. If death and Juan Manuel were to fight, for example, and remember Juan Manuel is almost a baby, but still, if death fought Juan Manuel, Juan Manuel would be bound to win. But she doesn't think this. Because she thinks with words. And words don't mean anything. Nothing means anything. Except for that electricity that comes from the eyes and the heart. Aurora is going to Ushuaia for the funeral of the mother of her friend Blanca. And she's taking Juan Manuel too. Death and life produce movement. It's as simple as that, as immutable, as fundamental. The noise of the plane is deafening. The plane is on its descent. It feels as if it's going to miss. The town is in miniature. The airport, pathetic. The plane seems enormous, much bigger than the town. 'There is nothing more beautiful than the plane landing in Ushuaia, my son,' Aurora says to Juan Manuel. The noise of the plane is deafening. The plane is on its descent. Ushuaia, her son, her friend, her friend's mother, death, life. There's nothing original. The only original thing is everything.

Part Two

12.

What is a giraffe? Who laid the egg for the world? What are the interior and the exterior? Blanca sets herself the task of drawing a map of Ushuaia as a present for her friend Aurora, who lives in Buenos Aires. But she doesn't want to do a map of present-day Ushuaia, which would be easy. She is looking to create a plan that reconstructs in perfect detail the Ushuaia of when they were both girls. So, Blanca dedicates months to this fruitless task. The real Ushuaia changes, grows, contracts, distorts. The one in her memory, the Ushuaia in Blanca's map, is more perfect every day. Reading is an art of response. Reality is not the objective of a representation, Ushuaia in this case. Ushuaia is not what is real. What is real is the place in which a fantastic world finally happens.

What's an elephant for? What is the use of a fruit? What was love created for? Love is catastrophe, panic, structure. Aurora will write a secret diary. Love is ascension, a horror film, look what you're doing to me. Blanca will also write a secret diary. Love is I adore you, plenitude, I'm desperate. Love and secret diary are synonyms for Aurora and for Blanca. And a secret diary is like a map. The city is life itself: always changing, always false, always strange. The secret diary is the model; inalterable, microscopic, complete. To narrate is to transmit an emotion. With the progress of the secret diary, Aurora and Blanca will begin to live the secret diary, and this secret diary will replace life itself. The imagination is autobiographic.

The elephant is the biggest land mammal. They are particularly intelligent animals. This is due, in large part, to their large brain, home of the famous 'elephant's memory'. An elephant never forgets. The herds are exclusively formed by the females and their calves, and one of the adult females leads them. Suffice it to say, Blanca never gave the map as a present to Aurora, since she has still not managed to finish it. Aurora and Blanca always lived on the same street, called Sarmiento. Everything we can imagine exists somewhere.

13.

Aurora's Diary

19 July: This is not a secret diary. This is terror. Manifest terror. The attempt to domesticate terror through language. I must be honest: I'm in love with a man. He is a writer in the literary gathering I attend. He's a tall, strong man, with black hair and a black beard, a full mouth, he dresses formally – with shirts and pullovers – and at times he puts the colours together badly. His name, paradoxically, is Ulysses. I already loved a Ulysses. A dog. And now this. An aberration of a duplication. This Ulysses is not a dog. This Ulysses is the Devil. I haven't slept for three nights. My son doesn't deserve this. Neither do my students. And, well, then there's Juan Carlos. Love is a monster. A monster that only produces horror and sadness. Why is this happening to me? Why me?

22 July: Today I told Ulysses, 'Very well, I'll have a coffee with you.' He said why don't we walk, because he had the spirit of a *flâneur*. And I said, 'No, no walking. Coffee or nothing', and so we had a coffee. The evening was short but correct. We talked about books, as always. When we were saying goodbye, Ulysses said to me, 'You know that I've fallen in love', and I said, 'With what?' He smiled and closed the door of my taxi.

3 August: I took Ulysses the dog out for a walk and I realized that I'd like to walk with the other Ulysses. But I also realized something more important: the love of Ulysses the dog is the perfect love. Juan Carlos's is so calm it's boring. Ulysses the writer's love produces so much anxiety in me that it's bad for me. While Ulysses the dog is demonstrative, noble, loyal, affectionate. Why don't humans love like dogs? If we were better, we'd be better.

8 August. Today I saw Ulysses. We walked for hours. He knows my situation. He also knows that we shouldn't let it get late but nevertheless it got late. At dinnertime I announced, well, 'I'm going to get a taxi, Ulysses', and he took me by the hand, very sure, and he kissed me long and deep. I kissed him shyly, a bad kiss. I acted like a girl. For dinner I made sausages and mash. That simple dish is Juan Carlos's favourite.

30 August: At the end of the literary gathering, Ulysses invited me to his apartment. I said no, what was he thinking of. He said, 'I want to fuck you.' I slapped him, turned around and left.

5 September: I don't know what it is, that feeling they call Love. What I feel is a combination of marvellous emotions and others that are dreadful, all together undifferentiated. I realize that I am writing all this so as not to write what really happened. I went to bed with Ulysses, and it was unforgettable. With Juan Carlos it was always correct, I can't say it wasn't. But well. This is what happened. I agreed to visit Ulysses's apartment. It's an old building. The apartment is small and the only things in it are books, a typewriter and a bed. Ulysses read me a book by a poet from Corrientes, a friend of his. When he finished reading, he said: the future of Argentine literature is surrealism, and he started kissing me. Then he took out his penis and put it in my mouth without a word. I'd never done that. With Juan Carlos, never. I started

to kiss his penis as if the penis itself was my boyfriend and I was kissing him passionately. I liked it. Kissing his penis was like kissing his soul. 'This cock is yours, do what you want with her,' he said. Cock, her? It sounded strange to me. A feminine cock. Then he said to me, 'Read poetry to me and don't stop', and while I was sucking his penis I was reciting, 'I want to captivate your desperation, oh monkey farewell; you tremble so much in your dark islands, oh monkey farewell.' Then he put me against one of the bookshelves and he penetrated me. It was intense, short and profound. We came together. Then we hugged, as if we'd scored a goal. Then he kissed me and looking me in the eyes he said, 'Aurora you're for real.'

28 September: Today, Ulysses, I thought about killing you. Why do you exist? Then I thought about leaving my husband and son and running away with you. Then I thought about suicide.

30 September: I wrote a poem for Ulysses, a poem I will treasure like a secret. But isn't a poem always written to be shared? And a secret diary. Is a secret diary written to be shared, or just for yourself?

Love

White pollen of worlds, sweet milk of ice
I wish to drink you like a thing from the skies.
Oh, to be a butterfly gigantic and divine
To plunge my head in your dust sublime!

The blood boils, a liquid of fire
bursts from my lips where it feigns desire.
Longing from the skies, yet what I would give
so that on my head that milk might drip.

1 October: Ulysses left me. He's an imbecile.

2 Ocober: I'm going to abuse my body and, know what, it's all because of you. I'm going to take a mountain of tranquilizers and a bottle of cheap cognac that I've just bought at the supermarket. I'm going to turn myself inside out. It's all over for me. It's done.

5 October: The suicide attempt cost me dear. I had diarrhoea for three days. Juan Carlos behaved very well, making me soup and giving me medicine. That's it. This ridiculous end is quite enough. There are no metaphors. I wanted to die for love, and I ended up shitting all over myself. I'll never fall in love again.

1 December: I'm writing this diary again because tomorrow I'm going to see Ulysses again. He left the literary gathering and we've not seen each other for two months. But there will be no sex tomorrow. Tomorrow we'll talk. We'll be friends.

2 December. The underground train that I took to get to him left me four blocks away and I walked those blocks trying to control my anxiety. I got there at ten to the hour. I sat down. I asked for a tea. I made as if to open a book, but I couldn't read. Couldn't concentrate. My heart was thumping. And when it was exactly on the hour, I saw him

appear in the door. Absolutely on time. He looked taller. Very tall. And his beard looked longer. He looked like a different man. A new man. Even more handsome than Ulysses. Yet he was still Ulysses. He sat at the table. He looked at me. I love you, Ulysses, I said. And I started to cry. Shall we go to my house? he said. He didn't even ask for his whisky. We left. We went to his house. And we made love. But this time there was nothing weird. We made just that. Love. We Made Love. Now we've made it for always.

3 December: Juan Carlos: I love another man. If you ever read this diary, have the decency to: a) walk out on me, and leave me with my son and my life; or b) not say a single word.

5 December. Yesterday Ulysses persuaded me to have anal sex. The whole time I felt as if I was going to defecate on his penis. I don't understand the pleasure of this experience.

8 December: Why have I fallen in love with this man? Why would a woman ever love a man? Women are better. They've got it right, those women who go with women.

16 December: I can't go on living like this. I can't. I'm a monster. I'm an egotist. I don't deserve anything from anyone. I should tear my eyes out. My son's a saint. My husband's one too. And I allow myself all sorts of perversions with this egomaniacal satyr. This has to stop.

24 December: I'm done. I can't go on. I'm at my wits' end with nerves and desperation. I don't sleep at nights. And I even think I've lost weight. I have to put an end to this. To my life. To everything. I'm going to turn the oven on. I'm going to put my head in the oven. My last Christmas. I'm going to commit suicide. The way poets commit suicide. None of this makes sense.

24 December. Later: I can't. Not in the oven. It's too cruel. Or I'm not brave enough. I'm going to set fire to myself. That's what I'm going to do. Set fire to me, my house and this diary. I can see Ulysses. Ulysses the dog. I'll die with him too. A semantic suicide. Die with the canine double of my lover. I love you too, dear animal. Let's give ourselves up. He doesn't know that he's going to die. That's what they say. I try to think like him. Make my mind go blank. I'll light a paper. And the house will go up in flames. And with it my dog and my heart and my life. Let's burn, beloved hound. We'll burn in the fire of desperation. We've had enough.

1 January: It's a miracle I'm alive. My dog Ulysses saved my life. It seems that while the kitchen was burning, I fell unconscious because of the smoke, lying on the kitchen floor, but the dog worked out how to open the front door, come back to the kitchen and drag me out through the house is if I were its pup. Or a stick like the ones he plays with. God knows what the animal thought he was doing. Maybe people have got it wrong, maybe dogs do know about death, and that's why Ulysses saved me. He saved me from death. He said, 'You've got to carry on living, Aurora.' The God dog. Anyway, after dragging me out, he started howling in the corridor with me lying there unconscious, and along came a neighbour who asked for the public telephone and called the Fire Brigade. We survived the fire, my dog and I. And so did this diary that

I hide so that nobody can read it. This diary that I couldn't destroy. I wanted to kill myself for one Ulysses and another Ulysses saved me. Love has no metaphors. I'm going to stop all this. This time, forever. I'm going to run away. I love you, Ulysses. Forget me if you can. I won't be able to. Now and forever and for all eternity . . .

2 January: The image we have of the countryside is always slightly anachronistic. When you get as far as Patagonia the sky is green like cement and the sea is like kerosene. I'm a fugitive who writes as she travels on a train with a dog and a child. I feel undone. And yet I feel beautiful. Beautiful like Judas Iscariot. I betrayed my husband. And I want to leave an account in this diary of the scene of my betrayal. Because what I did was, I sat Juan Carlos in the dining room, and I told him the whole truth. 'I screwed a guy for months. I don't love you anymore. I'm leaving. I'm taking your son and your dog.' I'm a bitch. I'm repugnant because I wanted to be. I'm not a good Argentine woman. He cried. Juan Carlos cried. Me, nothing. I am one holy bitch from hell. 'Don't cry, Juan Carlos, you're a grown man,' I said. This is just the way it is. The struggle for life: some regenerate and others fall by the wayside. And then he got angry. He shouted at me. He'd never shouted at me. I stood up to him and he backed down at once. He's a wimp, Juan Carlos. He cried again. 'You're killing me,' he said. I didn't say anything else. I couldn't. I grabbed a bag, picked up the baby and grabbed the dog's leash. I bumped into a chair . . . and I left. I'm not anybody's plaything anymore. I'm going to stop writing this diary. Now I start a new life, which is really the same life as ever, but new. I'm going back to Ushuaia. I'm going to open up my father's bookshop. And my best friend needs me. That's how things grow in the wind. Twisted but well rooted in the earth.

14.

Blanca's Diary

AUGUST. MONDAY
I'm starting to write a secret diary. On the advice of my friend Aurora. She told me that writing a diary might be good for getting through the storm. The death of my mother has left me very sad. And it's incredible: I see written, now in this diary, the word 'sad', and I am aware that it doesn't represent me. 'Sad', and I see a series of drawings thrown together by chance on a piece of paper. 'Sad' is said of a person of a melancholic character or temperament. 'Sad', and that is not how I feel. I feel truly sad. And my 'sad' would be something like: suffering, confused, anguished, relieved, lost, disconsolate, dissolute, indignant, ill, sad, a mess, a wreck. I don't understand what there is now. In my life. What is there? I don't understand. I lived my whole life with my mother. And now I'm asking: what now?

WEDNESDAY
In her agony, my mother wrote me a letter. She expressly asked me not to open it until after her death. And I still can't bring myself to open it. Tonight, I am going to buy myself some booze to give myself courage, and I am going to read that letter.

SAME DAY, AT NIGHT
The only good thing that we could say about my mother's agony was a man I met. I want to leave an account in this diary of the scene of how we met, so that I never forget a single detail. A man helped me get my mother into the hospital. I say to him thank you, sir. And he says be welcome, miss, my name is Klaus. I say to him hello Klaus, and he says to me Klaus Henriksen from Norway. And I say to him, Blanca, white, like the colour. And he says to me Blanco and I say to him, no, Blanca, with an 'a', Blanca. Planca, says he. I say to him Blanca and he says Planca and me Blanca and him Planca. Then he says I'm a marine biologist, I come Yujuaiah for study species of animals from here and compare to Norway. And I say to him but here in the hospital there are people not animals, Klaus. And he says to me that here in the hospital they lend to me instruments. Instruments he said. As if he was a musician. I laughed. But respectfully. And he laughed too. Why are you laughing, Klaus? And he says: since you have laughed, ha, ha, ha, since you have laughed. I was happy. I don't know why. Then he stops laughing and he says how is your mother? And I say no, Klaus, no, no, no, it's very difficult with Mum. And he puts his hand on mine, and I grab it, and he puts his other hand on top, making a sandwich of my hand, and he says, be strong, Planca. And his eyes were watering, a tear falling over his very very blond beard. I cried too. We'd only known each other for five minutes and we'd already laughed and cried together. It was a lot more than in the five years with Alberto.

FRIDAY
Klaus isn't taking any notice of me. I still haven't opened my mother's letter. I don't really feel like writing this diary. Who am I writing for? If it's only for me, isn't living my life enough? Why do I need to leave a record of things that are happening to me?

SATURDAY

I want him to love me. I want him to fall in love with me. To love me madly. To say Blanca. Blanca, when he dreams. To say it properly, for once and for all. Not Planca. Blanca. With a B. It's got to work out for me some time. Just once, for fuck's sake. That this guy falls in love with me. Loves me. Loves me properly. Kisses me. Holds me tight. Touches my tits. Asks me to do dirty things. Has an endless hard-on. Looks at me and, says, I love you like fuck. Robs my underwear from my drawer. Watches me pee after we've had sex. That we brush our teeth together. That he wakes up with a hard-on every day. Looks at me with pride. Even cries at times because he loves me so much. And I say what a wimp that Norwegian is. But I'd only say it to look good, because really I'd love him. I love him. I love you, Klaus. You bloody bastard. I love you. Love me. Come on, God, just once. Just once, let it be. For fuck's sake, Klaus. Come on God. What's the matter? Look over here a bit. I do everything right. I deserve it. Now yes. Now. Now.

SUNDAY

Sometimes I'm a bit flighty, that's true. But sometimes let's say that it's circumstances that fluster me. It so happens that Klaus finally came to have tea. The guy drinks tea. Not mate or café. Tea. Well, the tea's coming and going and, all of a sudden, he grabs my hand, Klaus grabs my hand. I look at him. He looks at me. I look at him. He looks at me. Slow, Klaus, always slow. Or maybe he's not slow, maybe it's that Norwegian speed is another speed, slower than ours in Argentina. And he says to me, I, Planca, he says, I am feeling very close to you. That's what he said. And I started to cover him with kisses, his little yellow and red beard, his mouth, everything. It was beautiful. Yes. It was a beautiful kiss he gave me. His tongue is as cold as ice. And he tastes gorgeous. Well, if we were going to be precise, we'd have to say that I kissed him. But no. A kiss is between two people. He gave and I gave, it was a kiss. Klaus kissed me.

TUESDAY

Today I will definitely open the letter. Once and for all. No booze or anything, Klaus's kiss gave me courage. Tonight, I will read my mother's letter.

WEDNESDAY

I have a father. The letter tells the whole story. That my mother left Salta and went to live in Buenos Aires and lived in a boarding house, and there was a young man there, younger than her, who was studying medicine. And they got together, and my mother worked so that he could study. And that man was my father. And it seems that this man who was a doctor was doing something that wasn't allowed, that's how my mother writes it, he was getting rid of the babies of the women who didn't want to have them. But it seems that, once, a woman who didn't know what she was doing but was doing the same as him had a problem and called this man who it seems was my father to help her with a girl, and this man couldn't save her, and the girl died. And, so, he was charged, and they ended up sending him here to prison in Ushuaia and that's why we live here. And that's the story. But it doesn't end there: it turns out that one day my mother goes to the prison out of the blue and found the guy with another woman. Because it seems that my father had had a lover for a while, and he was going to leave my mother then the accident happened and, well, this lover had managed to get money together to come and see him here in prison in Ushuaia. So, my mother never saw him again, she was stubborn, that woman. Anyway. I come out of that mess. My father is called Dr Emilio Fierro, and he lives in Río Grande. And I want to meet him.

SATURDAY, RÍO GRANDE
Klaus managed to get a doctor in the hospital to lend him his van and we went to Río Grande to see Dr Fierro. The journey was a real adventure. Klaus drove in silent concentration. I was excited. We got to Río Grande. We found Doctor Fierro's house. We knocked on his door. And there he was. Tall, dark, old by now, but healthy. 'Are you Dr Fierro?' I said to him. Yes. 'I am your daughter,' I said to him. And he invited me in for tea. As if it was nothing. Dr Fierro also drinks tea. He told me that he'd been the doctor in Río Grande for years but doesn't practise much anymore. He lived with the woman of the surprise visit until a year ago, when she died. He is well-mannered. And a bit strange. He said he'd come and visit me often, that we could be friends. Klaus says we're very alike. I can't imagine this man being my mother's boyfriend.

SEPTEMBER. MONDAY
Something beautiful happened. Klaus has to go to Antarctica for his research, and he's invited me. We're going in a week. I'm mad with joy. 'Planca, don't you want to come to Antarctica with me?' he said. And I said to him, Klaus, what is Antarctica? And Klaus smiles all white and pink, ha ha ha, ha ha ha, Antarctic is love. Is love a giant frozen desert, Klaus? I thought, but I didn't say anything because I saw he was so happy, poor thing.

MONDAY
First day in Antarctica. The place is fabulous like a fabulous dream. I said to Klaus, 'Hey, Klaus this place is like a fantasy place' and he said, 'No, this place is real, Planca.'

WEDNESDAY
Third day in Antarctica. It turns out that Klaus is wagging the tail of half the planet, because the Norwegian Polar Institute sent him to see if they could put a base here. Because it seems that lots of countries have bases. We stayed at an American base. So, Klaus spends his time speaking to the Americans and I know hardly any English. But I watch and I learn things. Klaus doesn't say anything to me. He only talks to me when we get up and before we go to sleep. This morning, he said, 'When I am small my grandfather read to me *The Odyssey* so I love the world.'

SATURDAY
Sixth day in Antarctica. Today was an important day. Klaus took me to see some seals. They're called Weddell seals. They're grey with little black faces. And it seems that these seals dive very deep in the sea. Then Klaus showed me his little trick, 'Come here, put your ear here,' he said. And I pressed my ear against the ice, and it was incredible. There was this incredible music. Music as if robots were making music. But they weren't robots. They were seals.

MONDAY
Eighth day in Antarctica. Klaus is an underwater diver. News to me. All of a sudden, I saw him with an astronaut's helmet and tight leggings clinging to his body. So, this is how it is: Klaus plunges into the depths to look at little animals. Not fish. Even smaller things. It seems that there is a whole universe under the sea. Creatures with enormous tentacles, worms with deformed jawbones, violent and bloodthirsty marine monsters, but the whole horror film is a miniature that only Klaus can see with his instruments. I like his stories. He's tired of the Americans and he's paying me more attention. Yesterday I said to him: and what are you looking for so much under the water, Klaus? And he said to me: Klaus looks for the origin of life.

THURSDAY
Today is the last day in Antarctica. In all of the time I've been here I've not had a period. I saw a group of penguins all walking together in the same waddling way and one that went the other way. Klaus explained that instead of going to the water it was going towards the interior of the continent, so it was going to certain death. Let's save it, Klaus. 'No, you have to let it be,' he said. And then he said: I think I am going to go back to Norway to give my reports in the university, then I return to Ushuaia and we marry, and then we return and live in Oslo, Norway. That's what he said to me. It turns out that Klaus proposed marriage. But, in fact, he didn't propose. He just told me. Like telling me something that didn't have any importance. Then he said: male penguins incubate the eggs as well as the female penguins. Did you know that, Planca?

NOVEMBER. MONDAY
I'm taking up this diary I had abandoned, because there's wonderful news in my life, and I want to register here. I am going to have a baby. I'm very happy. I hope Klaus gets back soon from Norway. He left a few days after the news, and I miss him already. Although he is a strange man. I'm getting to be quite friendly with Dr Fierro, my father. Although he too is a strange man.

DECEMBER. TUESDAY.
What I most feared has happened. I lost my baby. The end. Now everything is sad. 'Sad' and I feel a music that destroys my heart. 'Sad' is said of a person of a melancholic character and temperament. 'Sad' and that is how I feel. I don't believe in life anymore. I want to run, but don't know where. I wring out my life like a mop and nothing comes out. I'm dried up. My father says that it's unlikely I can have children now. The sun's shining outside. I cry all day long.

THURSDAY
Klaus should have come back a month ago. I'm beginning to get the feeling that he's left me. I'm broken. I have the word unhappiness written on my heart forever.

FRIDAY
I go to the chemist's a lot. At siesta time. The son of Arias the chemist quite likes me, so he sells me whatever I want. I'm taking pills for everything. Pills for the pain. Pills to sleep. Pills to get up. Pills for looking at the horizon on a rainy day. Pills for

thinking. Pills for not thinking. Pills for my cough. Pills for my stomach. Pills for my eyes. Pills for my arms. Pills for my legs. Pills for my sadness. Pills for eating. Pills to be dead. Pills to live. There's no psychology. How good it would be to live a normal life.

SUNDAY
I wrote a poem I would be embarrassed to share, but since it seems to me that it's a good poem, I am going to write it down here. It's called 'Last night' because it's what happened to me last night, although I wrote it today.

Last night

Last night
I mixed pills and alcohol again.
It's because I'm depressed.
I know it's bad.
I invited the chemist to my house.
He's called Víctor.
He wants to look after me.
Fuck me, Víctor, I don't need to be looked after,
I said.
I felt stupid.
I drank.
I danced.
I even cried a bit.
Víctor looked on silently.
I don't know, Víctor.
Sometimes I apologize.
I'd like to be stronger.
I don't know what metonymy is.
I say All and Nothing a lot.
I have problems with my self-esteem.
I always think I'm not loved.
I tend to fight with people.
I should try to fall in love.
Do you know what I mean, Víctor?
It's something here in the middle of my breast that's like I don't know what.
Why don't you try to calm down?
Fuck me, Víctor, because if you don't, I'm going to feel worse.

MONDAY
Malign forces take over me. I walk through the centre of the town. And suddenly, I feel a need. I go into the town hall. And I go mad. I become a whirlwind. I see red. And I destroy the place. I start to knock over desks. I throw paper, pens, lever arch files in the air. I start to take the typewriters apart. I am absolutely out of it. Stop her, I hear. But nobody can stop me. I'm possessed. I have the strength of an army. Destruction. Just because. For the injustices, the sadnesses, the suffering, the rage. I break everything with an almost joyful fury. More than disorder what I am making is

a fantastic dance. The furniture and equipment of the town hall fly from my body and crash against the windows. There is a fabulous rain of glass. It's a festival of revenge. I want to destroy my city. I want to destroy the nation, and with it I want to destroy me. The treasurer tries to stop me, and I break his nose with my elbow. I hear a baby cry. Wuahwuahwuah. I am wearing a white dress that is now half black with ink and half red with blood. I am barefoot. Lying on the floor. Dishevelled. And I even think I peed myself. I don't shed a single tear. I look up and see the faces of terror and fear around me. Sorry sorry. I say. I went too far. They wanted to arrest me or put me in an asylum. Because they've known me since I was a girl, they gave me another chance. Someone needs to look after her, they said. And Víctor Arias saved me. I can be her therapeutic companion, he told them. And now he's going around telling everyone that he's my boyfriend.

SATURDAY
I am going to put an end to this diary. As if it were a book that I finish and close. If this diary had to have a name, it would be 'Blanca's Torment'. But diaries don't have titles, or the title is 'Diary of' and the name of the person. But here it couldn't be called 'Diary of Blanca', no. Because I am a person undone. My name is no longer Blanca Fierro. I am now Blanca Darkness. I am in despair. I wrote a letter to Aurora. I need her, I need her to come and save me. I have no strength left. I've lost my way in this life. The roaring of sirens, whistles, fireworks, corks bursting from bottles, shots fired into the air, the sirens of fire engines. It must be exactly midnight. Happy New Year.

Part Three

15.

Everything's done, God heard them tell him, and he hadn't yet created the world. Any multiplication is still a multiplication. Nothing is created from nothing.

For example, the word reproduce. Produce again or produce anew. Or referring to living beings, it is to engender and produce other beings with the same biological characteristics.

For example, human beings. We wouldn't be here if our parents hadn't had sex in that exact and precise second. And if our grandparents hadn't had sex in that precise second. And if we go back four hundred years, our existence depends on fifteen thousand people having had sex, on the exact day and the exact moment. For example, Aurora. The knowledge was revealed to her in a book. Aurora understands that whatever destiny, no matter how long and complicated, consists, in reality, of one single moment: the moment in which a woman knows for ever who she is. For example, Blanca. A brave woman in an indecipherable darkness. Blanca felt like a woman in a hole waiting to be rescued by a wolf. And Aurora understood her intimate destiny as a wolf.

The two women met again after years, but for them it had only been minutes. 'Women are born to suffer,' Aurora said to Blanca. And at that Blanca understood that one destiny is not better than another, but that you must make the most of the destiny you carry in your heart. And in that very instant, almost like a miracle, both thought – at the same time – about the day they met. They were girls. They were looking at the moon. It was as simple as that. And then came everything else. Life. Everything is beginning. Always. For ever. Sometimes God appears and puts things in their place. 'Life is always life, Aurora,' says Blanca. And Aurora answers, 'Life is always life.'

16.

Blanca Are you the daughter of the man with the bookshop?
Aurora Yes.
Blanca What's your name?
Aurora Aurora.
Blanca Hello, Aurora, my name's Blanca.
Aurora Hello.
Blanca I'm five, how old are you?
Aurora Yes.
Blanca Yes?
Aurora Five. Yes.
Blanca You're always reading books, aren't you?
Aurora Yes.
Blanca Do you like reading books?
Aurora Yes.
Blanca I like drawing and writing.
Aurora Writing?
Blanca Yes. I write. Things. Anything.
Aurora Ah. I've never thought about writing.
Blanca You can. You write and it's written down.
Aurora Yes.
Blanca I want to tell you a secret.
Aurora What?
Blanca The moon follows me.
Aurora What?
Blanca Yes. The moon follows me.
Aurora What are you saying?
Blanca It's a discovery.
Aurora A discovery?
Blanca Don't be jealous, Aurora.
Aurora Why would I be jealous?

Blanca You live shut up reading books and then I appear and I bring you the moon.

Aurora   I don't understand what you're saying.

Blanca Come here. Give me your hand. Mine's clean. Give me yours.
Look. Can you see it? Can you see it, Aurora?
Look now.
Can you see it? Can you see it, Aurora?

Aurora   Yes.
Yes.
Yes, Blanca, yes.

17.

Blanca Your bookshop is beautiful.

Aurora Yes. A little rundown. There's no electricity.

Blanca The thing is, your aunt's senile, you knew that.

Aurora Yes, I knew that.

Blanca And we left her looking after Juan Manuel and the dog.

Aurora So, that Doctor Fierro turned out to be a piece of shit. 'I want to live.' That's what he said, those were his exact words?

Blanca Yes. 'I'm going to Buenos Aires. I want to live.' That's what he said. Well, he wrote it, really, in a letter with horrible handwriting.

Aurora He's an idiot, that man.

Blanca He's harmful.

Aurora We have to dust the shelves, put up new shelving, and get some new books.

Blanca It's going to be the most beautiful bookshop in the world.

Aurora Yes. Although it will take a lot of work.

Blanca Well, we're both pretty determined.

Aurora Yes, we'll make it happen.

Blanca Of course. Of course we will.

Aurora Shall we go? It's cold.

Blanca I'm proud of you, my friend.

Aurora Why are you proud of me? I haven't done anything yet.

Blanca Ah no, but I'm proud of you because you're my friend.

Aurora I'm proud of you too, Blanquita.

Blanca That's it. I know what it is. Friendship, us. I know what the lesson is.

Aurora What's the lesson, Blanca?

Blanca No, no, what do I know.

18.

What is the mystery? Why does the sky change colour? What is normality? They teach us that the sky is blue. It seems that there are things that exist just because. But no. The colour of the sky is a result of the interaction of solar light with the atmosphere. Strength is always unpunished. The sky of Ushuaia had dawned pink. Pink like white mixed with red, pink like a pink fish, pink like fantasy, pink like nothing. And how to explain this strange pink zenith in Ushuaia? Science offered an explanation, which was also a threat. The reason was two asteroids that would crash into planet Earth, more precisely into the southern town of Ushuaia. The fatal event would happen in the next forty-eight hours. The organism affirmed that it did not know the exact trajectory the asteroids would follow, and that there was the possibility that the collision would not happen, given the peculiar course that the two strange visitors would be following. The most astonishing events never need an explanation. Said asteroids, following tradition, were baptized with names alluding to Greek mythology. They've been given the names Philomela and Procne.

19.

Blanca In the house there are twenty geese eating wheat soaked in water and I'm looking at them, there's nobody else, I'm alone in the house with the geese and, all of a sudden, an eagle appears and begins to break the geese's necks one by one, get it: a psychopathic eagle. Then the eagle looks at me and says, come on, chin up, this isn't a dream, child.

Aurora Was the eagle Spanish?

Blanca I don't know. The point is that you appear.

Aurora And what did I do?

Blanca No, I don't know. That's when I woke up.

Aurora Well, you're going to make Juan Manuel's birthday cake.

Blanca Yes. Tomorrow I'll buy everything. I want to write something for him on the cake.

Aurora What do you want to write?

Blanca I want to write: Juan Manuel.

Aurora I thought you were going to write something else.

Blanca No. Juan Manuel. And five little candles.

Aurora Yes.

Blanca And I also want to make a cake to celebrate the publication of the *Anthology of Patagonian Women Poets*.

Aurora And are you going to write something on that cake?

Blanca Yes. I'm going to write: Poetry.

Aurora Put a lot of caramel spread in my cake.

Blanca What does the dream mean for you? The dream I've just told you.

Aurora It feels to me that it's got something to do with death.

Blanca With death?

Aurora Yes. I don't know. I don't know anything about dreams. I never understand them, or I understand them badly.

Blanca I usually make up any old thing.

Aurora And in this case, what would you say, for example?

Blanca I'd say that it's about death.

Aurora But that's what I said.

Blanca Do you know what I'd say about the dream, Aurora? Life is passing by, isn't it, and people are dying and it's very sad. Because you go on living with those dead people inside you. And you talk to the dead. Hello, Mum, I did such and such. Here, Aurora's dad would have said such and such. We're all going to die, Aurora. With all my deaths, I give myself up to death. Let's die. The wind's getting up.

Aurora   The word death should be replaced by the word poetry.

20.

There was a spine-chilling silence. You could feel in the air that something was about to happen. But saying 'something' wasn't right. 'Something' wasn't going to happen. 'Something' is a neutral pronoun. 'Something' designates an indeterminate reality. 'Something' was not a good use of the word in this case. Because something wasn't going to happen, the End of the World was going to happen. The worst had been confirmed: the asteroids would put an end to humanity, Philomela and Procne each have a diameter of thousands of kilometres, and they expand as they get closer to Earth. People flee from Ushuaia, desperate. But there is nowhere to run to. The world is all that exists. There is nothing left. All that's left is to pray. And Aurora and Blanca are not going to pray.

21.

Aurora   What will the day you'll die be like? Will it be sunny? Will it be raining? What will that last day be like? That definitive day? Will it be in your house or in a hospital? Will it be alone or accompanied? Who do you want to die with? Do you want someone to see you die? Or would it be better to be found dead? What will you think about in that last moment? Who?

22.

Let's suppose that a country, Argentina for example, were an invented country. That a whole system of books created what we call Argentina. What, then, would the end of the world be, in a country invented by books? It would be a metaphor, one more step, an operation that this fiction called 'Argentina' would make on 'reality', which would be the rest of the world. But no. Argentina was real, as real as the rest of the world, or maybe more. So, now it is night. Aurora and Blanca decided to go and shut themselves in the bookshop. They wouldn't have known where else to go. Juan Manuel is sleeping. Ulysses the dog is sleeping. Aurora and Blanca are sitting, one beside the other. They don't say anything. Only the two of them. Reading. In the light of a candle. Their austerity is in contrast with the exuberance of the sky: two orange, or golden, balls move around the sky, as if in an inexhaustible choreography. Aurora and Blanca, impassive, follow the thread of their reading. There is nothing worse than being interrupted when you're reading, even if it is the End of the World. And then suddenly, the two orangey blobs direct themselves, speedily, furiously, beautifully towards Ushuaia. They are like two fantastic rays, like two blond youngsters, like two bees. Their flight is furious, delirious, incredible. Strangely, they travel determinedly directly over the bookshop. The visual phenomenon is marvellous. Before crashing into the little shop, ostentatiously, the two asteroids change colour. As if they didn't know what to do to attract attention. They are blue, red, golden, with the face of a founding father, of a fruit, of a labyrinth, with the form of Argentina, of a tiger, golden again. It is a Big Bang in reverse. Two vainglorious monstrosities offloading forever on a small bookshop. But regardless. Aurora and Blanca carry on reading. And in that precise instant, the End of the World happens.

Outro: On Futures

As we reach the end of *Latin American Plays in Translation*, we encounter another ending. After six years of projects, programmes, podcasts and plays, the Global Voices Theatre team have made the decision to close our company.

For our small team, it has come to a point in our journey where we are pursuing other avenues in arts, theatre, publishing and research. Throughout our time as Global Voices Theatre, we have worked towards these main aims:

- To amplify theatre and performance work by underrepresented global artists
- To decolonize local theatre structures
- To advocate for international artistic practices
- To contribute to the professional development of artists across borders

But there is much work still to be done. We applaud the work of groups and individuals who continue to strive for these changes in our industry, and we hope to contribute to this work in our roles outside of Global Voices Theatre.

Since 2018, we have had the pleasure of collaborating with hundreds of brilliant artists from across the world. In this time, we have had the opportunity to produce ten flagship events at venues including Arcola Theatre, Bush Theatre, the British Library, Rich Mix and the Roundhouse; two podcast series that interview international playwrights, and explore the wider social and political contexts of the plays showcased; three Anti-School courses and events, creating spaces for non-hierarchical learning with renowned international artists; and three published anthologies with Oberon Books and Methuen Drama, including *Global Queer Plays*, *Global Jewish Plays* and the volume you currently hold.

We wish to thank our brilliant steering group: Fauve Alice, Malú Ansaldo, Taghrid Choucair-Vizoso, William Gregory, Ruba Huleihel, Madeline Sayet and Africa Ukoh; all of whom have offered invaluable support and guidance. We also wish to thank every one of the excellent curators, designers, directors, facilitators, performers, photographers, producers, readers, sound designers, stage managers and multidisciplinary artists who have contributed to Global Voices Theatre.

Although our time as a company has come to an end, we urge readers to continue seeking out narratives across borders, in translation, and to support international and migrant writers and artists. At a time when international collaboration and storytelling remains a radical act, let's keep forging these bridges between us.

With love and solidarity,
Lora, Robin and Zhui Ning
January 2025

Acknowledgements

The Global Voices Theatre team would like to thank the following individuals and organizations who helped bring to life the original readings of *Global Latin American Voices* and *Global Female Voices* 2.0. In no particular order:

Malú Ansaldo, Carla Zúñiga, Francisca Olivares Medina, Julieta Kilgelmann, Pepa Duarte, Xavier Villanova, Roberto Cavazos, Paulina Lenoir Guajardo, Drew Paterson, Ricardo Gilfillan, Juan Aguilera Justiniano, María José Andrade, Natalia Knowlton, Diego Poupin, Francisco Diaz, Sebastián Eddowes-Vargas, Almiro Andrade, Julene Robinson, Cinthia Lilen, Franko Figueiredo, Mariano Tenconi Blanco, Laura Guidi, Miguel Hernando Torres Umba, Ellen Victoria, Florencia Cordeucuccia, Fauve Alice, Susana Torres Molina, María Claudia André, Barbara Younoszai, Betsy Picart, Hari MacKinnon, Sami Edris, Samah Sabawi, Belinda Clarke, Sami Edris, Lauren Santana, Kheira Bey, Faezeh Jalali, Filiz Ozcan, Sanee Raval, Reema Chandarana, Nina Mitrović, Emma Linley, Mark Grindrod, Olga Dimitrijević, Ksenija Latinović, Ifewumi Fagunwa, Sheree Kane, Trine Garrett, Professor Catherine Boyle, Vanessa Gabriel-Robinson, Andrea Peláez and Nicolle Smartt.

With gratitude to the Arcola Theatre, Arts Council England and Roundhouse for hosting and supporting our projects.